Dealing with Mission Drift in Parachurch Agencies

An Analysis of Holistic Mission of Christian Non-Governmental Organizations and Non-Profit Organizations

Israel K. Kombaté

© 2025 Israel K. Kombaté

Published 2025 by Langham Academic
An imprint of Langham Publishing
www.langhampublishing.org

Langham Publishing and its imprints are a ministry of Langham Partnership

Langham Partnership
PO Box 296, Carlisle, Cumbria, CA3 9WZ, UK
www.langham.org

ISBNs:
978-1-83973-936-1 Print
978-1-78641-136-5 ePub
978-1-78641-137-2 PDF

Israel K. Kombaté has asserted his right under the Copyright, Designs and Patents Act, 1988 to be identified as the Author of this work.

All rights reserved. No part of this publication may be reproduced, stored in a retrieval system or transmitted, in any form or by any means, electronic, mechanical, photocopying, recording or otherwise, without the prior written permission of the publisher or the Copyright Licensing Agency.

Requests to reuse content from Langham Publishing are processed through PLSclear. Please visit www.plsclear.com to complete your request.

Scriptures taken from the Holy Bible, New International Version®, NIV®. Copyright © 1973, 1978, 1984, 2011 by Biblica, Inc.™ Used by permission of Zondervan.

British Library Cataloguing-in-Publication Data
A catalogue record for this book is available from the British Library

ISBN: 978-1-83973-936-1

Cover & Book Design: projectluz.com

Langham Partnership actively supports theological dialogue and an author's right to publish but does not necessarily endorse the views and opinions set forth here or in works referenced within this publication, nor can we guarantee technical and grammatical correctness. Langham Partnership does not accept any responsibility or liability to persons or property as a consequence of the reading, use or interpretation of its published content.

Contents

Dedication and Gratitude xi

Abstract xiii

Chapter 1 1
Introduction
    1.1 Short Description of Key Terms 4
        1.1.1 Agencies 4
        1.1.2 Parachurch NGOs/NPOs or CFB-NGOs/NPOs 4
        1.1.3 Holistic Mission/Transformation 4
        1.1.4 Mission Drift 5
        1.1.5 Mission Statement 6
        1.1.6 Paradigm Shifts 7
    1.2 Background: Significance of the Study 7
    1.3 State of Research and Research Problem 8
        1.3.1 Preliminary Literature Study 8
        1.3.2 Evaluation of the Research Problem 10
    1.4 Research Questions 11
    1.5 Research Procedure 13
    1.6 Scientific Aim of the Research 13
    1.7 Research Limits of Scope 15
        1.7.1 Limitations of This Research 15
        1.7.2 Delimitations of This Research 16
    1.8 Assumptions of This Research 17
    1.9 Overview of the Following Chapters 18

Chapter 2 21
Literature Review
    2.1 Origination of the Concept of Mission Drift 22
        2.1.1 Defining Mission Drift in Hybrid Ventures 23
        2.1.2 Understanding Mission Drift in Microfinance 24
        2.1.3 Causes of Mission Drift 26
        2.1.4 Consequences of Mission Drift 27
        2.1.5 Defining Mission Drift in Parachurch Agencies .. 28
        2.1.6 The Challenge of Mission Drift in Parachurch Agencies .. 31
    2.2 What are Parachurch NGOs/NPOs? 32
        2.2.1 Defining Parachurch Agencies: NGOs/NPOs 33
        2.2.2 Defining Parachurch Microfinance in Mission 35

        2.2.3 Why CFB-NGOs/NPOs? 40
        2.2.4 Characteristics of Parachurch NGOs/NPOs 41
        2.2.5 CFB-NGOs/NPOs in the Light of the Holistic
              Ministry of Jesus 44
        2.2.6 Evangelical Humanitarian NGOs/NPOs Under
              Challenge...46
    2.3 The Holistic Mission Debate in Missiology 50
        2.3.1 A Controversial Debate 50
        2.3.2 Holistic Mission: The Concept of *Missio Dei*......................56
        2.3.3 Lausanne Movement: The Two-sided Coin of
              Holistic Gospel..63
        2.3.4 Public Theology of Holistic Mission 69
    2.4 An Exegetical Study on the Holistic Ministry of Jesus 76
        2.4.1 Biblical Foundation of Holism 77
        2.4.2 Exegeting Matthew 9:35–38..81
        2.4.3 Exegeting Luke 4:18–19..86

Chapter 3 99
    Research Methodology
        3.1 Multiple or Collective Case Design 101
            3.1.1 Selection of Cases 105
            3.1.2 Data Collection 108
            3.1.3 Research Analysis of Data 110
            3.1.4 Reliability and Validity of This Empirical Research..........112
            3.1.5 Selection of Interviewees 117
            3.1.6 The Role of Cultural Interpretation in the Research
                  Questions..120
        3.2 Commitment to Research Ethics 121
            3.2.1 Informed Consent 122
            3.2.2 Permission to Conduct the Interview 123

Chapter 4 125
    Empirical Findings
        4.1 Case Studies: Holistic Mission Background 125
        4.2 Research Outcomes from the Analysis of Seven Case Studies...129
            4.2.1 Findings in Relation to EU: Parachurch Agencies
                  and Mission Drift 129
            4.2.2 Findings in Relation to RQ1: Holisticalization 135
            4.2.3 Findings in Relation to RQ2: From Internal
                  Secularization to Humanitarization 139
            4.2.4 Findings in Relation to RQ3: Paradigm Shifts 141

    4.2.5 Findings in Relation to RQ4: Causes and
        Consequences of Drifting 145
    4.2.6 Findings in Relation to RQ5: Holistic
        Contextualization 148
    4.2.7 Summary of the Key Findings 150
  4.3 Triangulating the Study Results: Avoiding Mission Drift 152

Chapter 5 157
Research Discussion

  5.1 CFB-NGOs/NPOs Facing the Crisis of Mission Drift in
      Their Identities 159
  5.2 Secularization and Humanitarization: From Christian
      Agency to Humanitarian NGO/NPO 162
  5.3 Paradigm Shift Versus Mission Drift 165
  5.4 Praxis of Parachurch Agencies' Contextualized Holistic
      Mission 168
  5.5 Postmodern Trends and 'Critical-Holistic'
      Contextualization: A Societal Challenge to CFB-NGOs/
      NPOs' Mission 171
  5.6 Mission True Agencies: The Pursuit of Holisticalization
      and Biblical Holism...178
    5.6.1 Staying 'Mission True': The Challenge of the Holistic
        God-given Missionary Vision..179
    5.6.2 A Holistic Proclamation of the Gospel.............................181
    5.6.3 Holistic Mission Spirituality of CFB-NGOs/NPOs:
        A Solution to Mission Drifting? 189
  5.7 Mission Drift Exposures 191
    5.7.1 Fundraising and Ambition for Growth:
        Susceptibility to Drifting? 191
    5.7.2 Hiring Unbelieving Professionals as Co-Staff:
        A Christian Identity Drift? 195
  5.8 Applying Matthew 9:35–38 and Luke 4:18–19 to the
      Present Study..198
  5.9 Applicable Guide: A Theoretical Framework Emerged
      from the Results 205

Chapter 6 209
Interconnected Theories And Spectrums

  6.1 Theory Analysis 210
    6.1.1 Organization Theory 210
    6.1.2 Isomorphic Theory 213
    6.1.3 Normative Theory 216

      6.1.4 Coercive Theory 217
      6.1.5 Conformism and Mimetic Theory 219
  6.2 Spectrum Analysis 221
      6.2.1 Spectrum of Bureaucratization 222
      6.2.2 Spectrum of Professionalization 225
      6.2.3 Spectrum of Dechristianization 229
  6.3 Mission Drift: A Symmetric Idea, a Binary Theory and/or
      a Snowballing Spectrum? 232

Chapter 7 235
Conclusion
  7.1 Reflecting on Research Methods 235
      7.1.1 What have I Learned? 236
      7.1.2 Challenges of Multiple Case Study? 236
      7.1.3 Benefits of Multiple Case Study? 236
  7.2 Implications 237
      7.2.1 Biblical-Soteriological Implications 237
      7.2.2 Missiological Implications 238
      7.2.3 Socio-Humanitarian Implications 240
  7.3 Recommendations 241
      7.3.1 Minimizing the Risk of Drifting 241
      7.3.2 Setting Organizational Goals:
          "Beingness in Doingness"..242
      7.3.3 Further Research 243
  7.4 Research Summary 244

Appendix 247
Interview Questionnaire

Bibliography 251

List of Tables

Table 3.1: Reliability and Validity Criteria 113

Table 3.2: Profile of the Interviewees 118

Table 3.3: Profile of the Parachurch Agencies 119

Table 4.1: Overview of the Seven Cases' Mission Statements and Objectives 128

Table 4.2: Overview of Mission Drift Occurrences 135

Table 4.3: Overview of the Paradigm Shift Motive 144

Table 4.4: Overview of Mission Drift's Causes and Consequences 147

Table 5.1: Domains of Authority in Contextualizing CFB-NGO/NPO's Mission 174

Table 5.2: Comparative Chart: Mission True vs. Mission Drift 181

List of Figures

Figure 1.1: Schematic Theoretical Framework and Overlapping Domains 14

Figure 2.1: The Church's Internal Holistic Theology as a Focal Point 71

Figure 2.2: Church's Neighborhood Holistic Theology 71

Figure 2.3: Church's Public Holistic Theology 72

Figure 2.4: Gospel's Theology of Holistic Mission 73

Figure 2.5: Spectrum of Public Theology of Holistic Mission 75

Figure 3.1: Schematic Overview of the Research Design 100

Figure 3.2: Purposive Sampling Technique 106

Figure 3.3: Population of Parachurch Agencies – Purposive Sample of Seven Cases of Study 107

Figure 3.4: Synthesis to Interpret Data and Analysis Through Triangulation ... 109

Figure 4.1: Schematic Overview of the Concept of Mission Drift 129

Figure 4.2: Schematic Overview of Participation 150

Figure 4.3: Schematic Overview of the Research Findings 151

Figure 5.1: Causative-Determinants Conceptual Framework 160

Figure 5.2: Sequential Progression Schematic Framework 162

Figure 5.3: Schematized "Growth-first Strategy" 193

Figure 5.4: Schematized "Powerful Demand-Pull" for Growth 194

Dedication and Gratitude

This study is appreciatively dedicated to my heavenly father and sovereign God who has enabled the realization of this doctoral work. He has graciously provided and been my great succour.

To my sweetheart, gorgeous and darling wife Esther Kombaté, who over the years has been my backbone, and our dearly loved children Johëlle Yendubé, Anaëlle Yenpiny and Raphaël Yendupo. I am grateful for their daily prayer, understanding, patience, and immeasurable love.

Esther encouraged and supported me spiritually, morally and, equally important, financially. Had it not been for her understanding and stamina, it would not have been possible for me to reach this level.

To my parents-in-law (Ruedi and Susanne Frösch) who supported me spiritually and in many other ways, to my friends John Duncan (who has happily edited my drafts) and his wife Patricia, to my former professors/mentors Dianne Wood (who has delightedly proofread my thesis) and her husband Darrell, to my uncle Peter Bandim who has done the second proofreading, and to the Lachat family (Yvette, Anne-Claire and François) through whom God provided all the finances needed for this study.

To my supervisor, Prof. Dr. Bernhard Ott, for his encouragement, wise instruction and scholarly comments without which I would have certainly given up. I also want to thank Prof. Dr. Lukwikilu Credo Mangayi for his constructive inputs.

> Not to us, LORD, not to us,
> But to your name be the glory
> because of your love and faithfulness,
> (Ps 115:1).

Abstract

This study investigated seven parachurch agencies with a holistic approach to Christian mission in order to study the concept of mission drift. Mission drift is a phenomenon where Christian faith-based mission agencies drift away from their God-given vision, original holistic mission objectives and Christian identity towards socio-humanitarian purposes. The multiple case study of the seven NGOs/NPOs is purposefully presented as a useful contribution to the discussion of the phenomenon. The study is aimed at presenting a deeper assessment of the concept of mission drift in parachurch NGOs/NPOs in the light of the holistic nature of the earthly ministry of Jesus, as exemplified in Matthew 9:35–38 and Luke 4:18–19. It also aims to develop a greater understanding of the challenging forces that can lead to mission drift among parachurch agencies, and to provide some steps that these holistic organizations can take to minimize the pressures towards drifting.

    The research reviewed a variety of literature describing mission drift, parachurch agencies, and the holistic mission debate, as well as presented an exegetical study of the ministry of Jesus. The research design reveals and supports the outline of the conceptual nature of this thesis. The study is therefore positioned within the larger field of empirical research, with a multiple case study approach, in order to grasp deeper real-life situations and to develop a better understanding of susceptibilities to mission drift. The research is then structured by combining empirical techniques with traditional bibliographical research methods in order to report and discuss the empirical data collected. This study's outcome has shown rates of 63 percent of holisticalization, 9 percent of internal secularization and 28 percent in the occurrence of mission drift in the seven agencies studied and from the material given by the thirty-two interviewees. These findings resulting from the research questions were then discussed and analyzed along with theories and spectra affecting CFB-NGOs/NPOs. This study has concluded its analysis by setting up practical implications to minimize mission drift. Mission drift is certainly a constant threat to any parachurch organization that is trying to remain 'mission true' and 'holistically relevant' in this post-Christian society.

Key Words: Mission drift; Parachurch agencies; Christian NGOs/NPOs; Holistic mission; CFB-NGOs/NPOs; Church-related organizations; Faith-based agencies; Holisticalization; Earthly ministry; Social action; Socio-humanitarian; Original mission.

CHAPTER 1

Introduction

Parachurch agencies (NGOs/NPOs) are part of the umbrella of development and welfare organizations. A present concern of Christian faith-based agencies is the observable occurrence known as 'mission drift'. This is the gradual drifting away of a faith-based mission organization from its original strong Christian founding values, God-given vision, mission objectives and Christian identity. The issue of mission drift has been previously identified in 'World Vision,' investigated by Lin;[1] 'Young Men's Christian Association' (YMCA), explored by Edwards and also by Rice;[2] and the universities of Harvard and Yale, pinpointed by Greer and Horst,[3] in order to better understand the phenomenon. These previous studies are the point of departure for this thesis. The rationale of this current research concerns only international Christian faith-based organizations that have communicated that they are doing holistic mission, not every existing Christian agency. I have identified relevant aspects of these sample cases, using multiple case technique to do the study. In this research, I am dealing with mission drift in parachurch agencies in the first place, and then looking at the phenomenon from a biblical perspective (using Matthew 9:35–38 and Luke 4:18–19 as an integral mission standard) in the light of the earthly ministry of Jesus. Jesus's ministry, as captured in these verses, gives me the framework for my analysis and evaluation of my case studies.

---

1. Lin, "Countering Mission Drift."
2. Edwards, "Faithfull Innovation"; and Rice, "Towards a Framework."
3. Greer and Horst, *Mission Drift*, 15–56.

The holistic nature of the earthly ministry of Jesus is of great importance to the theme of this research. It is obvious that his ministry included acts of salvific grace and deeds of merciful humanity. The gospels in general, but more especially the writings of the evangelists Matthew (9:35–38) and Luke (4:18–19), have repeatedly recorded in detail Jesus's acts of holistic and humble earthly service. And it is notable that, when studying the missional development works of Christian Faith-Based Non-Governmental Organizations (CFB-NGOs), there is certainly a link with Jesus's own mission in terms of giving his life as "a ransom for many" and of service (Matt 20:28, Mark 10:45, John 13:1–17). It is for this reason that Rowdon argues,

> Just as there would have been no need of a real Incarnation if God was interested only in redeeming the spiritual element in man (as is almost implied when we speak about 'souls being saved'), so there would have been no need of a ministry devoted to meeting the human needs of men and women (or, for that matter, of teaching and preaching).[4]

One of Bosch's remarkable descriptions of holistic mission emphasizes the following points: "Mission is a multifaceted ministry, in respect of witness, service, justice, healing, reconciliation, liberation, peace, evangelism, fellowship, church planting, contextualization, and much more."[5] Holistic transformational Christian mission is supposed to be multidimensional if it seeks to be true and reliable, impacting and fulfilling its original character of transforming people's lives by meeting people's spiritual, physical and social needs. Resembling Christian churches in their nature, parachurch agencies or Christian organizations can be a fountain of holistic innovations in mission. But these faith-based agencies also can face distinct challenges that may constrain them from working holistically according to Jesus's model of earthly mission, which restrains them from the essence of their original mission. When Christian Non-Governmental Organizations (NGOs) or Non-Profit Organizations (NPOs) shift their mission focus from integral mission approaches to solely social and development activities, they create unfamiliar paradigmatic situations for which the example of Jesus may not be pertinent.

---

4. Rowdon, "Holistic Mission," 35.
5. Bosch, *Transforming Mission*, 512.

Connections can be made between parachurch agencies and social entrepreneurship specializing in helping the poor by accessing small loans in microfinance and working with a hybrid ideal in their approach to social mission. It is well known that social entrepreneurs, in line with their philosophy of hybridity combine commercial activities with social mission. Hybrid ventures are Non-Profit Organizations, as Battilana, Lee, Walker and Dorsey, have outlined below, in pointing out the phenomenon of mission drift in the sector of social enterprise:

> Like hybrid species in nature, hybrid organizational models can be a fountain of innovation. But they also face distinct challenges that may prevent them from thriving. When organizations combine social mission with commercial activities, they create unfamiliar combinations of activities for which a supportive ecosystem may not yet exist. Hybrids also must strike a delicate balance between social and economic objectives, to avoid 'mission drift' – in this case, a focus on profits to the detriment of the social good.[6]

In this research study, parachurch holistic mission is seen to an extent as being parallel to hybrid ventures in social entrepreneurship and microfinance or microcredit. With regard to hybridity and holistic mission strategies, the question was whether Christian faith-based development agencies can achieve the delicate balance between social and spiritual objectives in order to avoid mission drift. This question has been investigated within Christian NGOs/NPOs in order to try to understand the theory of mission drift. In this case, I therefore suggest that a focus on integral mission in development works needs to be supported. The research study seeks to investigate wheither holistic mission is to the detriment of the exclusively social and humanitarian good. This study has drawn its conclusions and relevant recommendations from the study of seven parachurch agencies (enumerated in section 1.5) used as case studies.

---

6. Battilana et al., "In Search of," 51.

1.1 Short Description of Key Terms

1.1.1 Agencies

Christian agencies are local, national, or international organizations that provide Christian faith-based holistic services to people in need. In this study, a Christian agency is a non-profit institution for the poor that works to spread the goodness of God through the message of the gospel. The values and identity of a Christian agency are rooted in its scriptural convictions of God's love for humanity and are based on its understanding of compassion theology, which asserts that the followers of Jesus are called to be the expression of God's mercy to the poor and the oppressed in a holistic manner. For the sake of this research, the words agency (or agencies) and organization(s) are used interchangeably in talking about one or several Christian NGOs and/or NPOs.

1.1.2 Parachurch NGOs/NPOs or CFB-NGOs/NPOs

In this empirical research study, the abbreviation 'CFB-NGOs/NPOs' designates the Christian Faith-Based Non-Governmental Organizations. It is used alternatively with parachurch agencies or organizations. Likewise, NGOs stands for Non-Governmental Organizations and NPOs for Non-Profit Organizations.

1.1.3 Holistic Mission/Transformation

Holistic is a Greek term which is significantly employed in mission studies and works. It comes from the primitive adjective ὅλος (holism, transliterated *holos*) and denoting all, entire, complete, total, and whole. It refers to the expression 'integral mission' or 'all-inclusive mission' in both Christian and secular contexts and does exist in some modern dictionaries. Kesis indicates that "the word holistic seems to be quickly replacing the word wholisitic, both in dictionaries and usage."[7] The word holism – according to the lexicographer Gove – was coined by Smuts[8] in 1926, although the philosopher's connotation totally differs from the contemporary notion of holism.[9] In his understanding,

---

7. Kesis, "Wholistic or Holistic?," 63.
8. Jan Christiaan Smuts was a prominent British Commonwealth statesman and a South African philosopher and military leader.
9. Gove, *Webster's*, 1080.

Smuts describes the term holism as being the "fundamental factor operative towards the creation of wholes in the universe."[10] In this sense, Smuts, Gove and Kesis converge in their construal of the word holism.

In a Christian context, holistic transformation, also known as wholistic development, refers to the church's integral mission as well as the holistic mission of Christian organizations and agencies, which consists of meeting people's needs in a multidimensional way and thus transforming people's lives holistically. In the light of this understanding, Waweru argues that holistic mission, also referred to as Christian integral mission, is an all-inclusive transformational mission, involving an active multifaceted approach to evangelism and social development.[11] The description of Christian distinctiveness, has led to the phrase 'holistic transformation' or 'holistic development', commonly called 'holistic ministry'. Chester describes that "the term affirms a concern for the whole person – involving the physical, social, emotional and spiritual – and an approach to ministry that addresses all these various dimensions."[12] The ambiguity is that 'holistic' is nowadays equally used in other disciplines to refer to different things, even by secular welfare organizations, and no longer distinctively defines the nature of the Christian approach to welfare.

Therefore, holistic transformation or wholistic development involves combining different aspects, such as the organization's missiological concept, original intentions, and current practices as well as its ministry's impact, so that they work together, transforming people's lives and developing communities as a whole. The holistic works of the Christian NGOs/NPOs are one of the ways through which God still carries out the earthly ministry of Jesus as an expression of the creator's compassion for those who are poor in spirit and needy in physical and material things.

1.1.4 Mission Drift

In this research, "mission drift" refers to any Christian faith-based organizations that have drifted away from their founding mission, their purpose of existing, and their Christian identity, and have never returned to their original intent and founding mission statement. It happens either when the

---

10. Smuts, *Holism and Evolution*, 85.
11. Waweru, "Integral Mission," 13–18.
12. Chester, "What makes Christian Development," 5.

leadership finds that they have moved away from the agency's own mission or they consciously drift into a new direction, thus getting off-message from its unprecedented mission statement.

This may happen when the organization accepts funding from external sources (secular financial institutions or governments), and then compromises its organizational Christian mission, values, objectives and mission statement, and moving in a secular humanitarian direction. It may be considered as a gradual organizational backsliding from Christian faith similar to that of a believer who deserts his belief. Thus, a mission drift refers to the moving away from the founding purpose and the original mission statement towards becoming a secular agency with fewer and fewer Christian values.

1.1.5 Mission Statement

For parachurch agencies, a "mission statement" is a statement that clearly states the agency's belief, ideology and purpose, what the agency does, and how and for whom it does it. It may include why the NGO/NPO works and where it operates; thus, providing clarity for people who may want to work for, volunteer with, collaborate with, or donate to it, as well as for anyone who considers requesting assistance from the organization. The mission statement provides a clear description of exactly what the agency is involved in doing. Mission drift occurs when such an agency moves away from its original mission statement.

With regards to the mission statement, mission drift happens either when the leadership finds that they have moved away from the agency's own mission or when they consciously drift into a new direction, thus going 'off-message' from the original mission statement. The mission of a CFB-NGO/NPO determines the essence of what the agency does, why and for whom. For a parachurch agency, "a mission statement expresses the core values of an organization, while the 'vision statement' shows where it wants to go."[13] "Paradigm shift" will occur when the agency consciously reviews some strategies or implements new programs, yet does not go "off-message" from the agency's initial mission statement.

---

13. Shingadia, "Modern Canadian Universities," 3.

1.1.6 Paradigm Shifts

In this research, Paradigm Shifts describes the fact that a Christian organization makes a fundamental change in its way of doing mission: it may change its concepts, programs, and methods for the sake of contextualization but keep the essential values of its Christian identity. The concept aims to provide a framework for ideas to bring a breakthrough in holistic development strategies for the revitalization of mission. It is from this perspective that Bush argues that God is calling believers and Christian institutions to revitalize mission.[14] The purpose of a paradigm shift within a Christian NGO seems to be the re-examination of the agency's work of holistic transformation with the aim of avoiding mission drift. Thus, paradigm shift refers to the fact that an organization strategically adjusts the original mission in order to focus on one aspect of its vocation with the purpose of existential survival or to become more impactful, while keeping in sincerity the organization's 'Christianness'.

1.2 Background: Significance of the Study

Having been a missionary working with Christian international Non-Governmental Organizations (NGOs) and having also served as a pastor in a local church, I have developed a passion for this holistic kind of mission/ministry. While in the missions I believed in integral mission and served holistically. In my reading of the gospels, especially Matthew 9:35–38 and Luke 4:18–19, it appears that Jesus ministered all-inclusively and that his desire is geared towards the all-inclusiveness of mission. The holistic nature of the ministry of Jesus seems to me to be exemplified in the gospels (i.e. Matthew and Luke for the sake of this study). Therefore, it became obvious that in order to enhance my teaching ministry, I needed to engage in a research project at PhD level to investigate the concept of mission drift in Christian NGOs/NPOs on the basis of their missional holistic transformations and wholistic developments in the light of the all-inclusive ministry of Jesus on earth as a mission in the gospels. This is the reason why I decided to undertake this missiological research on Christian NGOs and NPOs' mission drift, thus assessing the holistic missional transformations and developments of these organizations among the poor.

---

14. Bush, "Paradigm Shifts," 111–118.

Since these empirical research investigations have revealed the presence of mission drift, I dealt with the issue by finding out how Christian faith-based agencies are dealing with the concept in their mission of holistic welfare, transformation and development among the poor. Equally, in considering the presence of mission drift in parachurch agencies (see chapter 4), the study explored ways to avoid 'drfiting' (see section 4.3).

1.3 State of Research and Research Problem

1.3.1 Preliminary Literature Study

This preliminary literature review is further developed in chapter 2 of this thesis. However, there are five main categories of literature that I have consulted to conduct this research project. Firstly, literature focusing on the issue of mission drift and its potential causes and consequences, both in past and present Christian faith-based organizations and institutions. Bennett and Savani; Copestake; Edwards; Eurich; Greer; Jones; Ma, Jing and Han; Pallant; Lin; and Ronsen and Woolnough point out the unspoken crisis of mission drift that Christian faith-based institutions, such as evangelical missions, churches and Christian charitable organizations are facing in today's mission work,[15] while Ott stresses the paradigm shift in the theology of mission.[16]

The second group of literature that I used for this analysis focused on the exegetical commentaries on the gospels in order to investigate the extent of the holistic nature of the mission of Jesus on earth. To do so, I have chosen Matthew 9:35–38 and Luke 4:18–19 as a biblical framework for this research analysis. The choice of texts from Matthew and Luke seemed to me to be summarizing and adequately presenting Jesus's holistic mission, integrating both the spiritual and social aspects of what he performed during his earthly service. I have justified the selection of these two passages in section 2.4 of this empirical research study. The following are the key commentaries I have

---

15. Bennett and Savani, "Surviving Mission Drift," 217–231; Copestake, "Mission Drift," 20–25; Edwards, "Faithfull Innovation," 1–153; Eurich, "Diaconia under Mission Drift," 58–65; Greer and Horst, *Mission Drift*, 15–67; Jones, "The Multiple Sources," 299–307; Ma, Jing, and Han, "Predicting Mission Alignment," 24–33; Pallant, *Keeping Faith*, ; Lin, *Countering Mission Drift*, ; Ronsen, *Mission Drift?* ; and Woolnough, "Christian NGOs," 195–205.

16. Ott, *Beyond Fragmentation*, ; Ott, "Evangelical Theology" 141–154; Ott, "Matthew 28:16–20"; and Ott, *Understanding and Developing Theological Education*.

consulted amongst others: Allison; Bruce; Butler; Longman III, Garland, Carson, Wessel, and Strauss; Clarke; Davies and Allison; Fitzmyer; France; Gooding; Green; Hahn; Keener; Koech; Lange and van Oosterzee; Tannehill; Uwaegbute; Weber; and Weren.[17] These commentaries brought in some context to enhance understanding of biblical holism and especially holisticalization regarding Jesus's earthly ministry as reported by Matthew and Luke.

The third group I chose from the literature consulted emphasizes the current debate on biblical holism, particularly discussions pertaining to the 'Lausanne Movement' and explores John Stott's writings; Birdsall and Brown; Dahle, Dahle and Jørgensen; Davies-Kildea; Fujino; George; Heldt; Kesis; Kuhn; Pope Francis; Ott; Tizon; Unruh and Sider; Steward; and Woolnough.[18] This group of literature also includes the WCC publications, which promote world evangelization and urge the necessity of the church and parachurch NGOs/NPOs to witness the full and holistic gospel to the entire world.[19]

In addition, I drew my attention to the fourth category of literature focusing on contextualization of the gospel's holistic message relating to the paradigm shifts engaged by Christian organizations in order to evaluate their

---

17. Allison, *Studies in Matthew*; Bruce, *The Synoptic Gospels*; Butler, *Holman New Testament Commentary*; Longman III et al., *The Expositor's Bible Commentary*; Clarke, "Faith Matters"; Davies and Allison, *A Critical and Exegetical Commentary*, ; Fitzmyer, *The Gospel According to Luke*, France, *The Gospel of Matthew*; Gooding, *According to Luke*; Green, *The Theology of the Gospel*; Hahn, *Matthew*; Keener, *The IVP Bible Background Commentary*; Koech, "The Spirit Motif 154–176; Lange and van Oosterzee, *A Commentary on the Holy Scriptures: Luke*; Tannehill, *The Shape of Luke's Story* ; Uwaegbute, "A Challenge of Jesus," 143–159; Weber, *Holman New Testament Commentary: Matthew*; Weren, *Studies in Matthew's Gospel*.

18. Stott, *Christian Mission in the Modern World*; Stott, *The Lausanne Covenant*. See also Birdsall and Brown, "The Cape Town Commitment," 165–224; Dahle, Dahle and Jørgensen, *The Lausanne Movement*; Davies-Kildea, *Faith in Action*; Fujino, "Lausanne III"; George, "Joined and Knit Together," 397–409; Heldt, "Revisiting the '*Whole Gospel*'," 149–172; Kesis, "Wholistic or Holistic?," 63–70; Kuhn, "Toward a Holistic Approach,"; Francis, "*Evangelii Gaudium*,"; Ott, "Matthew 28:16–20"; Tizon, *Transformation After Lausanne*; Tizon, *Whole and Reconciled*; Unruh and Sider, *Saving Souls, Serving Society*; Steward, *Biblical Holism*; Woolnough, "Christian NGOs" 195–205.

19. The WCC (World Council of Churches) is a worldwide Christian interchurch, ecumenical and non-governmental organization of social interest and of a denominational character, founded in 1948, in Amsterdam, Netherlands, which sees itself as a "fellowship of churches which confess the lordship of Jesus Christ as God and Savior according to the Scriptures and strive to respond together to their common vocation for the glory of the one God: Father, Son and Holy Spirit." (Harmon, *Ecumenism Means You too*, 97; see also Roberson, *Oriental Orthodox-Roman Catholic Interchurch*, 81). The objective of the WCC is harmony among Christians through a common witness, *concrete* joint achievements and Christian services. See therefore, Keum, *Together Towards Life*; Gros, Best and Fuchs, *Growth in Agreement III*.

holistic missional development. This literature includes Bosch; Escobar; George; Gustafson; Heldt; Hesselgrave; Kuhn; Myers; Newbigin; Padilla; Hesselgrave; Russel; Torry; Woolnough; and Wright.[20] And lastly, I consulted literature focusing on the theories and spectrums related to, and having a high propensity to triggering the occurrence of mission drift, as follows (Barnett and Stein, Bess and Dee, DiMaggio and Powell, DiMaggio, Jacobs, Jakobs, Scott).[21] This fifth category of literature are chiefly employed in chapter 6 of this book in discussion with the findings of this research.

1.3.2 Evaluation of the Research Problem

I have undertaken this research in order to assess the concept of mission drift in Christian faith-based NGOs/NPOs in the light of the holistic nature of Jesus's earthly ministry. In this analysis, I wanted to study the holistic mission of Christian NGOs/NPOs in relief and development in order to evaluate the claim that contemporary Christian mission is in crisis and that missionary organizations slowly slide away from their core purpose and inevitably are carried away from their identity, as Greer and Horst[22] describe the concept. According to Ronsen's claim, "Some Christian mission organizations have become relatively unrelated to the Christian context and the proclamation of the gospel and thus drift away from integral mission objectives,"[23] which consist of serving the poor while proclaiming the Word.[24] Thus, Jørgensen argues, "In the course of the century, mission has increasingly struggled with how, on the one hand, to be relevant to and involved in the world and, on

---

20. Bosch, *Transforming Mission*, Escobar, *The New Global Mission*; Escobar, *La Mission*; George, "Joined and Knit Together," 397–409; Gustafson, "The Church and Holistic Ministry," 80–85; Heldt, "Revisiting the *'Whole Gospel,'*" 149–172; Hesselgrave, and Stetzer, *Mission Shift*; Hesselgrave, and Rommen, *Contextualization*; Hesselgrave, *Communicating Christ Cross-Culturally*; Kuhn, "Toward a Holistic"; Myers, *Walking with the Poor*; Newbigin, *The Pen Secret: An Introduction*; Padilla, *"Holistic Mission,"*; Russell, "Christian Mission Today," 23–98; Torry, *Managing Religion,*; Torry, *Citizen's Basic Income*; Woolnough and Ma, *Holistic Mission*; Wright, Brown, and Newman, *John Stott: Pastor, Leader and Friend*.

21. Barnett and Stein, *Sacred Aid*; Bess and Dee, *Understanding College and University*; DiMaggio and Powell, "The Iron Cage Revisited," 147–60; DiMaggio and Powell, *The New Institutionalism*; DiMaggio, "The New Institutionalisms," 696–705; Jacobs, *Mapping Strategic Diversity*; Jakobs, *Corporate Standardization*; Scott, *Institutions and Organizations*.

22. Greer and Horst. *Mission Drift*, 18.

23. Ronsen, *Mission Drift?*, 3.

24. Hoover, *Mapping Church Missions*, 23; and Unruh and Sider, *Saving Souls, Serving Society*, 132.

the other hand, how to maintain its identity in Christ."[25] This seems to be an ongoing challenge.

It can be presumed that the central aspect of the problem of mission drift has evolved from the development of a diversity of 'mission theologies'. These are probably the product of two controversial schools of thought: the Evangelization-Only school, and the Humanitarization-Only school. Seen from a biblical perspective (e.g. Matt 9:35–38 and Luke 4:18–19), these schools appear to have formed their theologies with no regard for using the exemplar of the holistic earthly ministry of Jesus as the mission guideline 'par excellence' (see my arguments in sections 2.4, 4.2.2, 5.6 and 5.8). This concept of mission drift needs to be critically assessed to determine whether it is a phenomenon that could plunge Christian NGOs/NPOs into a missional and existential crisis. Therefore, I have delt with mission drift in NGOs/NPOs by analysing their various mission statements and how they deal with the concept/issue in bringing hope and relief to the poor. In order to do so, I took the earthly ministry of Jesus as a standard to evaluate the issue of mission drift and the holistic welfare, transformations and developments intended and provided by Christian faith-based agencies. I have therefore analysed and criticized both the original mission statement and the current practices of Christian organizations in light of the earthly ministry of Jesus. Aware of contextual issues that these international church-related agencies face wherever they serve, I have dealt with them in chapter 4.

1.4 Research Questions

At the outset of this empirical research, the following guiding questions were articulated; however, I found it legitimate to be open for other aspects that could emerge in the process of investigation. This research aims to contribute to scholarship by seeking to find answers to the following Empirical Unknown (EU) and to the auxiliary Research Questions (RQ):

EU: In what ways do parachurch agencies face the crisis of mission drift in their mission activities? I thereby wanted to investigate the holistic missional commitment of Christian relief and development work among the poor in bringing hope to the world, and then evaluate the concept/crisis of mission

---

25. Fagerli, Jørgensen, and Thoresen, *Witnessing to Christ*, 5.

drift among those Christian faith-based NGOs/NPOs. Provided that mission drift is verified, the investigation also sought to analyze if the organization has deliberately or non-deliberately shifted away from its original mission objectives. The main research question (EU) and secondary research questions (RQs) are dealt with in chapters 4 (Empirical Findings), 5 (Research Discussion) and 6 (Interconnected Theories and Spectrums). Secondary questions have not been the focus of a chapter because of the structure of this empirical research at hand.

RQ1: Do Christian faith-based international mission organizations subscribe to biblical holism, implement and practise the holistic-incarnational mission as exemplified in Matthew 9:35–38 and Luke 4:18–19? Through answering this study question, I intended to find out what parachurch agencies say about the evangelistic-missionary and socio-humanitarian works of Christian mission among the poor.

RQ2: Have these Christian organizations changed their mission statements, lost their Christian faith-based identity, compromised on their mission objectives, and become humanitarian agencies? I would like to evaluate this concept to determine if there is an issue of internal 'secularization'.[26] The study is to be done in a way that Christian NGOs/NPOs can explain how they may struggle with mission drift issues looking at their mission statements.

RQ3: Are these Christian faith-based NGOs/NPOs constrained to undergo the challenge and issue of mission drift, or are they delighted to assume it as a paradigm shift in their mission objectives? Through this question, the purpose was to examine the various prospects, opportunities, constraints and challenges that Christian relief and development workers face and what their analysis of the concept of mission drift is.

RQ4: Do Christian missionary NGOs/NPOs identify potential causes and consequences of mission drift on the organization's holistic missional values, Christian identity, and original mission objectives?

---

26. The term 'secularization' denotes the historical process through which the church and parachurch agencies (and religions in general) lose their spiritual, biblical, and cultural meaning, values, purpose, and relevance in modern societies. As a result, the significance and role of faith becomes restricted, unwanted, and unidentifiable in a 'Post-Christendom' societal context. Therefore, secularization occurs within a Christian NGO/NPO when spiritual relevance, biblical values and Christian identity are replaced with irreligious ideologies compromising their God-given vision and original holistic mission objectives.

RQ5: What do these organizations say about contextualization in relation to making decisions about paradigm shifts and how do they integrate Jesus's holistic mission concept (evangelistic and socio-humanitarian) in their Christian mission identity, praxis and objectives in order to avoid the crisis of mission drift?

1.5 Research Procedure

I decided that the appropriate research technique to conduct this empirical investigation was 'multiple case design,' using an interview guide, which consisted of a questionnaire of fifteen questions (see appendix 1). The procedure involved an in-depth empirical qualitative sampling study. This has been comprehensively detailed in chapter 3. The sampling study involved the following seven parachurch agencies: Compassion International, Latin Link International, Medair International, MEOS Interkulturelle Dienste, Mercy Ships International, Service de Mission et d'Entraide (SME), and Youth With A Mission (YWAM). All of these were investigated using a multiple case-study approach.

1.6 Scientific Aim of the Research

This research aimed to investigate the susceptibility of parachurch agencies to mission drift when operating strategic paradigm shifts, when confronted with threats to its existential survival, when engaging in fundraising and partnership with the non-Christian world, and when desiring growth. Therefore, the study has examined ways to deal with the issue in the light of the earthly ministry of Jesus as recorded, for instance, in Matthew 9:35–38 and Luke 4:18–19.

Answering these research questions would take me a step forward towards verifying or falsifying the theory of mission drift in Christian faith-based NGOs/NPOs. Since the phenomenon of mission drift was proven to be real by the study, then it would help scholarship through understanding the concept and suggesting some recommendations towards dealing with the issue. The introduction of a new study with its recommendations concerning the relationship between the organization's 'Christianness' (its Christian identity) and its holistic works of transformation and development can also enhance knowledge and schorlarship's ability to describe and analyse occurrences of mission drift within faith-based agencies. Ultimately, an analysis of mission drift investigated in the light of the earthly ministry of Jesus can also be useful to parachurch agencies, including their founders, leaders, workers and donors. The study can certainly help them realize when their agencies are particularly susceptible to mission drift and suggest measures to deal with the issue and minimize the risk of 'drifting'.

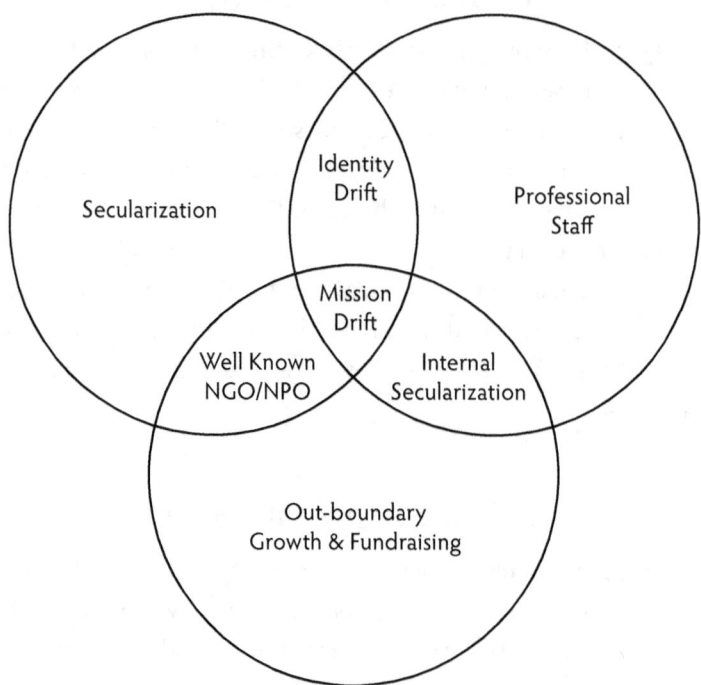

Figure 1.1: Schematic Theoretical Framework and Overlapping Domains

Based on a comprehensive literature review from various experiences of mission drift in CFB-NGOs/NPOs by Ronsen, on pioneering theoretical work by Greer and Horst, and on recent empirical research works by Gallet, Edwards and Lin,[27] this study has contributed to an understanding of a phenomenon in the Christian milieu that is little understood. The following diagram schematizes the present research theoretical framework. It

---

27. Ronsen, *Mission Drift?*; Greer and Horst, *Mission Drift*; Wilma Gallet, "Christian Mission"; Edwards, "Faithfull Innovation"; and Lin, "Countering Mission Drift."

introduces the overlapping domains and interrelated concepts (secularization, non-Christian professional staff, out-boundary growth and fundraising) that guided this study and determined the things I was looking for and therefore wanting to measure.

1.7 Research Limits of Scope

The limits of a qualitative research study come from its shortcomings, influences, conditions, and flaws. These may result from a small sample size, unavailability of sources, or flawed methodology. No research study, including this thesis, is completely limitless. In this regard, I made choices to delimit this research boundaries. Any identified potential limitations that might influence the results of this investigation are mentioned below. In addition, I have set vital delimitations for the success of this research study.

1.7.1 Limitations of This Research

Although the impact of Christian organizations in Global South countries is known to be significant, the author of this study is limited by the fact that he cannot travel to those nations to conduct studies alongside the beneficiaries. This is chiefly due to time factors and limited financial resources that have compromised any possibility of my travelling to interview the beneficiaries where the selected agencies operate. Also, internet-based interaction with people on site is uneasy. Therefore, this study on "Dealing with Mission Drift in Parachurch Agencies" was not able to take into account on-site interviews and field investigations such as *interactionism*[28] with the recipients across the globe.

Due to the fact that the topic is sensitive and thought-provoking, the selection of samples has been extremely challenging. Some large, well-financed and well-known parachurch NGOs/NPOs which in my view could have benefited from the investigation on mission drift, have simply disallowed participation in the study. In some cases, even when the organization is favourable to the study, some individual participants within the NGO/NPO withdrew after

---

28. Interactionist perspective studies how individuals are shaped by Christian missionary organizations in a particular society.

having read the questionnaire, making collaboration with them and the data collection process even more complicated.

Multiple case design undeniably has common limitations in its consistency. The outcome results cannot fully be generalized to the wider population of Christian faith-based organizations. This could result in rendering replication difficult, primarily because the researcher's bias and his own subjective feeling,[29] may influence the findings of the study, and, secondly, because the participant agencies and the interviewees were identified through the personal networks of the researcher. However, due to the considerable advantages[30] that multiple case research techniques offer in studying the "complex and relatively unstructured and infrequent phenomena,"[31] the choice of this method was justified as worthwhile.

Obviously, another limitation is that, of the informants used in this research for data collection and documentation, the greater proportion are Europeans and Africans, rather than from other parts of the world; with the exception of a few from Latin America, which could have had a catalytic effect in terms of insights. The only way to avoid all potential sampling bias and personal values would have been to extend the identification process of parachurch agencies and interviewees beyond correspondence to on-site interviewing of all existing church-related agencies in the whole world. Manifestly, this would be unfeasible, given the scope of this research.

1.7.2 Delimitations of This Research

This multiple case study research limited itself to the seven parachurch agencies chosen (regardless of their denominational or theological traditions) as a target population for this research because I wanted to understand how to

---

29. John W. Creswell, *Educational Research*, 263, 280 and 284.

30. Multiple case research design offers considerable advantages that include the following: (1) The collection of more detail not easily obtainable by other experimental designs. (2) Richer and more extensive data than can be collected by other case research techniques. (3) A tendency to create a more convincing theoretical base and quality of investigation in "rare cases where large samples of similar participants are not available" (Eisenhardt and Graebner. "Theory Building from Cases, 27). (4) They provide, within the case study, the possibility of scientific experiments being conducted. (5) Case studies can help experimenters adapt ideas and produce novel hypotheses which can be used for later testing" (Eisenhardt and Graebner, 27). (6) They allow wider exploration of theoretical evolution and research questions (Eisenhardt and Graebner, 27). This list is not exhaustive.

31. Andrew Bennett and Colin Elman, "Case Study Methods," 171.

deal with the phenomenon of mission drift in order to improve standards of Christian holistic mission services. The study did not include investigations into other religions' involvement in socio-humanitarian missions or the impact on their beneficiaries because it does not help to understand mission drift from a Christian perspective. Likewise, the research did not purpose nor propose to evaluate non-Christian or secular humanitarian organizations except for those with Christian-faith-based beginnings. The present research was done within the boundary area of European, African, and Latin American Christian faith-based NGOs/NPOs whose founding objectives are based on holistic mission. Additionally, the researcher was not able to travel across the world to conduct a survey by the beneficiaries because this option would be too costly and financially unfeasible.

Further delimitation for this study is that the research interview excludes closed-ended questions (see section 1.9) from the investigation because they only give the interviewee the chance to answer with a simple "yes" or "no" indicating the extent to which he/she agrees or disagrees with a real-life situation. Such answers are not pertinent to this research. Despite geographical restriction and procedural boundaries, both the objective of the study and the exhaustiveness of the research were not affected because the impact evaluation on the receivers was not part of the purpose statement of this study.

1.8 Assumptions of This Research

Following Ronsen, Wittberg, Edwards and Gallet's arguments, as outlined below, I based the present underlying hypothesis for this study: All parachurch agencies to some degree face the disturbing phenomenon of mission drift and need to deal with it before their Christian identity is weakened. Mission drift is a phenomenon that can affect today's church-related mission agencies, which "may become relatively unrelated to the Christian context and the proclamation of the gospel and thus drift away from integral mission objectives, which are both to serve the poor and to proclaim the Christian gospel."[32] Wittberg cogently argues for the theory that when parachurch agencies take on potentially incompatible mission obligations, Christian identity

---

32. Ronsen, *Mission Drift?*, 3.

is likely to become confused and weakened.[33] It can also be presupposed that the necessity and pressures of fundraising, threats to the agencies' existence, and complicated and potentially compromising relationships with unbelieving donors have the potential to compromise the organization's Christian identity (Christian worldview) and lead to a gradual mission drift (this is further described in Literature Review under sections 2.1.2, 2.1.5; Empirical Research Findings 4.2.1, 4.2.4, 4.2.5, 5.7.1 and Research Discussion 5.1, 5.3). A widely accepted truth is the notion that "if church-related organizations are to avoid mission drift when accepting government funding, they need to continually revisit their *raison d'être* to ensure that there is synergy between the agenda and purposes of government and their church's mission."[34] This synergy needs to be discussed with respect to the organizational standards and based on biblical values.

Another noteworthy assumption is that employing unbelieving co-workers in a Christian faith-based organization can gradually lead to internal secularization, especially if they are involved in decision-making at management level. The challenges associated with employing unbelieving or non-Christian leaders who are not committed to the Christian organization's mission are that it will at some point result in Christian identity drift and lead to secularization;[35] this is explained in sections 2.2.5, 4.2.5, 4.3, and 5.7.2. And last but not least, I have hypothesized that focusing the church-related agency's mission statement as well as its field-services on the earthly ministry of Jesus as a holistic model based on the Scripture and framed by a Christian worldview would help remedy the issue of mission drift. This last assumption is substantiated more deeply in section 2.4.

1.9 Overview of the Following Chapters

Having introduced the research project in chapter 1, I followed this with the Literature Review, in chapter 2, in which I looked at scholarly descriptions of the phenomenon. I prefaced this review by giving a short overview of each

---

33. Wittberg, *From Piety to Professionalism*, 59.
34. Gallet, "Christian Mission." 91; see also Ray Cleary, *Reclaiming Welfare*; Judd, Robinson, and Errington, *Driven by Purpose*.
35. Gallet, 125–26; see also Edwards, "Faithfull Innovation," 9–13.

chapter of this empirical research. In chapter 3, I have shown systematically why multiple case study methods provided the most suitable research design for conducting this qualitative empirical investigation, which consisted of analyzing seven parachurch NGOs/NPOs working holistically (named in section 1.5). The results of this empirical investigation are presented in chapter 4 and discussed in chapter 5. As I have indicated earlier, in Chapter Two, I have reviewed literature and detailed the results of my study of previous empirical researches, publications and non-published documents related to the subject of mission drift in hybrid/holistic institutions.

In chapter 6, I identified several theories and spectrums emerging from this empirical research and showed how they interconnect with existing theories that specifically explain the circumstantial factors favourable to the development of mission drift in holistic parachurch organizations. Conclusions, implications, and recommendations were then summarized and communicated in detail in chapter 7.

CHAPTER 2

Literature Review

This chapter's first aim is to review the origin of mission drift in social entrepreneurship and in the mission of parachurch agencies by looking at how the concept is defined in hybrid ventures and church-related agencies, how scholars describe it in microfinance and in CFB-NGOs/NPOs, as well as the causes, consequences and challenges related to 'drifting.' Its second aim is to take hold of a thorough definition of what holistic parachurch agencies are, why they exist, their characteristics as Christian faith-based organizations, and their mission in the light of the holistic ministry of Jesus, and the challenges evangelical humanitarian NGOs/NPOs are confronted with in their attempt to offer Bible-based mission. Thirdly, it seeks to investigate the holistic mission debate in missiology, the implications of the concept of *Missio Dei* and the impact of the Lausanne Movement. This debate concerning missiology includes discussion of the 'evangelism-only' school as a mission in which 'soul-winners' operate, as well as the 'humanitarian-only' school as a mission where 'social-gospellers' are active. This description is helpful to understand the context in which parachurch agencies serve the poor holistically. Finally, the chapter aims to review exegetically the holistic earthly ministry of Jesus, using Matthew 9:35–38 and Luke 4:18–19 as a biblical framework. These biblical foundations are the point of reference for the assessment of the holistic activities of CFB-NGOs/NPOs and how an organizational identity can be formed based on Scripture. This consideration of identity formation in Jesus Christ is useful in understanding the concept of mission drift in parachurch organizations. Throughout the chapter, different theoretical frameworks are reviewed to create an understanding of mission drift.

2.1 Origination of the Concept of Mission Drift

In the area of social financial entrepreneurship (hybrid ventures), some scholars[1] have argued that Muhammad Yanus[2] was the first to pioneer the concept of hybrid microfinance[3] with the purpose of lending "tiny sums to the poorest of the poor, who were shunned by ordinary banks."[4] Some studies[5] have revealed that a significantly increasing number of hybrid entrepreneurial organizations (with a strategic combination of dual dimensions; social mission and revenue objective) are falling into mission drift and moving away from their social mandate towards a greater emphasis on profit, financial stability and efficiency.

There is a general consensus among scholars of social/financial entrepreneurship that the concept of mission drift – as championed in the empirical studies conducted in the area of hybrid organizations/ventures – is an important issue.[6] During recent decades, there has been an unprecedented explosion of articles and academic empirical research into examples of social entrepreneurship,[7] commonly known as hybrid ventures. All these studies have been done in non-Christian social/entrepreneurial organizations but,

---

1. Gurus, "Bio Professor Muhammad Yunus."

2. Professor of economics at Chittagong College and MTSU Tennessee, Dr Muhammad Yunus was a Bangladeshi Cabinet Minister, Banker, Chairman of Yunus Centre, Civil Society Leader, and Social Entrepreneur "who was awarded the Nobel Peace Prize for founding the Grameen Bank and pioneering the concepts of microcredit and microfinance." Andrea Bocelli, "CV of Professor Muhammad Yunus."

3. Microfinance is understood to be a category of financial services rendered to the poorest of poor people, especially women and small businesses who are unable to qualify for traditional banking services. In other words, microfinance offers financial services to social enterprises, thus providing small loans (microcredit) to poor clients, microinsurances, payment systems as well as savings and checking accounts. While targeting entrepreneurs who are too poor to access conventional bank loans, microfinancing includes microcrediting.

4. Lessing and Elkington, "Banker to the Poor."

5. Doherty, Haugh and Lyon, "Social Enterprises as Hybrid Organizations," 1–21; and Haigh et al., "Hybrid Organizations," 5–12.

6. Hybrid ventures are non-profit organizations such as social entrepreneurships that operate in microfinance while strategically combining social services and economic objectives with purpose to alleviate poverty.

7. James Copestake, "Mainstreaming Microfinance," 1721–1738; Jones, "The Multiple Sources," 299–307; Kar, "Sustainability and Mission Drift"; Dempsey, "Microfinance Mission Drift"; Shingadia, "Modern Canadian Universities,"; Chambers, "Growing a Hybrid Venture"; Rabi, "How Social Enterprises"; Jeter, "Exploring Mission,"; Roche, "The Hybrid Nature"; Battilana, "Cracking the Organizational Challenge," 1278–1305; Bergin, "A Dual Mission"; and Ma, Jing, and Han, "Predicting Mission Alignment," 24–33.

significantly they reveal the same phenomenon as in holistic parachurch agencies. Consequently, this concept is pertinent to this current empirical study and equally related to Christian faith-based organizations whose work is informed by certain notions of hybridity (spiritual-evangelistic and socio-humanitarian), namely the holistic approach to Christian mission.

2.1.1 Defining Mission Drift in Hybrid Ventures

To the question of what mission drift is, existing literature is unanimous in defining the concept. According to Potocan and Nedelko, the phenomenon occurs when there is "an inadequate situation for a non-profit organization (NPO), in which the trade-off (required by the need to generate its own revenue through social entrepreneurship, or to secure the funding from external sources) compromises the initial organizational objectives and mission."[8] For Armendáriz and Szafars, mission drift in microfinance institutions is an occurrence whereby a hybrid venture increases its normal loan size in order to reach out to richer customers/clients to the detriment of the poorest unbanked microfinance customers[9] for reasons that relate neither to cross-subsidization[10] nor to progressive lending.

Scholars have argued that mission drift occurs in hybrid ventures from the time when the original announced mission statement becomes unaligned with the organization's profit maximization objective, thus showing a visible reorientation from poorer to richer customers among existing consumers or a gradual and yet tangible shift in the composition of its new customers.[11] Jones describes how "a mission drift occurs when an organization compromises one of its missions to the benefit of profit. Usually this happens when a hybrid

---

8. Potocan and Nedelko, *Handbook of Research*, 21.

9. Armendáriz and Ariane Szafars, "On mission drift."

10. Cross-subsidization is the fact that a microfinance enterprise strategically charges higher prices or loan mortgages to wealthier clients or consumers in order to artificially offer lower prices or rates to the poorest customers. In other words, Engels explains that "an increase in average loan sizes may result from progressive lending, whereby microfinance clients reach out to higher credit ceiling based on their performance and demand. Also, average loan sizes may be higher resulting from cross-subsidization. Cross-subsidization means that an MFI (microfinance institution) reaches out to the wealthier unbanked, using larger average loan sizes, in order to finance a larger pool of poorest unbanked, using small average loan sizes." Engels, *Mission Drift*, 41.

11. Cull, Demirguç-Kunt and Morduch, "Financial Performance," 123; Mersland, and Strøm, "Microfinance Mission"; Engels, *Mission Drift*, 41, 50–51; and Kar, "Sustainability and Mission Drift," 11–12.

organization loses its focus on its mission and concentrates its efforts on making profits."[12] Following the same line of thought, Copestake defines mission drift as a retrospective conversion/alteration that consequently changes the stated mission objective and operational preferences to fit spontaneous performance outcomes.[13] Although hybrid institutions cope with both social mission and generating revenue/profit they may drift away if they follow only one aspect of the two mission dimensions,[14] as Jones explains. On the other hand, several scholars have mentioned that a hybrid organization may risk the opposite: the possibility of 'revenue drift,'[15] meaning that the agency is so focused on its social mission that it falls into economic mismanagement in order to sustain its operations.

2.1.2 Understanding Mission Drift in Microfinance

In the context of hybrid organizations, there is a plentiful amount of well researched studies on mission drift – studied in the context of social non-profit agencies. In hybrid NGOs, mission drift is often linked to growth-based and fundraising decision making, where the leaders decide to "focus on profits to the detriment of the social good."[16] For example, this happens when, while trying to grow, microfinance organizations shift their focus from a social mandate to more conventional business priorities.[17] Scholars unanimously report that resource providers and market conditions often drive hybrid ventures toward mission drift,[18] as echoed by Austin, Stevenson and Wei-Skillem:

> Social entrepreneurs and their organizations are often pulled into rapid growth by pressure from funders, demand for their products or services, and pushed by their social missions to meet those needs ... A key challenge for social entrepreneurs is to resist the powerful demand-pull for growth, and to be more

---

12. Jones, "The Multiple Sources," 304.
13. Copestake, "Mission Drift," 23, 25 and Copestake, "Mainstreaming Microfinance," 1725.
14. Jones, "The Multiple Sources," 299–307.
15. Trones, "Hybrid Organizations," 14; Jones, 305; and Ebrahim, Battilana, and Mair, "The Governance," 81–100.
16. Battilana et al., "In Search of," 51; and Ronsen, *Mission Drift?*, 89.
17. Battilana et al., 89; and Fritsch, Rossi and Hebb, "An Examination."
18. Hockerts and Wüstenhagen, "Greening Goliaths," 482; Nazarkina, "The Big Green," 9; and Mennillo, Schlenzig, and Friedrich, *Balanced Growth*, 11.

deliberate about planning a long-term impact strategy ... In some cases, growth may not be the best approach to achieve the organization's goals or to have the greatest social impact. Growth for the sake of growth has the potential to squander organizational resources and can actually detract from the organization's overall impact.[19]

According to Cornforth and Kar, mission drift is to be understood as the divergence from the NGO/NPO's main mission or purpose due to certain factors.[20] It is viewed as a process of major organizational change that the NGO/NPO undergoes. All microfinance enterprises, regardless of size and type, "have a mission which they seek to fulfil," and most hybrid venture models are designed to help reach this objective.[21] Nevertheless, Cornforth goes on to clarify the point that these changes happen most frequently in NGOs/NPOs that have a "social mission," such as "voluntary and non-profit organizations, social enterprises, hospital and educational bodies that diverge from their original mission."[22] This understanding of Cornforth goes in line with the preceding viewpoints.

It can therefore be theorized that hybrid ventures are not charitable organizations that fortuitously added a commercial aspect to their activities, but they are purposeful enterprises that have been created and designed to address social micro-financial issues,[23] to draw on the exposés of Jeanne Roche and Muhammad Yunus. Roche has suggested that "mission drift in a hybrid entrepreneurship context is best understood as a concept belonging to the field of organizational theory ... which supposes that both aspects of the hybrid nature are vital to the venture."[24] To further emphasize the point, Roche, while referring to other writers for support, points out that both the charity and business forms are vitally indispensable to hybrid ventures, "Neither can be

---

19. Austin, Stevenson, and Wei-Skillern, "Social and Commercial," 7.

20. Cornforth, "Understanding and Combating," 4; and Kar, "Sustainability and Mission Drift," 11, 110.

21. Rabi, "How Social Enterprises," 15.

22. Cornforth, "Understanding and Combating," 4.

23. Roche, "The Hybrid Nature," 44; Muhammad Yunus, *Creating a World*, 77–78; and Yunus, *Building Social Business*, 61.

24. Roche, "The Hybrid Nature," 43.

dismissed without a fundamental change to the model,"[25] and therefore their sustainability as hybrids depends equally on their business performance and on the development of their social mission[26] – a view well supported by Jeter, Battilana and Lee, and Cornforth.

Using this approach, Roche then redefines mission drift as the result of the inability of a hybrid venture to achieve its social mission or inversely its business goal.[27] In this context, the importance of social and business aspects of hybrid ventures are interdependent, as evidenced in the literature. This leads to the conclusion that the mission of a hybrid venture is not only about the impact of its socio-humanitarian and poverty-reduction activities but also its sustainability, a good way to avoid destructive causes which inevitably drive to mission drift.

2.1.3 Causes of Mission Drift

Mission drift occurs in hybrid ventures mainly because of strategic factors of a lucrative nature. These involve particular forces generated by the sources of funding (shareholders, owners, foundations, etc.), and are due to particular styles of governance and structure and the wider organizational culture and operational priorities,[28] argues Cornforth. Rabi asserts that "the friction in many cases, though, is the source of the funding."[29] From the same perspective, Jones outlines how mission drift arises from activities that are liable to cause a diversion of money, time and energy from the main mission of a hybrid venture.[30] Considering this change in direction or diversion in mission to be caused by environmental forces, Young argues that these forces compel hybrid organizations to consider "lucrative strategies which allow them to survive and grow."[31] In fact, hybrid ventures can be "tempted by financial pressures to shift their activities toward goals favored by various sources of

---

25. Roche, 43.

26. Jeter, "Exploring Mission"; Battilana and Lee, "Advancing Research," 397–441; and Cornforth, 3–20.

27. Roche, 44; see also Battilana and Dorado, "Building Sustainable Hybrid," 1419–1440; Kar, "Sustainability and Mission Drift"; Battilana and Lee, "Advancing Research," 397–441; Ebrahim, Battilana, and Mair, "The Governance," 81–100.

28. Cornforth, "Understanding and Combating," 4.

29. Rabi, "How Social Enterprises," 15–16; see also Young, "The State," 24.

30. Jones, "The Multiple Sources," 300.

31. Young, "The State of Theory," 24.

income,"³² says Young, because each donor expects compliance with his/her own criteria before he/she will finance an organization.

However, Young concludes that while funding is not the sole cause of whether mission drift happens in a hybrid venture, it remains a key determinant of mission drift.³³ Moreover, Rabi also adds that financiers of all stripes may claim influence and prerogative in the governance of an organization through "seats in the board or in a similar fashion."³⁴ Involving "different individuals with different competencies" may certainly lead to unnecessary influence, which may distract from the organization's original mission,³⁵ argues Billis. Rabi believes that a board made up of different competencies may direct the hybrid venture in a way that prioritizes their own economic interests, something evidently detrimental to social duty.³⁶ Due to the complexity of running a hybrid venture as it is, the presence of these investors as board members would constitute a challenge to the governance structures of the organization and its effectiveness,³⁷ as Young maintains.

Therefore, hybrid ventures are well advised to avoid the influence of these lucrative investors who come with expectations that the organization should comply with their own criteria. This may be achieved by a greater focus on the hybridity in terms of the equilibrium of the value generation aspect of the organization. The number of undermining influences within the organization has a direct bearing on the gravity of its problems and the consequences that flow from them.

2.1.4 Consequences of Mission Drift

Why is mission drift an issue in hybrid ventures? Mission drift can lead to unwanted consequences if the tangible benefits associated with pursuing a social mission are not in place, which could cripple and ultimately result in the failure of the hybrid venture. Both Chambers and Rabi have stated that mission drift can tarnish the reputation of an organization, threaten organizational culture, and jeopardize future funding since social-finance and

---

32. Young, 33.
33. Young, 30.
34. Rabi, "How Social Enterprises," 16.
35. Billis, *Hybrid Organizations*, 48–56.
36. Rabi, "How Social Enterprises," 16.
37. Young, "The State of Theory," 27.

grant-giving foundations may not agree with the newly redirected mission of the venture.[38] This could lead to the complete abandonment of the original mission or goals, thus creating internal friction within the organization. It can be summed up from the literature that mission drift in microfinance or hybrid ventures results from a clash between business value generation and social value generation. Rabi argues that the organization will end up "leaning further toward either one – which brings with it distinct and tangible benefits in one aspect, and detrimental losses in the other aspect."[39] In the literature, as Kar asserts, the concept of mission drift is frequently expressed as a phenomenal concern that unbalances the very heart of the organizational mission,[40] leading to the destruction of the essential nature of hybridity.

2.1.5 Defining Mission Drift in Parachurch Agencies

What is mission drift in CFB-NGOs/NPOs? In answering the question from a Christian organizational standpoint, I must start by looking into how parachurch agencies advertise their missions. What is the organization's mission statement? If I assume that a particular NGO/NPO states that its main mission or objective is to show God's love socially and spiritually, and therefore in a holistic manner, then instead of asking what mission drift is about, one may ask: what prompts the agency to focus so much on the socio-humanitarian dimension of its mission to the detriment of the spiritual, or the other way round? To answer this question, scholars provide two straightforward phrases to describe the phenomenon.[41] Firstly, "progressive and unintentional drifting," which relates to the view that the agency unwillingly and unwittingly but gradually moves away from its own mission statement. Secondly, "sudden and intentional drifting" which pertains to the idea that the leadership has decided to change direction for the purpose of growth and fundraising. These two descriptions are in line with the understanding of mission drift in parachurch agencies, even though the sudden form of mission drift does not often occur, as can be noticed in the literature.

---

38. Chambers, "Growing a Hybrid Venture," 37; and Rabi, "How Social Enterprises," 17.
39. Rabi, 17.
40. Kar, "Sustainability and Mission Drift," 11–12.
41. Ledesma and David-Casis, *Mission First*, 6; Ronsen, *Mission Drift*, 101; Grimes, Williams, and Zhao, "Anchors Aweigh," 29; Lin, "Countering Mission Drift," 25; and see also Chambers, "Growing a Hybrid Venture," and Cornforth, "Understanding and Combating,".

Relatively, mission drift refers to a phenomenon whereby a parachurch organization progressively "moves away from its original founding mission."[42] Scholars describe mission drift as an unspoken crisis facing Christian mission[43] that parachurch NGOs/NPOs have been shown to experience,[44] and as such "a phenomenon where faith-based organizations will inevitably drift from their founding mission, away from their core purpose and identity."[45] In an e-mail exchange, professor Bernhard Ott argues that the concept of mission drift refers to the problem of Christian Non-Governmental Organizations (NGOs) and/or Non-Profit Organizations (NPOs) having focused on human needs in the context of a firmly Christian view of holistic mission, 'drifting away' from their Christian and missiological foundations and thus becoming purely humanitarian relief agencies.[46] Furthermore, while drawing on the example of Harvard University and Yale University,[47] Greer and Horst describe how mission drift advances gradually like a current, pervasively carrying Christian agencies/institutions away from their core identity and purpose.[48] Edwards explains that for a parachurch NGO/NPO, the gradual and slow shift might open up possibilities for 'secularization' (see definition in section 1.4).[49] Moreover, since the drifting of an agency is hardly intentional but rather a slow process that often manifests itself in a subtle way through small graduated changes, management might not even realize the changes that are triggering the mission drift.[50] Greer and Horst describe the following with regard to the unintentionality of drifting:

---

42. Lin, "Countering Mission Drift," 25.
43. Greer and Horst, *Mission Drift*, 15.
44. Lin, "Countering Mission Drift," 25.
45. Greer and Horst, *Mission Drift*, 15.
46. Bernhard Ott, e-mail message to author, 03 October 2019.
47. See the histories of these two universities on their respective websites. In the vein of these examples, Greer and Horst reported that "at the 350th anniversary celebration of Harvard, Steven Muller, former president of Johns Hopkins University, didn't mince words: 'The bad news is the university has become godless'" (*Mission Drift*). Moreover, Summers adds that "the president of Harvard confirmed Muller's assessment, acknowledging, 'Things divine have been central neither to my professional nor to my personal life.'" (Summers, "Convocation of the Divinity School of Harvard University.")
48. Greer and Horst, 18.
49. Edwards, "Faithfull Innovation," 7.
50. Edwards, 7.

Most organizations have not willingly, consciously, changed direction. Most have not volitionally chosen to soften their Christian distinctiveness. Neither Harvard nor Yale held a 'mission change day' where they mapped out their new identity. Instead, they drifted quietly, gradually, and slowly. And one day, they hardly resembled the institutions their founders intended.[51]

Far from being isolated incidents without consequences, scholars reveal that the changes over time at Harvard and Yale Universities have, regrettably, had a dramatic effect on the institutions, which have irreversibly become secular. Remembering the past of these universities, Greer and Horst state that "only 80 years after its founding, Harvard's identity was shifting."[52] Ringenberg argues that a group of New England pastors, having realized that Harvard had drifted too far away from its original mission and being concerned by the secularization they sensed at Harvard, counterattacked in 1701 by establishing a new college, which was viewed as a stronghold of Christian higher education.[53] Greer and Horst, recalling that history, state:

> Clergyman Cotton Mather approached a wealthy philanthropist who shared their concerns. This man, Elihu Yale, financed their efforts in 1718, and they named the college after him, the institution today known as Yale University. Yale's motto was not just *Veritas* (truth) like Harvard, but *Lux et Veritas* (light and truth). These pastors hoped to avoid the drift they saw at Harvard. But today, neither Harvard nor Yale resembles the universities their founders envisioned . . . Their founders were unmistakably clear in their goals: academic excellence and Christian formation. Today, they do something very different from their founding purpose. What happened to Harvard and Yale reflects the reality of Mission Drift.[54]

---

51. Greer and Horst, *Mission Drift*, 22.
52. Greer and Horst, 17.
53. Ringenberg, *The Christian College*, 39; see also Yale University's history on its website.
54. Greer and Horst, *Mission Drift*, 18.

The concept of mission drift in parachurch agencies is not simply the concern of practitioners,[55] as Reimer and Eurich state, but has been argued about and studied by many erudite minds. Apart from the continual occurrence of mission drift, scholars also point out the more sudden effect of the phenomena that brings about secularization. Mission drift, therefore, also implies suddenly losing sight of fundamental purposes, mission concepts, values and culture, and dedicating resources to priorities alien to the original vision, thus upsetting the stability between values and mission,[56] affirms Shingadia. It has been concluded by both Shingadia and Phills that becoming aware of mission drift allows parachurch agencies to gauge the direction and the significance of an organization's mission in order to escape secularization.[57] Edwards – as well as Sommerville – declare that the danger of mission drift leading to secularization can loom over CFB-NGO/NPOs; the danger that they might be transformed into institutions with a totally secular worldview that denies their original purpose is part of the challenge.[58] How then can the challenge of mission drift in these agencies be met?

2.1.6 The Challenge of Mission Drift in Parachurch Agencies

Finding a good integration between evangelism and social action represents a real challenge for parachurch agencies. Chester suggests that in conflating "proclamation and social action, . . . the ensuing problem is that this usually ends up with one aspect – and it is usually evangelism, being lost . . . , we must not do social action without evangelism."[59] Padilla – as well as Bosch – claim that social works must always be connected to an invitation to faith and a call to repentance.[60] Hence, evangelism and proclamation are at the core of a parachurch organization's mission,[61] as Gros, Best and Fuchs affirm. This

---

55. Reimer, "How Do We," 171; and Eurich, "Diaconia under Mission Drift," 58.
56. Shingadia, "Mission Drift," 3.
57. Shingadia, 31; and Phills, *Integrating Mission*, 15.
58. Edwards, "Faithfull Innovation," 7; see also Sommerville, "Secular Society," 252.
59. Moreover, Chester argues, "The Lausanne process, by giving primacy to proclamation, established that the clearest defined need of the poor is to be reconciled to God. Social services, although valuable and able to demonstrate the gospel, may be like a signpost with no direction if there is no proclamation." Chester, *Good News to the Poor*, 65.
60. Padilla, *Mission Between*, 56; and Bosch, *Transforming Mission*, 415.
61. Gros, Best and Fuchs, *Growth in Agreement*, 282.

lays a sacred and irreplaceable duty upon the Christian mission to include them. Consequently, they are not an 'optional extra'.

Henceforth, the prevalent concern for mission drift is not a matter for speculation. Greer and Smith write that "the concept of mission drift is not something new, as many initiatives based on the Christian faith have gradually steered away from their initial mission objective and become unrecognizable when compared with their original mission."[62] Furthermore, the two scholars argue that the reason for this in our contemporary world (modern society) can be traced to the tendency to equate social service and proclamation.[63] In line with this thought, Ronsen maintains that when the positive relation between the two strands of holistic mission is lost, the predictable result may rightly be called mission drift.[64] This situation represents an important challenge that causes concern and constitutes a potential crisis constantly facing parachurch organizations.

2.2 What are Parachurch NGOs/NPOs?

Most scholars would agree with the fact that the development of Christian faith-based organizations was a significant part of the church's ministry from its beginning and throughout the centuries.[65] Newbigin and Jambrek, advocate that the term "parachurch NGO or NPO" began to be used in an all-inclusive sense, frequently along with the word "mission", and its gradual development coincided with "the fact that the concept of mission in the sense of Christianization came into vogue only gradually, beginning with the 16th century"[66] and "gained stronger momentum at the end of the 18th and the beginning of 19th century."[67] Woolnough notes that individual believers responded to the gospel's holistic message through the needs of a suffering world by founding parachurch NGOs/NPOs to tackle development and relief

---

62. Greer and Smith, *The Poor*, 195.
63. Greer and Smith, 195.
64. Ronsen, *Mission Drift?*, 29.
65. Anthony and Benson, *Exploring the History*, 343; Betz, *Religion Past*, 340; McGrath, *Christianity: An Introduction*, 171; Osborn, *The Faith*, 77 and see also Noll, Bebbington and Rawlyk, *Evangelicalism*.
66. Lesslie Newbigin, *Sign of the Kingdom*, 12.
67. Jambrek, "Christian Witness," 188.

problems around the globe on the basis of Christian convictions.[68] Responding to the American Society of Mission's views on Christian social development and humanitarian relief involvement, McGravran warns that many of the organizations that they represent have purposely lessened or denied the mandate of the Great Commission (e.g. to evangelize) and instead favored social humanitarian works.[69] McGravran's argument cautions against the danger of giving pre-eminence to improving human existence, which is seen as the 'lion' that threatens to devour the character and purpose of missionary work by deflecting attention away from propagation of the Christian faith in Jesus Christ as God and savior, and from discipling people.[70] Parachurch agencies have been described as "fundamental building blocks of modern society" and "basic vehicles through which collective action occurs."[71] They are categorized as goal-directed since they engage in social welfare and evangelism, build social systems, meet human needs and maintain the boundaries of spiritual values. This section outlined a definition, and various characteristics of parachurch agencies. I delineated their directions of travel towards fulfilling their goals, and their challenges in the pursuit of good among the poor, providing basic perspectives to be followed throughout this dissertation.

2.2.1 Defining Parachurch Agencies: NGOs/NPOs

As suggested by Brown and Silk the term "parachurch" is used to describe Christian faith-based agencies that serve outside the built and organizational structures of the church, to engage in evangelism and social welfare.[72] They are often national and/or international, and mostly evangelical or cross-denominational, seeking to come alongside the church, to provide services and missions that individual churches may not be able to engage in. There is a consensus among scholars, arguing that a parachurch agency is any faith-based organization that derives inspiration and direction from the biblical teachings and principles of the Christian faith or from a particular school of

---

68. Woolnough, "Christian NGOs," 195.
69. McGravran, "Missiology Faces," 335.
70. McGravran, 339; Escobar, "Missiology Faces," 339; Hesselgrave, "Missiology Faces," 349; and Scherer, "Missiology Faces," 347.
71. Aldrich and Ruef, *Organizations Evolving*, 1.
72. Brown and Silk, *The Future*, 28; see also Reid, *Introduction to Evangelism*, 283.

thought within Christian belief.[73] At a minimum, as Scott declares, Christian Faith-Based NGOs/NPOs must be in liaison with an organized Christian assembly either in the form of a particular faith ideology, or by drawing in leadership, staff and volunteers from a particular church.[74] Other qualities that qualify an NGO/NPO as a Christian faith-based organization are being initiated by a Christian foundation and having biblically oriented mission statements, or receiving substantial support from at least one particular Christian faith denomination.[75] It is important to note that parachurch organizations are influenced in their relief and development mission by the values of their sponsoring religious institutions,[76] declares Olarinmoye. Clarke classifies Christian faith-based organizations on the basis of function and/or objective and develops a five-fold typology as follows:

1. "Faith-Based Representative Organizations" also called 'Apex Bodies,'[77] which represent the members of the faith and defend them by arrangement with the state;
2. "Faith-Based Charitable or Development Organizations,"[78] which aim to mobilize the faithful in order to fund poverty alleviation initiatives and manage development activities. They are mostly related to faith-based representative subsidiaries and are the most easily visible form of parachurch institutions in the developing countries;
3. "Faith-Based Socio-political Organizations,"[79] which understand and deploy faith as a political paradigm: mobilizing and organizing social groups on the basis of faith while also pursuing impactful political ambitions, promoting faith as a socio-cultural paradigm and connecting various social groups on the grounds of religious cultural identities;

---

73. Olarinmoye, "Faith-Based Organizations," 3; Buckley and Dobson, *Humanitarian Jesus*, 15; and Clarke and Jennings, *Development*, 279.
74. Scott, *The Roundtable*, 2.
75. Scott, 2.
76. Olarinmoye, "Faith-Based Organizations," 3.
77. Clarke, "Faith Matters," 4.
78. Clarke, "Faith Matters," 4.
79. Clarke, 4.

4. "Faith-Based Missionary Organizations,"[80] which spread faith values by actively seeking converts, stimulating the faith, and who engage with and support other faith agencies on the basis of Christian values and principles;
5. "Faith-Based Radical, Illegal or Terrorist Organizations,"[81] which stimulate militant or radical forms of faith identity. They promote illegal practices on the basis of their beliefs and engage in violent acts or armed struggle, which they legitimize on the basis of faith.

Olarinmoye argues that organizations displaying a high-level of Christian faith involvement in their mission can be referred to as "faith-saturated" while those showing a low level of religious involvement are referred to as a "faith-secular partnership."[82] Moreover, Olarinmoye maintains that a healthy parachurch mission exists primarily to promote and carry on a 'Bible-based' ministry of the church outside of its physical structures and forms.[83] In the same perspective, Ferris states with conviction that Parachurch NGOs/NPOs are faith-based agencies that operate from a Christian religious point of view while seeing the need to work with the unchurched or non-Christian communities regardless of religious boundaries.[84] Based on what has been said, it can be concluded that the mission of these CFB-NGOs/NPOs is to serve by restoring the dignity of the poor regardless of their belief system, and by passionately bringing the easy yoke of Jesus to all facets of society.

2.2.2 Defining Parachurch Microfinance in Mission

By their inherent nature, parachurch microfinance organizations are different from the secular 'hybrid ventures' active in social welfare organizations. Microfinance in Christian mission aspires to have an effect on poverty. Scholars suggest that Christian microfinance shows its potential when viewed as a vehicle in parachurch holistic mission focusing upon community empowerment and social needs.[85] This sub-chapter in this review raises scholarly

---

80. Clarke, 4.
81. Clarke, 4.
82. Olarinmoye, "Faith-Based Organizations," 4.
83. Olarinmoye, 4.
84. Ferris, "Faith-Based," 317.
85. Backues, "Interfaith Development," 75; and Woolnough and Ma, *Holistic Mission*, 177.

concern about whether Christian microfinance has the potential to alleviate both spiritual and material poverty. The review aims to identify possible main drivers for mission drift in this context. An account of biblical-spiritual and socio-economic aspects of poverty as well as the role and performance of Christian microfinance in social action are going to be studied.

2.2.2.1 Christian Microfinance and a Biblical-Theological Perspective of Poverty

There has been a significant drift in microfinance industry in that, from being chiefly a charitable movement directed by NPOs, "It has now become a major industry so that multinational banks such as Citibank see microfinance as a profit opportunity."[86] Numerous microfinance organizations have been transformed from philanthropic to profit-oriented ventures. In this business framework, Christian microfinance NGOs/NPOs operate endeavoring to make a tangible difference while embracing and transmitting Christian values as a channel of holistic mission.[87] Literature defining the nature of poverty reports that "the poor are the main target group of Christian microfinances: its *raison d'être* is to improve the material and spiritual situation of the poor."[88] Therefore, to establish the occurrence of mission drift pertaining to this core objective of Christian microfinance, it is necessary to understand how the biblical-theological perspectives on the poor in relation to Christian initiatives are presented within the Christian microcredit community.

The poor, says Ronsen, are seen as being the first target group for Christian microfinance, and parachurch mission in general.[89] The priority of the poor, according to Ronsen, is emphasized by Jesus himself in the synagogue of Nazareth when he refers to Isaiah 61:1–2,[90] as related by the evangelist Luke: "The Spirit of the Lord is on me, because he has anointed me to proclaim good news to the poor. He has sent me to proclaim freedom for the prisoners and recovery of sight for the blind, to set the oppressed free, to proclaim the year of the Lords' favour" (Luke 4:16–19). The good news proclaimed by Jesus

---

86. Ronsen, *Mission Drift?* 39.
87. Ronsen, 40.
88. Ronsen, 41.
89. Ronsen, 42.
90. Ronsen, 42.

gave people a chance to escape from the "poverty trap, extended to them an opportunity to start anew with their lives"[91] and introduced the era of salvation as the cusp of the coming of the kingdom of God, as Green points out.

One of the charges against microfinance, as Ledesma and David-Casis argue, is that the client base progressively "tends to be better off than originally planned, and well above the absolute poverty line."[92] Nevertheless, Green explains that πτωχός (poor: transliterated *ptochos*) is not to be understood only as a reality in a socio-economic context according to contemporary measures for material poverty, but also as referring to spiritually poor people, destitute and excluded people with a dishonourable status in society.[93] In the context of microfinance (microcredit and microassurance), Ronsen concludes that the idea of mission drift describes how hybrid ventures in order to maintain financial stability often slowly drift away from serving needy people.[94] Furthermore, he employs an extended use of the term mission drift to "describe the extent to which microfinance activities run by Christian mission organizations may, for various reasons, also drift away from the integral mission objective of sharing the gospel of Christ and leading poor people into a process of spiritual transformation."[95] It can be observed, based on the preceding argument that the socio-economic aspects of poverty serve as a vehicle to enforce the holistic mission of parachurch microfinance organizations.

2.2.2.2 Socio-Economic Context of Poverty Facing Microfinance

Leading development experts such as Chambers and Friedman assign the term 'poverty' to households that are powerless and incapable of breaking out of the 'poverty trap', a reading that parallels the biblical understanding.[96] From the socio-economic perspective, Friedman carefully labels significant socio-economic boundaries that impact the absolutely poor in society. They are unable to improve their economic situation, whether that pertains to their skills, their possibilities and knowledge for self-development, or to instruments of work and livelihood, financial resources, social networks, or even

---

91. Green, *Theology of the Gospel*, 78.
92. Ledesma and David-Casis, *Mission First*, 6.
93. Green, *Theology of the Gospel*, 82.
94. Ronsen, *Mission Drift?* 101.
95. Ronsen, 101.
96. Chambers, *Rural Development*, 103; and Friedman, *Empowerment*, 26–29.

the use of their free time. In other words, "the poor are basically characterized by powerlessness and lack of access to social power."[97] Chambers, in his approach, suggests a description of the nature of poverty that designates five interlocking causes, each an aspect of the state of the poor:

> *Material poverty*, reflecting the lack of an asset base; *physical weakness*, reflecting lack of health services and so on; *isolation*, indicating that individuals are excluded from the educational and financial system; *vulnerability*, reflecting a high degree of sensitivity to changing circumstances, such as floods, and limited reserves and choices; and *powerlessness*, reflecting their lack of political influence in society and their exposure to exploitation.[98]

The various causes reinforce themselves and deeply trap individuals or households in a poverty cycle from which is hard to break out. Consequently, there appears to be a multifaceted description of poverty that involves a network of uneasy interlocking situations of life at both the personal and societal levels,[99] as Ronsen argues. He states that poverty might be viewed in terms of inequalities in the global systems that regulate financial flows, trade and investments, which affect the poor regardless of the country where they might be living and which makes the situation even more difficult.[100] In view of the preceding arguments, the mission of Christian microfinance NGOs/NPOs consists of responding to the socio-economical aspect of poverty while complementarily offering solutions to the spiritual needs of the poor.

2.2.2.3 Spiritual Context of Poverty Facing Microfinance

The nature and causes of poverty described above in section 2.2.2.2 show that poor people are in a cycle that is too complicated for them to break out of. Although poverty is defined in terms of the socio-economic context, scholars also explain that the poor do not rely uniquely on material improvement for happiness. Green explains that when Jesus proclaims "good news to the poor", this is not just related to helping the poor improve materially,

---

97. Friedman, *Empowerment*, 67.
98. Chambers, 103–104; and see also Ronsen, 46; Johnson and Rogaly, *Microfinance and Poverty*, 10; and Hulme and Mosley, *Finance Against Poverty*, 2.
99. Ronsen, *Mission Drift?* 47.
100. Ronsen, 47; see also Copestake et al., *Money with a Mission*, 25–27.

but in a broader sense "the good news" pertains to the bringing together of physical, social and spiritual release as a whole.[101] Moreover, he asserts that "the 'release' effect is of great significance in understanding Jesus's ministry, and that Luke portrays both forgiveness and healing in social terms to match their more evident spiritual and physical overtones."[102] Later, Green goes on to argue that the use of the term 'blind' refers to a much larger and deeper understanding than the literal physical condition; it is also used allegorically in terms of receiving salvation and release, which implies inclusion in God's family.[103] Therefore, the reality of poverty in a biblical context is obviously a multifaceted problem requiring spiritual, physical and material release,[104] Ronsen sums up.

Myers argues that the cause of poverty is basically spiritual and that, without a convincing theology of sin, it is hard to find a totally inclusive way to describe poverty.[105] He further maintains that sin has stained all relationships so that "poverty is the result of relationships that do not work, that are not just, that are not for life, that are not harmonious or enjoyable. Poverty is the absence of shalom in all its meanings."[106] Moreover, Myers shows that this has evident implication for those involved in Christian microfinance within the social services and strategies of NGOs/NPOs. Christian faith-based "transformational developmental work must also include the provision that people should in some form hear the good news of the gospel and be given the chance to respond."[107] Through the 'good news' Jesus proclaims, there is a real way to escape from sin and a personal transformation that yields the hope of breaking out of poverty. To sum up, the role and performance of parachurch agencies operating in microfinance are much broader than simply improving the material condition of the poor, which explains why Christian Faith-Based NGOs/NPOs may be essential.

---

101. Green, *Theology of the Gospel*, 78.
102. Green, 78.
103. Green, 79.
104. Ronsen, *Mission Drift?* 47.
105. Myers, *Walking with the Poor*, 88.
106. Myers, 86.
107. Myers, 88.

2.2.3 Why CFB-NGOs/NPOs?

The World Bank now admits that poverty cannot be fought without tending to the spiritual dimension of people and its many manifestations in faith-based institutions.[108] In a similar way, governments' commitments at UN conferences acknowledge that only initiatives with a spiritual vision can address spiritual needs in the context of relief and development. James considers that this acknowledgment of the fact that belief and spirituality play a crucial role in the lives of numerous peoples has "led to a reassessment of the role of faith in development and a move from estrangement to engagement."[109] According to Chester, the development practice of parachurch agencies should be set in the framework of a Christian/biblical worldview shaped by the story of salvation.[110] Woolnough argues that the real role of CFB-NGOs/NPOs is to tackle:

> the needs of the whole person, indeed the whole community, and recognizes that the needs of the world are not purely materialistic, dealing with poverty, disease and injustice, not even mental and emotional, but involve underlying spiritual causes. In an inextricably inter-acting fashion, the needs and the solutions in our lives and communities are holistic. Holistic mission seeks *shalom*, wholeness for all of God's creation. It seeks to further what we regularly pray for the Lord's Prayer, that His kingdom may come on earth as it is in heaven. The work of the church, indeed the work of CNGO's is done as part of God's all-embracing work in *Missio Dei*.[111]

Writing as an anthropology researcher at the London School of Economics, Freeman describes how parachurch agencies do not frame development only as a concern for human rights or social justice, but also as an issue of what God wants for the poor (in Africa).[112] According to James, faith-based organizations are more visible than secular NGOs in development work in a number of ways: reaching the poorest at the grassroots, delivering efficient professional welfare and development services, and providing an alternative

---

108. Barron, "The Role"; and Marshall and Keough, *Mind, Heart and Soul*.
109. James, *What is Distinctive*, 6–7.
110. Chester, "What Makes Christian?" 4.
111. Woolnough, "Christian NGOs," 196.
112. Freeman, *Pentecostalism and Development*, 2.

to a secular philosophy of relief.[113] Now the significant question to ask is: what characteristics of parachurch agencies distinguish them from the myriad of other organizations?

2.2.4 Characteristics of Parachurch NGOs/NPOs

There is a prevailing consensus among scholars that parachurch NGOs/NPOs have traditionally held a unique place in providing a wide range of relief and development services that respond to the emerging concerns of the poor in society.[114] In 2007, according to Duriez, Mabille and Rousselet, church-related NGOs accounted for 57.4 percent of the organizations affiliated with the United Nations.[115] The Industry Commission, Barnett and Stein, Klaits, and Steensland and Goff observed that church-related welfare NGOs/NPOs arose from the goodwill, compassion, discernment and sagacity of philanthropic women and men, based on religious convictions.[116] Following a similar logic, Putnam argues that parachurch agencies are frequently recognized as linking religion and altruism, embodying the power of faith values, and leading the way in addressing social needs, often ahead of government organizations and secular agencies.[117] Anthony John Abbott, speaking as an Australian Minister for employment, has stated that the distinctiveness of church-related agencies is related to their Christian convictions, which enables them to bring a unique dimension to welfare services. Afterwards, he went on further to suggest, "There is something extra about people with faith in their hearts and the love of God on their lips, that gives them that extra commitment to jobseekers."[118] According to Maddox, parachurch NGOs/NPOs are successful because they are prepared to spend the extra time and go the extra mile with the poor[119] in their social welfare services.

---

113. James, *What is Distinctive*, 7.

114. Gallet, "Christian Mission," 24; see also Dickey, *No Charity There*; Hughes, "Theology and Welfare," 1–20; Murphy, *A Decent Provision*; and Murphy, "Church and State," 261–285.

115. Duriez, Mabille and Rousselet, *Les ONG*, 31.

116. The Industry Commission, *Charitable Organizations*, xvi; Barnett and Stein, *Sacred Aid*, 125; Klaits, *The Request* 12; and Steensland and Goff, *The New Evangelical*, 84.

117. Putnam, *Bowling Alone*, 67; see also Breward, *A History*; Monsma, *When Sacred*; Cnaan and McGrew, "Social Welfare."; and Wittberg, *From Piety*.

118. Abbott, "Church, Civil Society," 4.

119. Maddox, "God, Caesar and Alexander," 9.

Church-related organizations are known to be active in nearly every country of the world. Ferris argues that Christian agencies seem to have a greater worldwide outreach, assisting the poor regardless of their religious affiliation, whereas Islamic and Jewish organizations primarily serve their own co-religionists.[120] Ayton, Carey, Keleher and Smith, and Mendes hold to the fact that the traditional values of CFB-NGOs/NPOs focus on creating a sense of community and belonging, as well as respecting the dignity of each individual person.[121] Catholic priest Peter Norden, having worked with Jesuit Social Services in welfare, stated the following, while describing the distinctive characteristics of parachurch welfare agencies:

> We are not just a welfare service; we are also a Christian ministry. So, we choose the young people we work with on the basis that they're most likely to fail, the most in need. You don't measure your success on numbers but what you're actually communicating to this person, a sense of care, respect and belonging.'[122]

Social capital experts – Howe and Howe, and Putnam – have suggested that the express role of church-related institutions in building community and creating a sense of belonging has contributed to the development of social welfare.[123] The fundamental difference between parachurch agencies and secular agencies lies in the attitude toward those who are to benefit and the manner of seeking all-inclusive transformation, rather than just economic development.[124] This implies catering for the poorest of the poor and for those in real need, not just the entrepreneurial poor; providing holistically, and not just for materialistic improvement; and aiming to help the whole community, rather than the individual. Woolnough argues that the guidance and strength experienced for the execution of projects is likely to be different because church-related agencies prayerfully seek strength and direction from God, unlike secular NGOs/NPOs.[125] Moreover, he maintains that "the impact

---

120. Ferris, "Faith Based," 316; see also Heist and Cnaan, "Faith-Based International," 17.

121. Ayton et al., "Historical Overview," 10; and Philip Mendes, "Empowering the Poor: Towards a Progressive Version of Welfare Reform," *Australian Quarterly* 75, no. 2 (2003): 23.

122. Howe and Howe. "The Influence," 330.

123. Howe and Howe, 331; Putnam, 72; and see also Berger and Neuhaus, *To Empower People*; Cleary, *Reclaiming Welfare*; Howe, "The Church"; Schneider, *Social Capital* .

124. Woolnough, "Christian NGOs," 200.

125. Woolnough, 200.

indicators will be different, leaving the outcomes ultimately in the hands of God rather than being shaped by some externally imposed target"[126] from donor organizations. Wink reminds us of Mahatma Gandhi's statement about the fact that we should hold "non-attachment to results as essential for the uphill struggle against entrenched evils: we must leave the outcomes in the hands of God. Yet, if we believe that God is the transformative power of justice in the world, we expect our invocation to make a difference."[127] Lin argues that "goal direction provides the *raison d'être* for the organization,"[128] and so influences the make-up of the agency and gives it features that characterize Christian CFB-NGOs/NPOs in contrast to secular ones.

In fact, parachurch NGOs/NPOs are described by some scholars – Putnam, Bielefeld and Cleveland, see also Beck – as being the contributing factor that glues and cements together civil society and its members.[129] However, other scholars – Bielefeld and Cleveland, and see also Bretherton and Howe – argue that parachurch agencies that contract with secular financial institutions and governments are likely to drift into secularism.[130] Many criticisms have been raised against parachurch organizations including a suggestion that partnerships and contracts with various governments draw them too closely to the priorities of the state, thus jeopardizing their position as outsiders able to render effective criticism,[131] as Austin and Gregg emphasize. Moreover, Bennett and Savani stress that when the priorities and activities of parachurch agencies are influenced or determined by governments, there is a high predisposition for mission drift to occur.[132] This 'drift' will have the consequence of definitely distancing them from the holistic ministry model of Jesus. This assumption is later addressed in chapter 4 of this dissertation.

---

126. Woolnough, 200.
127. Wink, *Unmasking the Powers*, 66.
128. Lin, "Countering Mission Drift," 49.
129. Putnam, *Bowling Alone*, 63; Bielefeld and Cleveland "Defining Faith-Based Organizations," 442; Beck, *A God*.
130. Bielefeld and Cleveland, "Faith-Based Organizations," 468; Bretherton, *Christianity and Contemporary Politics*; and Howe, "The Church and Markets".
131. Austin, "The Changing Relationship," 97; and Gregg, "Playing with Fire," 3; and see also Howe, "The Church and Markets."
132. Bennett and Savani, "Surviving Mission Drift," 278.

2.2.5 CFB-NGOs/NPOs in the Light of the Holistic Ministry of Jesus

The mission of parachurch agencies is to follow Jesus in working with the oppressed and marginalized poor in order to promote holistic transformation in people by seeking social justice and bearing witness to the good news of God's kingdom,[133] as Woolnough claims. Christian organizations are described as 'maintaining boundaries in Jesus.' Aldrich and Ruef stress that their purpose and direction are to carry on his holistic mission, and they use social models designed to meet human needs.[134] Likewise, as Lin, Aldrich and Ruef, Kühl, and Scott write, the practice of 'boundary maintenance' determines agency decisions on hiring co-religionists as co-workers and enforces membership distinctiveness.[135] Because parachurch agencies are uniquely motivated by faith-based convictions,[136] they are influenced by the teachings of Jesus and expected to be distinctive in the way they deliver services.

Several authors have indicated that the example of Jesus should be reflected in parachurch welfare services, responding compassionately to the most vulnerable and disadvantaged at the grassroots.[137] Bouma points out that another established feature of a parachurch agency is its position in advocating for a just and fair society pertaining to scriptural requirements informed by the person and teaching of Jesus.[138] Christian NGOs/NPOs will be able to deliver a higher quality of welfare service as they work in the light of the earthly ministry of Jesus, and as they respond to the scriptural injunction: "Whatever you do, work at it with all your heart, as working for the Lord" (Col 3:23, NIV).

However, there are other voices that speak to the problematic side of Christian faith-based socio-political mission. Scholars such as Bongmba; Harrison; Hastings, Mason and Pyper; Elphick and Davenport; and Byrnes have denounced the fact that Christianity (in the form of some church-related

---

133. Woolnough, "Christian NGOs," 204.

134. Aldrich, and Ruef, *Organizations Evolving*, 3.

135. Lin, "Countering Mission Drift," 49; Aldrich and Ruef, 4; Stefan Kühl, *Ordinary Organisations*, 18; and Scott, *Institutions and Organizations*, 96.

136. Gallet, "Christian Mission," 27.

137. Ayton et al., "Historical Overview," 9; Hugen and Venema, "The Difference," 405; Winkworth and Camilleri, "Keeping the Faith," 317; see also Davies-Kildea, *Faith in Action*; and Judd, Robinson and Errington, *Driven by Purpose*.

138. Bouma, "Religious Diversity," 285; see also Berthon and Hatfield-Dodds, "Standing for Truth."

organizations and church denominations) has played a significant role in the history of apartheid in South Africa by theologically supporting racial segregation, prejudice, inequality and subjugation, with only a few Christian denominations openly opposed to the powerful system.[139] Some churches (i.e. the Dutch Reformed Church) and parachurch agencies (such as those employing English-speaking missionaries), while helping the poor, still failed to confront the apartheid government. They addressed its effects through deeds of compassion (the diaconal dimension of holistic mission), yet they associated with the ruling socio-political systems and powers by refusing to acknowledge cause and effect until "the advent of contextual theology in the 1970s and 1980s in South Africa,"[140] as Rodriguez, Pauw, De Gruchy argue, which gave a theological basis to the resistance.

Some scholars have a more nuanced view, noting that a certain number of churches, though coming from the Reformed tradition, dared to oppose the 'apartheid imperialistic system' with its socio-political implications. Pauw, Rodriguez, Elphick and Davenport gave as examples: the Methodist Church, Presbyterian Church, Anglican Church, and Congregational Church.[141] Nevertheless, putting aside these shortcomings of Christian mission, some scholars acknowledge that there is a constant rise in the number of non-Christian officials, governments and institutional observers who recognize the superior quality of welfare services offered by CFB-NGOs/NPOs. The BBC reports that the Chinese government are happily and unprecedentedly supporting (by millions of dollars) the rapid growth of church and the development of parachurch institutions in China because "Christians worked better than non-Christians . . . Our goal in supporting these religions in developing religious education is that we hope they can train qualified clergy members so that their religions can enjoy better development."[142] In the same perspective, Parris, an atheist, in a recent review asserts from experience that Christian relief and development services in Africa, especially in Malawi, are revealed

---

139. Bongmba, *The Routledge Companion*, 400–403; Harrison, *South Africa's Top Sites*, 11–16; Hastings, Mason and Pyper, *The Oxford Companion*, 29; Elphick and Davenport, *Christianity in South Africa*, 11–15; and Byrnes. *Religion and Apartheid*.

140. Rodriguez, "Confrontational Christianity," 2, 44, 131; Pauw, "Anti-apartheid Theology," 59; and De Gruchy, "Grappling with a Colonial Heritage," 160–61.

141. Pauw, "Anti-apartheid Theology," 59–60; Rodriguez, "Confrontational Christianity," 11; and Elphick and Davenport, *Christianity in South Africa*, 155–60.

142. Landau, "China Invests."

to be far more efficient than those of the secular agencies.[143] The Disasters Emergency Committee (DEC) while reporting on different organizations and their involvement in relief and development in disaster situations often commend the outstanding work of Tearfund as a Christian agency.[144] As Christian faith-based agencies, as Woolnough says, we have the wonderful privilege of serving Jesus to the best of our ability while working in God's world in his strength.[145] NGOs/NPOs from evangelical churches face enormous challenges due to their stated willingness to be like Jesus in mission.

2.2.6 Evangelical Humanitarian NGOs/NPOs Under Challenge

Before going further, let me define my usage in this thesis of the following terms: "Evangelical", "Evangelism" and "Evangelization" according to recent scholarship, the sources of which are cited below. Generally speaking, "Evangelicals" are disciples/believers in Christ who form a transnational movement of the church and a worldwide trans-denominational Christian community. Stanley affirms that the evangelical movement originated in Protestant Christianity and is based on the belief that "the essence of the gospel consists in the doctrine of salvation by grace alone, solely through faith in Jesus' atonement."[146] In this sense, Stiller writes that, as Christians, evangelicals believe in the necessity of conversion, the centrality of being "born again" as a result of having received salvation, as well as in "the authority of the Bible as God's revelation to humanity, in spreading the Christian message,"[147] and in the teachings of Jesus Christ and not in human doctrines,[148] maintains Jambrek. The movement is also called "evangelicalism"[149] by some scholars such as Stanley, Noll, Treloar, Hutchinson and Wolffe, Wolffe, Ward, and Bebbington. The word 'evangelism' comes from the original Greek word

---

143. Mathew Parris, "As an Atheist."
144. Woolnough, "Christian NGOs," 204.
145. Woolnough, 202.
146. Stanley, *The Global Diffusion*, 11.
147. Stiller, *Evangelicals Around*, 28, 90.
148. Jambrek, "Christian Witness," 194.
149. Stanley, *The Global Diffusion*; Noll, *The Rise of*; Treloar, *The Disruption*; Hutchinson and Wolffe, A Short History; Wolffe, *The Expansion*; Ward, *Early Evangelicalism*; and Bebbington, *The Dominance*.

εὐαγγελίζω (*euaggelizó*: to evangelize, to preach or announce good news), which means the verbal proclamation of the gospel or the spreading of the message of God's kingdom, together with the adjective 'evangelist,' meaning a bringer of that good news of the kingdom; while 'evangelization' is a term that designates the combination of socio-humanitarianism and evangelism.

According to Steensland and Goff, contemporary evangelical humanitarian agencies are active in the field of social justice and thus relate to the 'Social Gospel Movement', emulating the life of Jesus by relating works of mercy with the message of salvation.[150] Moreover, they argue that the majority of evangelical humanitarian agencies reflecting these commitments were founded in the course of the twentieth century.[151] Among the most important parachurch agencies are World Vision International (1950), Samaritan's Purse (1970), Mercy Ships (1978), Prison Fellowship International (1979) and International Justice Mission (1997),[152] as Zoba writes. In some of these organizations, such as Mercy Ships and Youth With A Mission, all the staff are volunteers and, in addition to working for free, they even pay for their accommodation and food,[153] according to the report of the Radio Télévision Suisse (RTS).

The evangelizing aspect of evangelical Christians in humanitarian aid is strongly challenged and criticized by even other (traditional and/or liberal) Christian agencies as being evidence of an increasing presence of fundamentalism and a challenge for the faith-based humanitarian community,[154] as Ferris argues. Moreover, Ferris maintains that the Indonesian press reported in early 2005 that evangelical humanitarian groups were trying to bring the missionary message to Muslims affected by the tsunami through relief and development and that this "led to questioning and criticism of the work of all Christians."[155] Contrary to some stereotypes, many evangelical organizations do not combine humanitarianism and evangelism. Other evangelical humanitarian agencies consider that they cannot provide social assistance without evangelism. Verna says that the diversity of evangelical groups means

---

150. Steensland and Goff, *The New Evangelical*, 242–43.
151. Steensland and Goff, 244.
152. Zoba, *The Beliefnet Guide*, xx.
153. Radio Télévision Suisse (RTS), *Le navire-hôpital*.
154. Ferris, "Faith-Based," 323.
155. Ferris, 323.

that both scenarios are possible.[156] He also argues that, to certain evangelical agencies, in certain regions of the world such as the African continent, the cultural settings put a lot of importance on spiritual things, making it difficult for certain populations to accept or understand the work of humanitarian NGOs and NPOs that do not display their Christian faith-based identity.[157] Following Verna's argument, it might therefore be concluded that he shares the viewpoint evoked by Ferris.

Within the world of Christian NGOs/NPOs, Ferris argues that "there are sharp differences between those – primarily from Catholic and mainstream Protestant traditions, which separate assistance and evangelization, and those which, as primarily evangelical groups, see their humanitarian work as an integral part of their missionary activities."[158] Furthermore, he asserts without ambiguity that for that reason, some evangelical groups are frequently criticized in their humanitarian relief and development activities by traditional church-related agencies that are committed to respecting the religious beliefs of the people whom they serve.[159] Ferris believes that the work of evangelical humanitarian organizations that combine a missionary message with assistance can have consequences for all faith-based humanitarian organizations.[160] In Georgia for instance – declares Nodia – the humanitarian workers of evangelical groups (most especially Baptists and Pentecostals) suffer assault and violence from the extremist representatives of the Orthodox Church.[161] Likewise, Saidul upholds to the view that church-related NGOs/NPOs in Bangladesh are sometimes criticized for their evangelistic activities associated with social assistance.[162] Bosch, in his book entitled *Witness to the World*, points out ten areas of what he calls 'typical shortcomings' in the evangelical 'theology of mission' as follows:

1. Jesus is perceived as the lord of the church but not necessarily of all creation;

---

156. Verna, "Le comportement," 32–33.
157. Verna, 33.
158. Ferris, "Faith Based," 316.
159. Ferris, 316.
160. Ferris, 316.
161. Nodia, *Civil Society Development*, 50.
162. Saidul, "The Role of NGOs," 185.

2. Sanctification for some evangelicals is seen as withdrawal from everything that is worldly;
3. Social involvement is regarded as the means to an end, optional, or simply not a priority;
4. Evangelism as the mission of the church is primary over social service;
5. Sound doctrine is considered as different from its ethical application;
6. Personal conviction is equated with God's will;
7. One's own enterprise is identified with God's work;
8. Divine sanction is claimed for all personal ventures;
9. Everything in this world is viewed as temporary and relatively unimportant;
10. Above all, evangelicals "lament the increasing secularization of all areas of life, and yet, accept all the technical products and achievements of secularization as proofs of divine providence."[163]

Therefore, in addressing this issue, it might be fair to assume that Bosch held a holistic view of missions.

As a result, the evangelical humanitarian groups working in tsunami-affected areas were strongly sanctioned and the Council of Churches in Indonesia dissociated itself from them, underlining its respect for the religious beliefs of the people being assisted,[164] as Saidul writes. He further explains that since they are identified with the activities of evangelical Christians, local churches are unhappy that some evangelical organizations have many more financial backings than they do.[165] Moreover, Saidul describes the fact that Iraqi indigenous churches have found themselves targets of anti-Christian sentiment resulting from a reaction to the activities of foreign evangelical humanitarian groups.[166] What an enormous challenge this is! How can para-church agencies still exist and give their holistic assistance to the needy in a multi-religious world, given these varied and disunited interpretations of Christian witness?

---

163. Bosch, *Witness to the World*, 202–08.
164. Saidul, "The Role of NGOs," 323.
165. Saidul, 323.
166. Saidul, 232–24.

2.3 The Holistic Mission Debate in Missiology

There has been a critical disunity among scholars regarding the relationship between proclamation of the gospel and social responsibility that dates back to the 1970s – even before the "Lausanne Congress,"[167] which was held in 1974. Scholars not only disagreed on whether proclamation of the good news of God's kingdom is different from social responsibility, but also whether it is in any way different from holistic transformation through the gospel. Even though the argument still causes differences between scholars, there seems to be a growing consensus among Christians worldwide, as well as among the various church movements and traditions regarding holistic mission, that the mission of the church includes both evangelism and social welfare. This section provides further details on this controversial debate and on the understanding of the concept of *Missio Dei*,[168] which denotes the implication of holistic mission.

2.3.1 A Controversial Debate

The issue of how to handle poverty and the multiple interconnected problems of modern society divides scholarship into two groups. In his analysis, Hart notes that one camp, which he calls "soul-winners,"[169] builds a strong case for evangelism as the ultimate answer to the problem, while the other camp, which he labels the "social-gospellers,"[170] emphasizes direct social involvement.[171] According to Moberg, "Each accuses the other of being untrue to the essential nature of Christianity. Each feels the other is hypocritical. Each charges the other with bringing detriment to the kingdom of God and

---

167. The 'Lausanne Congress' also known as the 'Lausanne Covenant' or (by a number) as 'Lausanne I' produced the very first manifesto in modern evangelicalism promoting active worldwide Christian evangelization. This was promulgated at the time of the first 'Lausanne Movement' (International Evangelical assembly of representatives for discussion on World Evangelization) held in July 1974 in Lausanne.

168. The Latin term *Missio Dei* is a Christian theological expression rendered as the "mission of God" (God's mission) or a missiological concept that describes the integral mission of the church. It can also be translated as the "sending of God".

169. The soul-winners advocate the evangelism-only school as the ideal mission concept for *Missio Dei*.

170. The social-gospellers defend the humanitarian-only school as the appropriate theory for Christian mission.

171. Hart, *From Billy Graham*, 48.

to the cause of Jesus Christ."[172] Following this train of thought, Moberg, Rauschenbusch and Jambrek echo the view that the evangelicals (soul winners) emphasize evangelism, while the ecumenical wing of the Protestants in particular (social-gospellers) stresses social involvement.[173] Wright, Brown and Newman describe John Stott as the man who embodied the spirit of the "Lausanne Movement" and served both as chief architect of the "Manila Manifesto"[174] and as Bible expositor during the formation of the "Lausanne Covenant" and/or "Cape Town Commitments", a manifesto that aimed to promote active evangelization throughout the whole world (further developed in section 2.3.3).[175]

The definition of the church's mission has been a topic of endless discussion for roughly one century. Lewis, Crossman and Hoke state that the debate turns mainly on the relationship between what has been called "the *cultural mandate* and the *evangelistic mandate.*"[176] According to them, the "cultural mandate" can be referred to as Christian social duty, which goes back to the concept of neighbor in Matthew 22:39, and even further back as far as the Garden of Eden (Gen 1:20–31).[177] For Lewis, Crossman and Hoke, the doing of good to others and to society as a whole is a God-given responsibility and a biblical cultural mandate.[178] The evangelistic mandate is equally first seen in the Garden of Eden. Following Adam and Eve's sin, humans are not only doomed to death but have been separated from God's nature.[179] Lewis, Crossman and Hoke argue that the "evangelistic mandate" comprises the seeking and finding of lost women and men separated from God by sin, and that the bearing of "the gospel which brings people from darkness to light is fulfilling that mandate."[180] Lewis, Crossman and Hoke maintain that both the

---

172. Moberg, *The Great Reversal*, 14.

173. Moberg, 14; Jambrek, "Christian Witness," 191; and Rauschenbusch, *Christianity and the Social Crisis*, 349–50.

174. The Manila Manifesto also referred to as the "Manila Documents" is an elaboration of Lausanne II, which took place in July 1989 in the Philippines, 15 years after the first Lausanne Movement. It is the 2nd International Congress on World Evangelization.

175. Wright et al, *John Stott*, 6.

176. Lewis, Crossman and Hoke, *World Mission Manual*, 10–16.

177. Lewis, Crossman and Hoke, 15.

178. Lewis, Crossman and Hoke, 16.

179. Lewis, Crossman and Hoke, 16.

180. Lewis, Crossman and Hoke, 16.

cultural and the evangelistic mandates are essential aspects of the *Missio Dei* and of the church's biblical-holistic mission[181] – neither is optional.

The current debate, according to Lewis, Crossman and Hoke, involves the adoption of one of four positions (different models of relating to social action and evangelism):

1. That which would confer primacy to the evangelistic mandate over the social, physical and cultural;
2. That which would confer pre-eminence to the social or cultural mandate over evangelization;
3. That which would maintain the pre-Lausanne view that *Missio Dei* is the evangelistic mandate, and nothing else
4. And that which would give equal weight to both – even arguing that it is "illegitimate to divide them by using such terminology."[182]

In terms of such a theme, Bosch agrees with Lewis, Crossman and Hoke stating that the putative debate still critically opposes the modernists' social theology, which advocates radical changes in society, to the views of Protestant conservatives who call for individualistic and person-oriented perspectives.[183] The evangelicals do not form a monolithic block, since they constitute no less than six different groupings,[184] as Künneth and Beyerhaus acknowledge. The following are seen as the distinguishable groupings in evangelicalism that have varied interpretations of Christian witness: New Evangelicals,[185] Separatist fundamentalists,[186] Confessional Evangelicals,[187] Pentecostal and

---

181. Lewis, Crossman and Hoke, 17.
182. Lewis, Crossman and Hoke, 17.
183. Lewis, Crossman and Hoke, 14; and Bosch, *Witness to the World*, 30.
184. Künneth and Beyerhaus, *Reich Gottes*, 307–308.
185. The New Evangelicals are modernists who try to federate all evangelical forces and to accommodate Christianity to contemporary developments, a group that Billy Graham joined later on after reviewing his conversion-oriented position.
186. They were totally against any idea of liberalism in evangelicalism, resisted all secular engagement, and have formed a homogenous group along with organizations such as the Carl McIntire International Council of Christian Churches. Carl McIntire was an American minister and the founder of the 'Bible Presbyterian Church.' He also cofounded and presided for a long time over the International Council of Christian Churches (ICCC), which is known as a fundamentalist Christian group that is openly opposed to the more liberal wing of the World Council of Churches.
187. The Confessional evangelicals tend toward creedal aspects of evangelicalism like those associated with Presbyterianism, Anglicanism, Lutheranism, the Southern Baptist Convention, and the Westminster Seminary.

Charismatic evangelicals,[188] Radical evangelicals,[189] and lastly, the Ecumenical Evangelicals,[190] thus explaining the fact that the "Lausanne Covenant reflected not only one school of thought but, rather, a dynamic interaction between many different approaches."[191] According to Gatewood, the "soul-winner's faction," made up of the majority of churchmen, shared the same view as Billy Graham.[192] Referring to another view, Longfield considered the social gospel of the liberals to be no gospel at all and saw in the Bible only a good news that saves people, not one that redeems the social order.[193] Bosch suggests that evangelism and social works are to be viewed as a "two-mandate approach" with the priority given to evangelism.[194] Moreover, he affirms that "in the church's mission of sacrificial service, evangelism is primary . . . reconciliation with man is not reconciliation with God, nor is social-action evangelism, nor is political liberation salvation."[195] According to Sider, it is much easier to meet social needs than it is to meet spiritual needs, and he argues further that "many great social works that have been birthed out of evangelistic zeal" have often finished up as humanitarian projects.[196] In an extreme development of this view, Christian NGOs/NPOs risk drifting towards the humanitarization of their vocations.

In the evangelical-ecumenical debate, Ott argues that terms such as "integral mission" or "holistic mission" became famous in the twentieth century, creating a serious issue in mission definition.[197] The evangelical-ecumenical mission conferences of the 1970s and 1980s reflected the struggle within the evangelical community to accept the broader definition of mission, suggesting that "evangelism as the central focus of mission would be jeopardized."[198]

---

188. They believe the most in speaking in tongues, miraculous healing, and 'signs and wonders.'
189. They emerged especially during the Lausanne Movement.
190. They are open to the ecumenical movement.
191. Bosch, *Witness to the World*, 194; De Gruchy, "The Great Evangelical," 45; and Newbigin, *Sign of the Kingdom*, 30.
192. Graham changed his position during the Lausanne Movement.
193. Longfield, *The Presbyterian Controversy*, 87–88.
194. Bosch, *Transforming Mission*, 415.
195. Bosch, *Transforming Mission*, 415.
196. Sider, *Cup of Water*, 93.
197. Ott, "Matthew 28:16–20," 1.
198. Ott, 1.

Moreover, as Ott argues, many scholars and practitioners in the evangelical movement have adopted a broader description of mission with the inclusion of the formal formula of the World Council of Churches and a very strong declaration on evangelization.[199] Wietzke points out that nowadays the concept of holistic mission belongs to the meeting point between ecumenicals and evangelicals.[200] Seemingly, the disagreement between ecumenicals and evangelical mission theologians is currently still active.

Having lost the social dimension of mission, argues Ott, some German evangelical missiologists have become suspicious of expressions such as 'holistic mission,' 'social responsibility,' 'contextualization,' 'shalom' and 'God's kingdom.'[201] Sider notes that naturally, "Evangelism has a logical priority for *evangelical* social action. Far more importantly, its outcome – eternal life – is so momentous that nothing in the world can compare with it."[202] Nonetheless, Sider upholds the view that one must not invite the starving to accept Christ before being provided with food, nor the sick to pray the sinner's prayer before being prayed over for healing, or offered pain relief medication.[203] Moreover, he argues that in order for the church to be in a better position to reach out to the lost and heal the broken world, it is essential for the church to be united, and to genuinely present Jesus as the true answer to the toughest faith-related questions and social problems of today by sharing the love of God with the whole person in a combined evangelistic and social approach.[204] Attempting to play a 'bridging role', Sider denounces one-sided Christianity, which considers word proclamation and personal evangelism the only means of winning souls, and also the ultra-liberals on the other side, who favor social involvement and ignore evangelism.[205] He lays emphasis on the scriptural (and theological) basis for merging together evangelization and social transformation in the power of God's Spirit.[206] In addressing this issue, Birdsall and Brown suggest that "all local Christian

---

199. Ott, 1.
200. Wietzke, *Mission erklärt:*, 427–28.
201. Ott, "Evangelical Theology," 147 and Ott, "Matthew 28:16–20," 1.
202. Sider, *Evangelism and Social*, 173; and see also Anderson, *Wasted Evangelism*, 77.
203. Sider, *Evangelism and Social*, 173.
204. Sider, *Good News*, 172.
205. Sider, *Cup of Water*, 11.
206. Sider, *Cup of Water*, 11.

communities are to demonstrate respect for the unique dignity and sanctity of human life, by practical and holistic caring which integrates the physical, emotional, relational and spiritual aspects of our created humanity."[207] They further argue that the conviction and practice of integral mission as a vital component to and through the following generations will better position the church in world mission,[208] as Birdsall and Brown write.

It is in this perspective that Campbell declares that the church of Christ has never been confronted to such a great extent with the question of whether the 'good news' is about social or personal spirituality.[209] Before his shift of position during the Lausanne Movement, Billy Graham emphatically stated the following:

> This cause of evangelism to which I have dedicated my life is now suffering from confusion. There is confusion about evangelism among both its enemies and its friends. The enemies of biblical evangelism – which demands a personal confrontation with the claims of Jesus Christ – are keeping the name but substituting another practice. The 'new' evangelism says soul winning is passé. It wants to apply Christian principles to the social order. Its proponents want to make the prodigal son comfortable, happy and prosperous in the far country without leading him back to the Father.[210]

An executive statement of the Lutheran Youth Convention urges that the church of Christ must not embark on any form of social and secular politics because such involvement would invite the entrance of secularism into the church and, moreover, that modern social theology as advocated by some preachers is unsuitable in the church and aggressive to some churchmen,[211] as Moberg writes. The church's mission is solely for the salvation of souls, she is not called to redeem society; the latter will be a normal by-product

---

207. Birdsall and Lindsay, "The Cape Town Commitment," 195; and see also Dahle, Dahle and Jørgensen, *The Lausanne Movement*, 38.
208. Birdsall and Lindsay, "The Cape Town Commitment," 212.
209. Campbell, *Christian Manifesto*, 9.
210. Graham, "What we Expect," 4.
211. Moberg, *The Great Reversal*, 18.

of the proclamation of the good news.[212] In contrast, Newbigin, Gutierrez, Heldt and George advocate the notion that the two should be joined closely and firmly, as parts of the one Missio Dei assigned to the church.[213] Coming from the same viewpoint, Dahle, Dahle and Jørgensen conclude that "there has been a steady development in the *Lausanne Movement* towards a more comprehensive and holistic understanding of mission, reaching a climax in the *Cape Town Commitment*."[214] Following this perspective, how can one describe the concept of *Missio Dei* and its implication on holistic mission?

2.3.2 Holistic Mission: The Concept of *Missio Dei*

The term *Missio Dei* describes a trinitarian integral missional activity on earth that is strongly connected to the kingdom of God. Scholars argue that the concept of *Missio Dei* emphasizes the holistic mission of Jesus Christ and the Holy Spirit through God the father, a biblical mission that involves the church.[215] Bosch points out that the church, at most, sees itself as an illustration – "in word and deed – of God's involvement with the world."[216] *Missio Dei* is therefore viewed as a movement from the triune-God to the world and the church is seen as the instrument for that integral mission,[217] he further argues.

At this point, it is crucial to focus on the 'scholarly description'[218] of what they view as the connection between the verticalization[219] and the

---

212. Free Conference Told, "Church's Role," 16.

213. Newbigin, *Sign of the Kingdom*, 4–5; Newbigin, *The Pen Secret: Sketches*, 110–11; Gutierrez, *A Theology*, 176–77; Heldt, "Revisiting the 'Whole Gospel'," 150; and George, "Joined and Knit Together," 398.

214. Dahle, Dahle and Jørgensen, *The Lausanne Movement*, 36.

215. Bosch, *Witness to the World*, 75; Newbigin, *Sign of the Kingdom*, 11–12; Schulz, "Tensions in the Pneumatology, 102–03; Engelsviken, "*Missio Dei*," 485; Swart, et al., "Toward a Missional Theology," 75–87; Love, "*Missio Dei*," 56–64; Van Rheenen, "From Theology to Practice," 42; and Dahle, Dahle and Jørgensen, *The Lausanne Movement*, 127.

216. Bosch, *Transforming Mission*, 390.

217. Bosch, 390.

218. Claydon, *A New Vision*, 216; Erickson, *Christian Theology*, 903; and Holder, "A Vertical and Horizontal," 3.

219. Verticalization means the evangelistic effort, and the proclamation of the gospel that brings souls to salvation through Jesus Christ, in terms of entering of the kingdom. However, according to the messianic teaching of the good news, verticalization embodies only half of Jesus's message of God's kingdom.

horizontalization[220] of the good news as it defines the mission of the church. *Missio Dei* involves a relationship between the evangelistic-spiritual vocation and the social mandate or responsibilities of the church,[221] as John Stott puts it. He argues that holisticalization is "a public shift in mainline evangelical understanding of the relationship between evangelism and social concern."[222] Advocates of *Missio Dei* view holistic mission as an integral part of the kingdom or reign of God and as the source that drives a holistic understanding of Christian mission[223] in order to unfold God's plan for God's people.

In addition, Bassham indicates that the evangelical affirmation of mission as holistic mission or *Missio Dei* has broadened the focus of a significant number of Christians from evangelism to fully rounded mission.[224] Holisticalization as Russell sees it, is for a certain category of believers a time-draining distraction from the primary task of evangelism, whereas for others it is a 'wake-up call' and a battle cry declaring the true purpose of the *Missio Dei* for Christ's church.[225] Furthermore, he argues against the fact that "some lament the lack of emphasis on personal evangelism in missions today and criticize the tendency to consider all missionary endeavors as important as evangelism."[226] Woolnough and Ma, who refer to the fact that, by the power of the Spirit, "It is possible-not-perfectly,"[227] for the followers of Jesus to live in a mutual social compassion, aptly describe the horizontal meaning of the gospel of the kingdom.

---

220. Whereas Horizontalization, which is the other half, is all about Christian involvement in social issues to better people's conditions by demonstrating God's love to them: promoting the right social relationship to your neighbor through Jesus. Vertically, it consists of pointing people to Jesus by bringing them closer to God through the preaching of the word and horizontally, bringing Jesus into people's daily life by sharing God's love towards them through actions and deeds.

221. Stott, *Christian Mission*, 9; and Dudley-Smith, *John Stott*, 218.

222. Stott, 9.

223. Tizon, *Transformation After Lausanne*, 6.

224. Bassham, *Mission Theology*, 231.

225. Russell, "Christian Mission Today," 93.

226. Russell, 93.

227. To make their point clear, Woolnough and Ma advance the reality regarding forgiveness in the following terms: "According to Jesus, we cannot separate a right relationship with God from a right relationship to neighbour. Jesus' repeated linkage of God's forgiveness and our forgiving others underlines the point" (Matt 6:12–14; 18:21–35) . . . Jesus is not teaching that our good deeds earn God's favour. Woolnough and Ma, *Holistic Mission*, 20.

Woolnough and Ma, in following this viewpoint, advance the idea that the kingdom of heaven comes to us as a sheer gift and the believer enters not by social engineering nor by good deeds, but by repentance and acceptance of the forgiveness of God, graciously offered through Christ.[228] They support the view that throughout his successive parables, Jesus puts emphasis on God's acceptance of sinners, but not the sin nor the lifestyle of pharisaic self-righteousness (Luke 18:9–14).[229] In this respect, Woolnough and Ma advocate the idea that – mercifully, God forgives as in the picture of the prodigal son and his father (Luke 15:11–32).[230] They echo this construal, noting that Matthew points out that the vertical aspect of the holistic gospel requires only that each person come as a meek child with no claims, in order to be admitted into Christ's kingdom (Matt18:3).[231] When we do come as humble children with no presumption of right, then we experience the eager, merciful, and immeasurable "Father Heart of God" (Luke 12:32; Matt 20:28),[232] as Woolnough and Ma acknowledge. Following this train of thought, they maintain that the kingdom of God comes as gift, and believers enter it in vertical terms solely by pure divine forgiveness and the sheer grace of the sacrificial act of Jesus on the cross.[233] The idea of the "Father heart of God" helps to cast a light on the concept of the holistic gospel (holisticalization of Christian mission).

Referring to this, Padilla stresses that "the Lausanne Congress paved the way for the evangelical affirmation of a *Missio Dei* . . . In a way, the adjective 'holistic' only intends to correct a one-sided understanding of mission that majors on either the vertical or the horizontal dimension of mission."[234] According to Yeh, the relationship between evangelism and social involvement was still fairly undeveloped and thus became a point of discord at the Lausanne Congress revealing two streams of evangelical missiology, termed

---

228. Woolnough and Ma, 20–21.
229. Woolnough and Ma, 21.
230. Woolnough and Ma, 21.
231. Woolnough and Ma, 21.
232. Woolnough and Ma, 21.
233. Woolnough and Ma, 21.
234. Padilla, *"Holistic Mission,"* 216.

"holistic mission" and "frontier missions."[235] Following the above considerations, the question is: Why do Christians still hold such different views on such a practical and essential issue?

In his attempt to find an answer, Gustafson in the first place outlines the fact that most people in the Christian milieu have a "truncated concept of evangelism" and secondly, he points out the fact that "our focus is too much on the *proclamation* of the Gospel instead of the *transformation* that the verbal proclamation is supposed to bring about."[236] Moreover, he does not deny the necessity for verbal proclamation of the good news, but says it is not the complete picture of the gospel.[237] A certain category of believers has pointed to social ministry and evangelistic ministry as 'functionally separate', before stating that the two ministries are even more "integrated than that formulation would imply,"[238] as remarks Russell.

In this context, as Pope Francis argues, Christians can understand the command of the lord Jesus to his followers that states: "You yourselves give them something to eat!" (Mark 6:37) as underlining the fact that they must strive to promote the holistic development of the poor and to eliminate the structural causes of poverty.[239] Dahle, Dahle, and Jørgensen echo this Roman Catholic understanding of mission, noting that Scripture declares that the redemptive purpose of God for creation includes holistic mission, which "means discerning, proclaiming, and living out, the biblical truth that the gospel is God's good news, through the cross and resurrection of Jesus Christ, for individual persons, and for society, and for creation."[240] Furthermore, they argue that all three are broken and suffer the consequences of sin; they are included in God's redemptive mission; and all three must be integrated in the followers of Christ's comprehensive mission.[241] While addressing the social dimension of world evangelization Pope Francis, emphasizing on the

---

235. "By *Frontier Missions*; one should understand a Christian missiological term used to refer to the natural pioneering of the gospel among ethno-cultural and ethno-linguistic population segments where there is no indigenous church with emphasis on personal evangelism." Yeh, "Tokyo 2010," 5.

236. Gustafson, "The Church and Holistic Ministry," 84.

237. Gustafson, 84.

238. Russell, "Christian Mission Today," 95.

239. Pope Francis, *Evangelii Gaudium*, 61.

240. Dahle, Dahle, and Jørgensen, *Lausanne Movement*, 181.

241. Dahle, Dahle, and Jørgensen, 181.

Roman Catholic view of the all-inclusive mission declares that to evangelize consists of making God's reign present in this world because the richness of the holistic gospel implies the authentic and holistic meaning of the mission of world evangelization – the integral promotion of each person.[242] Likewise, he claims that Christian faith is no longer restricted to the private sphere of people and no longer exists only to save souls for paradise.[243] As disciples of Christ, says the Pope, Christians must know that God wants his people to be happy in this world, even though they are destined to be fulfilled in eternity, a fulfilment that also relates to social welfare.[244] As he gives his Roman Catholic perspective of the integral gospel and motivation for holistic mission, he states; "Our faith in Christ, who became poor, and was always close to the poor and the outcast, is the basis of our concern for the integral development of society's most neglected members."[245] In this respect, the concept of holistic mission is not foreign and unknown to the Roman Catholics.

Russell insists, "Evangelism is a means to the end of loving God – as is social ministry. He sustains the view that they are also both a means to the end of loving others. Finally, each is a means to the end of increasing the effectiveness of the other."[246] In this sense, Morley affirms that social action can be understood as a sort of duty stemming from the gospel and forming part of the Christian identity, as a support for evangelization.[247] Moreover, he adds that social action has always accompanied missionary works but that, quite often, missionary reports only focus on social activities, and say nothing of the fruits of evangelism and spiritual ministry.[248] Other scholars argue for the positive impact of socio-humanitarian works.[249] Thus Nsi, in putting

---

242. Pope Francis, *Evangelii Gaudium*, 57.
243. Pope Francis, 57.
244. Pope Francis, 59.
245. Pope Francis, 60.
246. Following Russell's argument, it might be fair to assume that the evangelistic ministry and social ministry are essentially interdependent parts of the Great Commission and are to be viewed as a greater whole of the good news of the kingdom. The two ministries are both ways to a variety of common objectives and ends – that of reaching out to individual lives with the Gospel. Russell, "Christian Mission Today," 95; and see also Padilla, *The Local Church*, 19–20.
247. A cet égard, "l'action sociale peut être comprise autant comme une sorte de devoir découlant de l'Évangile et participant à l'identité chrétienne, que comme un support à l'évangélisation." Morley, *La mission polaire évangélique*, 30.
248. "L'œuvre sociale accompagne les réunions d'évangélisation" Morley, 29.
249. Fath, *Une Autre Manière*, 416–422 ; and Luneau, *Paroles et silences*, 37–38.

emphasis on the fruits of socio-humanitarian works in mission, notes that the Catholic mission in Gabon was able to witness from a "socio-missionary enterprise" point of view, through the establishment of a local church in Gabon.[250] Some Christians even today show their disapproval of the gradual move towards a holistic *Missio Dei* in a variety of ways – through statements such as that holisticalization takes away time and resources for evangelism and confuses missionaries. Refuting the concept of holisticalization in the mission work of CFB-NGOs/NPOs, McGravran argues,

> As long as missiology straddles the fence; as long as missiology voices two opinions as to what its essential central task is; as long as missiology confuses helpful activity with the discipling of *ethnos* after *ethnos*, missiology will limp where it should run. Only by facing the 'lion', recognizing it as the enemy, and separating the science of missiology from it, will missiology achieve its true goal. Only so will missiology do the work to which God has so clearly called it. Missiology, the science of mission, is in reality the science of propagating the gospel, of discipling every piece of the vast mosaic of humankind.[251]

In the same line of thought, while referring to the substantial investment of resources in Christian mission to build hospitals and schools, Olson states that one might wonder if these resources could have been better spent in direct evangelism for conversion of souls.[252] This declaration brings confusion in ways that Little and Floyd denounce the disapproval of holistic mission.[253] Countering this view, Little argues that the church would do better to welcome these new paradigms of *Missio Dei* as good news because this shift will actually enhance the effectiveness of evangelism.[254] Considering such mitigating arguments against holisticalization, Russell concludes that some of the virulent criticisms are centered on the embryonic role of business in

---

250. Nsi, *L'Église catholique*, 127–28.
251. McGravran, "Missiology Faces the Lion," 340.
252. Olson, *What in the World*, 274.
253. Little, "What Makes Mission," 3; and Floyd, "Is Personal Evangelism," 56.
254. Little, "What Makes Mission," 80.

mission.[255] In terms of such a theme, Russell reports the following supporting argument:

> However, it should be noted that the Apostle Paul used business in missions. His reasons were not to make money; rather he had a strategic purpose. He argued passionately that he was entitled to financial remuneration (1 Cor 9:1–5). His purpose was to become 'all things to all people' (1 Cor 9:22). This phrase is often used to teach missionaries to identify with their host culture. However, it should be noted that in the context – it is Paul's culminating statement defending his practice of refusing financial donations. Rather than being forced into work out of some hardship, Paul had a three-fold purpose: 1) gain credibility, 2) model integrity, a strong work ethic, lay evangelism and 3) have access to people he otherwise would not have been able to reach. Paul did not view his tentmaking enterprise as a time-draining distraction, but rather as an enhancement to his goal of seeing lives transformed, churches planted and the Gospel spread around the world.[256]

At this juncture, it seems very important to take into account the contribution of the Lausanne Movement in this holistic mission debate (also called in this study the holisticalization of the Christian missions) because it underlines a worldwide Christian understanding of *Missio Dei* and the need of world evangelization (especially the evangelical position).

---

255. Russell, "Christian Mission Today," 95.
256. Russell, 95.

2.3.3 Lausanne Movement: The Two-sided Coin of Holistic Gospel

Evangelism and socio-humanitarianism have been considered in turn by both the "Lausanne Covenant (LC)"[257] and "Cape Town Commitment (CTC)"[258] as the two-sided coin of the gospel. One of the pioneers of integral mission, Sider wrote the following reflection shortly after returning from the Cape Town Congress: "At Lausanne III . . . the biblical obligation to combine evangelism and social action was assumed by almost everyone. A deep powerful longing to share the gospel with everyone who is not a believer pervaded the Congress. But so did the call to seek justice for the poor, care for the environment, combat HIV/AIDS, and work for peace."[259] In addressing this issue, Tizon argues that to younger evangelicals who read about the "fundamentalist-modernist split" that has afflicted much of the twentieth century as past history, Sider's reflection may appear somewhat congruous.[260] Moreover, Tizon goes on to say that the very fact that this newer generation of evangelicals views the 'social concern versus evangelism' issue as a curious debate of a time long past attests to the maturing of the Christian holistic vision.[261] This brings me to the question of how evangelism and social action relate to each other. The Lausanne Occasional Paper (LOP21) has identified three ways of relating social activity and evangelism:

1. Social responsibility is seen as a 'consequence of evangelism'– meaning that evangelism is a means through which God brings people to salvation (regeneration and new birth). Subsequently,

---

257. The Lausanne Movement (LM) is also known as the "Lausanne Committee for World Evangelization" or "Lausanne Congress". It is a worldwide movement that assembles and unites evangelical leaders to work in collaboration for world evangelization. The agreed vision of Lausanne at the original "Lausanne Congress" held in 1974 was and still is "the whole church taking the whole gospel to the whole world." In short, the "Lausanne Covenant" was produced at the first congress, the "Manila Manifesto" at the second gathering (July 1989) and the "Cape Town Commitment" out of the third assembly (October 2010).

258. The Cape Town Commitment (CTC) emerged from the 3rd Lausanne Congress, which gathered more than 4,000 evangelical leaders from 200 nations. These Christian leaders met in October 2010 in South Africa (Cape Town) to discuss critical Christian faith issues of postmodernism as they relate to world evangelization and the Church. This congress held in Cape Town outlined an "Evangelical Confession of Faith" and stated a "Call to Action" – enacted nearly 35 years after Billy Graham's call to the original Lausanne Congress in 1974.

259. Sider, "Evangelizing the World," 48.

260. Tizon, *Transformation After Lausanne*, 170.

261. Tizon, *Transformation After Lausanne*, 170.

their new life would manifest itself in their social involvement in helping others (Eph 2:10; Jas 2:14–26; Titus 2:14). Social action is therefore one of the major aims of evangelism because good deeds cannot save but serve as essential evidence of salvation.[262]

2. Social responsibility serves as a 'bridge' to evangelism because several holistic parachurch missions, through "social uplift", have been able to extend their diaconal and kerygmatic ministries to the poor in the light of Jesus, whose "words explained his works, and his works dramatized his words. Both were expressions of his compassion for people, and both should be of ours. Both also issue from the lordship of Jesus, for he sends us out into the world both to preach and to serve. If we proclaim the Good News of God's love, we must manifest his love in caring for the needy. Indeed, so close is this link between proclaiming and serving, that they actually overlap."[263]

3. Social responsibility not only follows "evangelism as its consequence and aim, and precedes it as its bridge, but also accompanies it as its *partner*. They are like the two blades of a pair of scissors or the two wings of a bird. This partnership is clearly seen in the public ministry of Jesus, who not only preached the gospel but fed the hungry and healed the sick. In his ministry, *kerygma* (proclamation) and *diakonia* (service) went hand in hand. For evangelism is not social responsibility, nor is social responsibility evangelism. Yet, each involves the other."[264]

Since the 'Great Reversal', defined by Tizon as "the move of evangelicals from spearheading social reform in the eighteenth and nineteenth centuries to retreating almost totally from mainstream society by the late 1920s," LM has taken the Christian social vision to unprecedented levels through a much larger emphasis on holistic transformation.[265] In this respect, it particularly applies to the "neo-evangelical wings" as Tizon points out. He notes that

---

262. Lausanne Movement, *Evangelism and Social Responsibility*.
263. Lausanne Movement, *Evangelism and Social Responsibility*.
264. Lausanne Movement, *Evangelism and Social Responsibility*.
265. Tizon, *Transformation After Lausanne*, 171, see also pages 22–23; and Moberg, *The Great Reversal*.

the holistic thrust as a whole has been driven by "Cape Town,"[266] making the good news of the kingdom the "two-sided coin" of the holistic gospel. Looking at the holistic understanding of mission, Dahle, Dahle and Jørgensen write that there has been a constant development in the Lausanne Movement towards a much more comprehensive approach to the gospel, reaching a climax in the "Cape Town Commitment."[267] However, it is from this perspective that they uphold the view that the "2010 International Congress on World Evangelization" also emphasized that there is a certain primacy for evangelism, chiefly founded on the fact that it relates to people's eternal destiny.[268] This notion of the "two sides of a coin" brings me to the issue of primacy in partnership, whether evangelism and social activity are equal or unequal. Are they identical, or does one take primacy over the other in importance? On this note, Bosch criticizes the Lausanne Covenant's statement (LOP21) on the partnership between social service and evangelism, which asserted,

> If social activity is a consequence and aim of evangelism, then evangelism must precede it. Moreover, evangelism relates to people's eternal destiny, and in bringing them Good News of salvation, Christians are doing what nobody else can do. Seldom if ever should we have to choose between satisfying physical hunger and spiritual hunger, or between healing bodies and saving souls, since an authentic love for our neighbour will lead us to serve him or her as a whole person. Therefore, a person's eternal, spiritual salvation is of greater importance than his or her temporal and material well-being (LOP21; cf. 2 Cor 4:16–18).[269]

Moreover, Bosch maintains that the LM has insisted that "the supreme and ultimate need of all humankind is the saving grace of Jesus Christ, and . . . therefore a person's eternal, spiritual salvation is of greater importance than his or her temporal and material well-being."[270] Dahle, Dahle and Jørgensen have pointed out that at that time, the Lausanne Movement particularly

---

266. Tizon, 171.
267. Dahle, Dahle and Jørgensen, *Lausanne Movement*, 36.
268. Dahle, Dahle and Jørgensen, 36.
269. Bosch, *Witness to the World*, 203.
270. Bosch, 203.

focused on "evangelization" as distinct from simple "evangelism."[271] The new term "evangelization" embodied the notion of holistic mission embracing both the evangelistic mandate (evangelism or word proclamation) of the gospel and the social mandate (then called "socio-political") and was viewed as the responsibility of Christians living in this fallen modern world,[272] as the three co-writers imply.

The "Lausanne Covenant" (LM) and its principles have promoted active worldwide evangelization and have laid emphasis on the need for the whole gospel (the holistic gospel) to be taken as a holistic mission to the whole world by the whole church,[273] as Fujino writes. He asserts that this has served as a guide to the global evangelical church for almost four decades in its practice of mission.[274] According to Fujino, even though word proclamation (evangelism) was unquestionably and outspokenly stressed during from the "LM manifesto" and the need for the unsaved to come to Christ was boldly declared, holistic mission prefigured the new term of "evangelization" and was "a new way of describing the two-sided coin of evangelism and social action."[275] Moreover, he describes how evangelism and social involvement are now literally "integrated" as an "inseparable reality of witnessing through a changed life that impacts society."[276] In short, the preceding views seem to be agreeing on the fact that the LM manifesto prefigured the holistic mission concept.

Keum echoes Fujino's elaboration on the "LM platform", observing that it "provides a structure for churches and mission agencies to seek ways of expressing and strengthening unity in mission."[277] Furthermore, he argues that as a fundamental part of world evangelization, the LM has been able to promote a holistic understanding of Christian mission – uniting churches and agencies from all over the globe from Roman Catholic, Orthodox, Anglican, Protestant, Evangelical, Pentecostal, Charismatic and Indigenous backgrounds.[278] Particularly, Keum maintains, the influential position and

---

271. Dahle, Dahle and Jørgensen, *Lausanne Movement*, 36.
272. Dahle, Dahle and Jørgensen, 76.
273. Fujino, "Lausanne III," 18.
274. Fujino, 18.
275. Fujino, 19.
276. Fujino, 19.
277. Keum, *Together Towards Life*, 24.
278. Keum, 24.

context of the LM and its manifesto have eased closer collaboration with the Roman Catholics. Furthermore, he argues that having acknowledged that together all churches share a common concern, the WCC urges that "the whole church should witness to the whole gospel in the whole world."[279] Moreover, Keum maintains that the increasing intensity of working relationships between evangelicals and members of other church movements (especially since 'LM for World Evangelization in Cape Town' and the formation of the World Evangelical Alliance) has also richly added to the development of an ecumenical-holistic theology of mission.[280] It is from this perspective that he goes on to state the following declaration:

> We affirm that dialogue and cooperation for life are integral to mission and evangelism. Authentic evangelism is done with respect for freedom of religion and belief, for all human beings as images of God. Proselytism by violent means, economic incentive, or abuse of power is contrary to the message of the gospel. In doing evangelism it is important to build relations of respect and trust between people of different faiths. We value each and every human culture and recognize that the gospel is not possessed by any group but is for every people. We understand that our task is not to bring God along but to witness to the God who is already there (Acts 17:23–28). Joining in with the Spirit, we are enabled to cross cultural and religious barriers to work together towards life.[281]

Sider concludes that the LM has been a major catalyst in this vital shift, saying that, "Lausanne III . . . reflected the huge change that has occurred among evangelicals all around the world. Holistic ministry – combining evangelism and social action – is now part of our spiritual DNA."[282] In this respect, Tizon goes on to show how transformation in integral mission has taken place, providing perspectives on transformational economics and thinking, and examining relevant Christian perspectives to improve the lives of the

---

279. Keum, 24.
280. Keum, 24.
281. Keum, 40.
282. Sider, "Evangelizing the World," 48.

poor holistically.[283] He further argues that "both freedom rights and sustenance rights are important, not grounded in social authorization but in God's creation of persons in the divine image."[284] In terms of such a theme, Tizon calls on radical Christians (those federated with Roman Catholic, Reformed, Wesleyan, Anglican, Anabaptist, and Evangelical background) to develop "a theology of radical orientation to faith and society, questioning injustice and social and economic disorder."[285] Dahle, Dahle and Jørgensen argue that holistic mission is the 'word proclamation' and 'deed demonstration' of the 'two-sided coin' gospel.[286] It is from this perspective that Tizon states that word and deed in holistic mission are to be viewed as the 'greatness' of the good news (especially of the Great Commission), which he calls the 'Whole Mission' of the gospel[287] – thus, inferring the holistic mission of CFB-NGOs/NPOs.

During 'Cape Town meetings', the representatives committed themselves to the holistic and dynamic implementation of all the dimensions of Christian mission to which Christ commands his followers and God calls his church,[288] as Dahle, Dahle and Jørgensen write. They describe how evangelism and social concern are not simply done alongside each other; the two are interrelated in such a way that evangelism has socio-humanitarian consequences as people are called to love in all areas of life. Moreover, Dahle, Dahle and Jørgensen state that the reverse of this is that social concern has spiritual-evangelistic consequences – as people bear witness to God's transforming grace through Jesus Christ.[289] While laying stress on CTC (the third Lausanne Congress on world evangelization) with its outline "Evangelical Confession

---

283. Tizon, *Transformation After Lausanne*, 78.
284. Tizon, 89.
285. Tizon, 3; see also Cueva, *Mission Partnership*, 203.
286. Dahle, Dahle and Jørgensen, *Lausanne Movement*, 55.
287. Tizon, *Whole and Reconciled*, 155–56.
288. Dahle, Dahle and Jørgensen, *Lausanne Movement*, 189.
289. Dahle, Dahle and Jørgensen, 55.

of Faith"[290] and statement "Call to Action",[291] Dahle, Dahle and Jørgensen conclude that if Christians ignore the world, they betray God's word that sends them out as disciples of Jesus to minister to the world.[292] It is equally true, as they write, that if the followers of Christ ignore the gospel, they have nothing substantial to offer to this world.[293] After outlining the impact of LC and CTC, let us see now how exegetical interpretation of these selected texts (Matt 9:35–38 and Luke 4:18–19) may contribute to understanding Jesus's holistic ministry/mission on earth and how it can be viewed as a manifesto for Christian agencies serving holistically.

2.3.4 Public Theology of Holistic Mission

Given the fact that parachurch NGOs/NPOs are an extension of the church working mostly in the public sphere, there is a need to discuss the interconnectivity between the church and its public theology focused on holistic mission. In an e-mail exchange, professor Lukwikilu Credo Mangayi expressed his view that the holistic aspect of public theology moves beyond the four walls of the church to reach out to communities.[294] In addressing this issue, he upholds the view that embraces God's doctrine of holism, with NGOs and NPOs taking it from the church into the public sphere.[295] YWAM is a good example; it started from the corners of the church and went out to reach the youth of the world,[296] as Mangayi says.

Hoek and Thacker make the same analysis of scriptural holism (also called biblical holism and described in detail in section 2.4.1) or the notion of

---

290. The Cape Town "Confession of Faith" is outlined in 10 points as follows: "We love because God first loved us. We love the living God. We love God the Father. We love God the Son. We love God the Holy Spirit. We love God's word. We love God's world. We love the gospel of God. We love the people of God. We love the mission of God" (Cape Town Commitments 2010).

291. The Cape Town "Call to Action" involved the following aspects: "Bearing witness to the truth of Christ in a pluralistic, globalized world. Building the peace of Christ in our divided and broken world. Living the love of Christ among people of other faiths. Discerning the will of Christ for world evangelization. Calling the Church of Christ back to humility, integrity, and simplicity. Partnering in the body of Christ for unity in mission" (Cape Town Commitments 2010).

292. Dahle, Dahle and Jørgensen, *Lausanne Movement*, 55.

293. Dahle, Dahle and Jørgensen, 55.

294. Lukwikilu Credo Mangayi, e-mail message to author, 17 March 2021.

295. Lukwikilu Credo Mangayi e-mail.

296. Lukwikilu Credo Mangayi e-mail.

holisticalization incarnated in the person of Jesus, recalling Micah's concept of a network promoting a public theology of holistic mission:

> Holistic transformation is the proclamation and demonstration of the gospel. It is not simply that evangelism and social involvement are to be done alongside each other. Rather, in integral mission our proclamation has social consequences as we call people to love and repentance in all areas of life. And our social involvement has evangelistic consequences as we bear witness to the transforming grace of Jesus Christ. If we ignore the world, we betray the word of God, which sends us out to serve the world. If we ignore the word of God, we have nothing to bring to the world. Justice and justification by faith, worship and political action, the spiritual and the material, personal change and structural change belong together.[297]

It is with this argument in mind that Jung challenges each church-related mission agency "to go beyond its one-sided reductionist attitudes and practices toward the holisticalization of mission, advancing God's Kingdom both in word and deed."[298] Following Jung's view, it can be noted that holisticalization, or "the public theology of biblical holism of the church," is merely fulfilling the *Missio Dei* through the acceptance of the *Pareo Dei*.[299] In addressing this concern for a public theology of holistic mission, Grigg uses a succession of illustrative figures to highlight his viewpoint.[300] The following graphic depicts the commonly accepted activities of the church, which are seen as its primary focal point.[301] Houston calls this "the traditional concept of discipleship."[302] Based on this construal, the primary responsibilities of the church consist of making disciples locally before going out to tackle its public holistic mission, as the graphic below shows.

---

297. Hoek and Thacker, *Micah's Challenge*, 17; see also Thiessen, *The Scandal of Evangelism*, 176.
298. Jung, "Toward A Theology," 281.
299. *Pareo Dei* in Latin means the obeying of God.
300. Grigg, *Companion to the Poor*, 81.
301. Grigg, 81.
302. Houston, "Biblical Holism," 11.

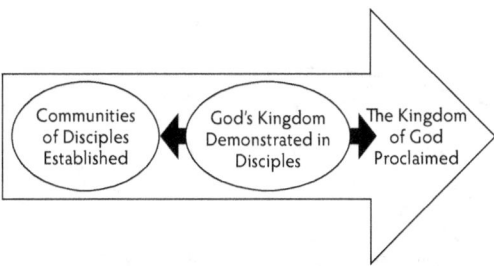

Figure 2.1: The Church's Internal Holistic Theology as a Focal Point

As holism grows internally – argues Grigg – the church then goes out to become influential by being "salt of the earth and light of the world"[303] (Matt 5:13–14). This biblical command of influencing the world holistically becomes real in the community where the church is located. The following graphic[304] shows this very well.

Figure 2.2: Church's Neighborhood Holistic Theology

To the general biblical principles illustrated in the previous figure, the third graphic adds specific biblical commands regarding spiritual salvation, physical welfare, economic development, social justice, and political action.[305]

---

303. Grigg, *Companion to the Poor*, 81.
304. Grigg, 81.
305. Grigg, 81.

Figure 2.3: Church's Public Holistic Theology

This illustration (including all the statements shown above) has scriptural and theological warrant and is part of the mission of the church as it goes out to reach the world.

Grigg goes further – as typified in the graphic below – to lay stress on what he calls "holistic discipleship", which consists of obedience to God (as in the traditional concept of discipleship) while also including spiritual salvation, physical welfare, economics and social-justice, which are the socio-political components of discipleship.[306] Following this train of thought, scholars such as English, Moon, Lynn and Hughes stress how 'holistic discipleship' transforms traditional Christian worldviews by integrating the deeds and words of Jesus into the church's public theology of holism with regard to community development activities.[307] According to Grigg (and Houston as well), the following graphic illustrates the insights that public theology brings to holistic mission, which proclaims repentance spiritually, economically, socially and, where necessary, politically.[308]

---

306. Grigg, *Companion to the Poor*, 79; see also Houston, "Biblical Holism," 11.

307. English, *Deep Discipleship*, 77–78; Moon, *Intercultural Discipleship*, 207; Lynn, *The DNA of a Disciple*, 23; and Hughes, "The Third Sector," 8.

308. Grigg, *Companion to the Poor*, 79; and Houston, "Biblical Holism," 11.

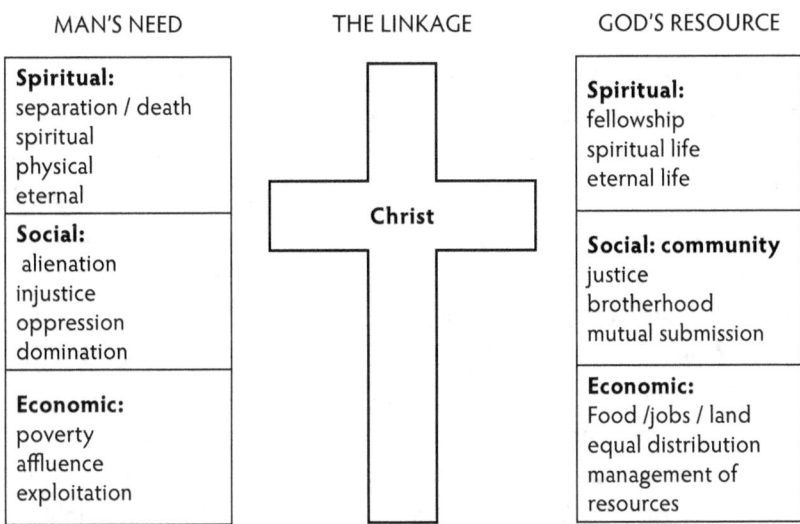

Figure 2.4: Gospel's Theology of Holistic Mission

With regard to the public theology of holism, Jerry Ireland, in the example he gives on "the Masai" women in Kenya, talks about the pursuit of holistic economic development, and calls this kind of action: "a microfinance ministry."[309] Furthermore, he explains,

> In the case of the Masai church, the women are engaging in a simple but powerful form of microfinance, a savings and credit association that has enabled the women to save and lend *their own money* to one another . . . this is a very poor church using its own spiritual, human, financial, and technical resources to restore oppressed women and then to send them out as missionaries to oppressed women . . . Group meetings consist of Bible study, prayer, singing, and fellowship, providing these 'second class citizens' with a profound encounter with the ultimate solution to all of our needs: Jesus Christ.[310]

With this perspective in mind, Dewitt and Prance propose that, with regard to the need for integrated transformation projects, the church must put

---

309. The Masai are "a semi-nomadic tribe in East Africa," mostly based in Kenya. Ireland, *For the Love of God*, 137.

310. Ireland, 137.

in place an economic support base viewed as a supply center for undertaking integrated holistic mission in the community, a sort of laboratory to incubate spiritual development and to be a tangible means for the community to experience God's grace in Jesus Christ.[311] Besides, as a resource center for cohesive holistic welfare development, Dewitt and Prance add, the church is the facilitator of God's grace in beginning to transform people and society into what they were created to be in Jesus Christ.[312] With respect to world mission and the church's public holistic theology, Yamamori and Eldred outline the idea that entrepreneurs in God's kingdom are business owners (though not salaried) who are divinely called to be engaged full-time in God's business.[313] They endorse the construal that while ministering through their own enterprises and parachurch agencies, "they are more like Aquila and Priscilla than like Paul,"[314] (Ac 18:1–5, 24–26). In a similar development of this view, Johnson lays stress on the fact that holistic practitioners must learn from the failures of colonialist and post-colonialist mission strategies, establishing holistic economic stimulus paradigms that involve holism – with mission-minded Christian entrepreneurs and businesspeople amalgamating the evangelistic component with a development component.[315] Thus, the *Missio Dei* and the *Pareo Dei* are intimately intertwined and imbedded in the public holistic mission of the church.

The next graphic, as Houston interprets it, shows how "*Missio Dei* is a shaft of white light refracted through the prism of the church in the world and which emerges as the spectral colors of the rainbow (violet, indigo, blue, green, yellow, orange, red) each of which represent different types of ministries."[316] This is ministry done to reach out to the world, as the graphic[317] by Houston illustrates.

---

311. Dewitt and Prance, *Missionary Earth*, 122.
312. Dewitt and Prance, *Missionary Earth Keeping*, 126.
313. Yamamori and Eldred, *On Kingdom Business*, 8.
314. Yamamori and Eldred, 8–9.
315. Johnson, *Business as Mission*, 34.
316. Houston, "Biblical Holism," 16; see also Bosch, *A Spirituality of the Road*, 392.
317. Adapted from, Houston, 16.

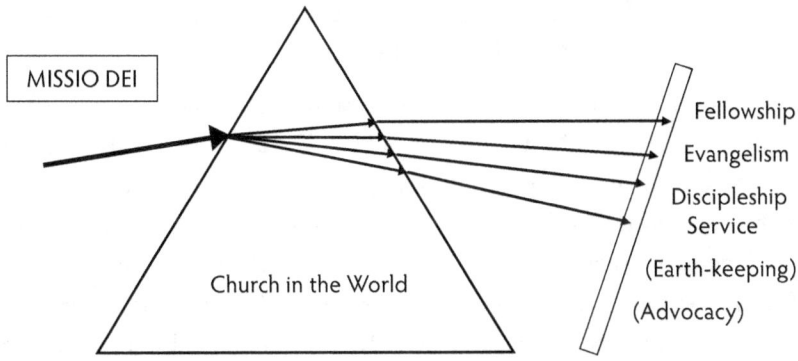

Figure 2.5: Spectrum of Public Theology of Holistic Mission

None of the above-mentioned colors is more significant nor has more temporal priority than the others,[318] says Houston, who further argues that each colour is a part and a dimension of the original white light that goes through the prism of the church and reaches out to the world. Socio-humanitarian and spiritual impoverishment are a reality in so many areas of the world and, through the prism of the church, solutions can be proposed. It can be assumed, based on the preceding arguments that parachurch agencies engaged in the world mission of the church must identify that problem of spiritual and socio-humanitarian impoverishment. They must therefore establish socio-economic paradigmatic projects, seeing this as both a responsibility and an opportunity to respond strategically to people's needs, and then offering a durable path to holistic development.

The public mission of the church, through its agencies, must definitely be to create a pathway along which hope is conveyed: hope that galvanizes people to want to improve socially and confronts them with the existence of God and his lovingly gracious acts manifested in Jesus Christ and made real for them through the holistic practitioners. In short, if a small church in Kenya such as the one Ireland mentions, in a single instance can have such a public holistic success and impact in using the initiative of women, then the larger body of Christ can also be more effective in such public holistic transformation. It is all a matter of vision, understanding and willingness. Every child of God is a missionary for the purpose of the church's world mission.

---

318. Houston, 17.

2.4 An Exegetical Study on the Holistic Ministry of Jesus

This section has the purpose of exegetically studying the understanding of the nature of the earthly ministry/mission of Jesus. The ambition of this inductive study is to come to a deeper understanding of Jesus's mission as portrayed by the evangelists Matthew and Luke. The study has exegetically analyzed two selected passages (Matt 9:35–38 and Luke 4:18–19) which seemed to effectively encapsulate and emphasize the nature of the ministry of Jesus on earth. Many other New Testament Scriptures could have also been subjects of the study, but it was the above two that show the wholeness of the ministry of Jesus on earth particularly well. The choice of these two passages was evoked and briefly justified in sections 1 (Introducing the Research Project) and 1.3.1 (Preliminary Literature Study).

Matthew's missionary vision (9:35–11:1) - as pointed by Bosch - motivates him to write his gospel in order to provide guidance to a Jewish Christian community on how it should understand its calling to mission.[319] Luke's rendering of the earthly mission of Jesus is based on Isaiah's prophecy (Isa 61:1–2 and Luke 4:18–19). Bosch refers to it as "the key text not only for understanding Christ's own mission but also that of the church."[320] The main reason for selecting Matthew 9:35–38 and Luke 4:18–19 is to be found in the fact that Luke 4:16–30 stands as a 'preface' to the entire holistic-public-ministry of Jesus. Scholars argue that it can even be seen as a summarized version of the gospel story as a whole, as well as a "programmatic discourse"[321] which accomplishes the same function in the gospel of Luke as "the missionary discourse"[322] does in the gospel of Matthew. Mainstream scholars recognize Matthew 9:35–38 as a seminal text and distinct unit speaking of a particularly significant moment in Jesus's earthly word-and-deed mission, and view 9:35 (see also 4:23) as the beginning of missionary discourse of Jesus (Matt

---

319. Bosch, *Transforming Mission*, 58.
320. Bosch, 85.
321. Ireland, *Stewardship and the Kingdom*, 168; Green, *The Gospel of Luke*, 197–198; and Van den Brink, van Staalduine-Sulman and Wisse, *The Spirit is Moving*, 320.
322. Green, *The Gospel of Luke*, 206–207; Tannehill, *The Shape of Luke's Story*, 29; Marshall, *New Testament Theology*, 132; Weaver, *Matthew's Missionary Discourse*, 182–183; and see also Dupont, *The Salvation*, 20; Anderson, "Broadening Horizons," 260; and Dillon, "Easter Revelation," 249.

9:35–11:1):³²³ a call bestowed upon the disciples and the church (10:1, 7–8, 40–42 & 11:1) to take up the mission of being, doing and telling.

This construal encapsulates the nature of the holistic earthly mission of Jesus and the very essence of holism embodied in his person. In addition, the apostle Matthew presents in a holistic manner the caring humanity of Jesus (9:35–38; 12:9–21), whereas Luke presents his attitude of servant-hood (4:18–19; 22:27). These two descriptions of Jesus's personality depict his inclination to the poor and his willingness to meet their needs holistically. These circumstances should, I believe, be sufficient reason to choose Matthew 9:35–38 and Luke 4:18–19 for the study of the holistic ministry of Jesus in this thesis because, based on the preceding arguments, they seem to best summarize and present the preaching and healing ministry of the Messiah – a ministry with the object of meeting every human need.

2.4.1 Biblical Foundation of Holism

This exposition on the biblical foundation of holism tries to bring scholarly answers to the question: *what is biblical holism and where does it start from?* Biblical holism is the foundation on which God's mission or *Missio Dei* is built. It highlights the fact that God's plan of salvation is revealed as being holistic, as is seen throughout the Scriptures. While the Bible does not outline a systematic treatise on holism, it offers a biblical vision and presents a deep paradigm within which holistic mission can be practiced, through several texts scattered throughout both testaments.³²⁴ Ajulu defines biblical holism as "everything God does in establishing his kingdom in the whole world in all its fullness" by seeing the integral wholeness of his creation and acting within a holistic development process, in order to meet whole needs within whole conditions, which brings this holistic impact to bear on human welfare, community sustainability and environmental durability.³²⁵ Glasser

---

323. Luz, *The Theology*, 39–55; Park, *The Mission Discourse*, 40–41; Green, *The Message*, 128; Luz, *Studies in Matthew*, 143; Turner, *Cornerstone Biblical Commentary*, 145; France, *The Gospel of Matthew*, 370; Talbert and Parsons, *Paideia Commentary*, 130; Flemming, *Recovering the Full*, 94; and Weaver, *Matthew's Missionary Discourse*, 183.

324. Genesis 1:26–31; Isaiah 61:1–8; Micah 6:8; Matthew 4:23; 10:1, 7–8; 22:34–40; 25:35–40; 28:18–20; Mark 3:7–8; 6:7–13; 10:45; 16:15–20; Luke 4:17–18; 9:1–2, 6; 10:1, 9; Acts 1:8; Romans 15:18–19; 1 Corinthians 2:4–5; 4:20; 2 Corinthians 5:18–19; Ephesians 2:10; 4:12; Colossians 1:20; Hebrews 10:24; 13:15–16; James 1:27; 2:15–18; 1 Peter 5:2–3; and etc.

325. Ajulu, *Development as Holistic*, 166.

and McGavran state that 'biblical holism' is defined by taking the *Missio Dei* across cultural borderlines to people who owe no allegiance to God and leading them to receive Jesus and become a viable part of his kingdom.[326] They further argue that biblical holism is working in God's kingdom as the Spirit leads and accomplishing God's will 'on earth as it is in heaven' through evangelism and social involvement.[327] Moon indicates that the practice of biblical holism is modelled on the incarnation, which shows God's concern for 'holistic discipleship' in the sending of his divine son to proclaim good news and to address spiritual and social issues.[328] After examining God's holism, Kuhn comes to the following engaging and helpful observation,

> "Holism" is the belief or theory that reality (things or people) is made up of organic or unified wholes that are greater than the simple sum of their parts. The term "holistic" has to do with holism, and as such it emphasizes the importance of the whole and the interdependency of its parts.[329]

Moreover, he points out that the foundation of holism goes back to the story of creation when God made mankind (both men and women) in his own likeness and image and assigned them to co-work with him as co-creators[330] (Gen 1:26–31). Following this logic, McConnell argues: "Creation begins in perfect harmony under the lordship of God, with human beings in relation to their creator as stewards of his creation."[331] In other words, in the creation account – God, the great developer – co-develops with human beings his holistic vision of the first great commission (Gen 1:28; 2:15) to that newly-created world but with a soteriological implication and an eschatological dimension,[332] as Miller writes. In expounding on holism in the Bible and the Christian missionary mandate, Steward argues with pertinence that those people lacking knowledge concerning eternity may first be attracted to the gospel through words, those who are sick and needy may respond to

---

326. Glasser and McGavran, *Contemporary Theologies*, 26.
327. Glasser and McGavran, 26.
328. Moon, *Intercultural Discipleship*, 207.
329. Kuhn, "Toward a Holistic Approach," 20.
330. Kuhn, 166.
331. McConnell, "Holistic Mission," 448–449.
332. Miller, *Discipling Nations*, 181 and 232.

the 'gospel-as-deeds,' and the demon-possessed may respond to the gospel's powerful signs and wonders through the holism of the triune God.[333] This revelatory understanding provides a foundational biblical framework for biblical holism and Christian holistic development work.

The prophet Micah gives a meaningful definition of the divine ideal of holism and our obligations to it as God's people (Mic 6:8).[334] Barker argues that this text stands as a motto for the holism of Christian religion.[335] Old Testament scholars writing in the twentieth century made deeply felt responses to Micah's declaration in their commentaries. For Smith, this is "the finest summary of the content of practical religion to be found in the OT."[336] Von Rad observes it is "the quintessence of the commandments as the prophets understood them"[337] and it moves Boadt to call it "a one-line summary of the whole Law."[338] Barker underpins the notion of "faithful covenant love" that is to act righteously, to be honest in dealings with others (Prov 21:21; Matt 7:12) by being merciful, showing genuine compassion and kindness to those in need, and by co-working with God as humble stewards of God-given resources.[339] Following this train of thought, Ajulu suggests the following view:

> Stewardship (in Holistic Christian mission) thus implies the ordering of life in the world with proper management of all God-given resources (natural resources, all human natural gifts, talents and spiritual gifts, land and environmental resources), not merely in relation to money budgeting, finances, or ordering of affairs of only one family unit.[340]

In this respect, Steward upholds the view that the implication of biblical holism is that holistic transformation through the agency of parachurches acknowledges the ultimate ownership of God over all resources and his

---

333. Steward, *Biblical Holism*, 170.

334. Micah's threefold definition of holism in God's eyes: "Act justly, love mercy and walk humbly with your God" (Micah 6:8).

335. Barker, *Micah, Nahum*, 113.

336. Smith, *A Critical and Exegetical Commentary*, 123.

337. Van Rad, *Old Testament Theology*, 186–187.

338. Boadt, *Reading the Old Testament*, 336.

339. Barker, *Micah, Nahum*, 114; see also Lange et al., *A Commentary*, 49.

340. Ajulu, *Holism in Development*, 46.

lordship over the entire creation, as well as all aspects of human life.[341] The book of Acts is notable for the way it makes this case. Acts 17:24 can be used to support the holistic perspective revealed in the Bible – i.e. "God who made the world is the Lord of heaven and earth,"[342] as Engel and Dyrness write. During the time of the Lausanne Covenant, Stott cited Acts 17:26–31, which he summarized as meaning that the triune God is the creator of culture and its ultimate judge – to reinforce a call to share God's "concern for justice and reconciliation throughout human society and for the liberation of men from every kind of oppression."[343] In biblical holism, "self-theologizing endeavors should be carried out in alignment with the biblical and holistic vision of God's salvation and mission. Otherwise, Jung pinpoints the loss of biblical fidelity ends by creating a contextual theology of the *Missio Dei* that fails to secure wholistic scriptural credibility even when applied to one's own cultural Christian group."[344] According to Mangayi, grasping the concept of biblical holism will fuel in holistic practitioners a conversion to becoming more and more kingdom-focused in their approach to Christian mission that embraces development[345] and welfare in the communities they serve.

Acts 6:1–7 shows the primitive church's concern to undergird biblical holism ("ministry of the Word and serving tables") and to show that social responsibility and evangelism are distinct aspects of holistic stewardship,[346] Stott and Dudley-Smith write. To this effect, Ajulu further develops this view, stating that God's people, in responding to their stewardship role vis à vis holism (viewed as a central concept in the Bible), are to extend holistic transformation to cover the whole world; this is to encompass both spiritual-everlasting and temporal-ephemeral dimensions – with full answerability to God.[347] Isaiah 52:7[348] echoes this view of spiritual-eternal and temporal-transient dimensions and informs the very meaning of biblical holism. Keil

---

341. Steward, *Biblical Holism*, 12.
342. Engel and Dyrness, *Changing the Mind*, 33.
343. Stott and Dudley-Smith, *Authentic Christianity*, 24.
344. Jung, "Toward A Theology," 273.
345. Mangayi, "Conversions in Context," 87.
346. Stott and Dudley-Smith, *Authentic Christianity*, 180.
347. Ajulu, *Development as Holistic Mission*, 167.
348. "How beautiful on the mountains are the feet of those who bring good news, who proclaim peace, who bring good tidings, who proclaim salvation, who say to Zion, 'Your God reigns!'" (Isaiah 52:7, NKJV).

and Delitzsch comment that in the first place, this verse refers to those who proclaimed deliverance to the captives of Babylon, but it also prefigures the announcement of salvation by the coming messiah, and the heart of its message is that "your God reigns," which is tantamount to proclaiming that "the kingdom of God has come to the earth."[349] Holism is also proclaimed through Jesus's synagogue sermon (Isa 61:1–2a; see Luke 4:18–19). The latter Scripture is extensively examined in detail in section 2.4.3. It is preceded by an exegetical consideration of Matthew 9:35–38 in section 2.4.2 and the practicality of both is defined in section 5.8.

2.4.2 Exegeting Matthew 9:35–38

This text introduces the mission discourse of Jesus and shows him in relation to his disciples. The followers of Jesus are to carry on his earthly ministry as he instructed them to do (10:40–11:1). Scholars argue that the disciples were to do the holistic works of Jesus by demonstrating the reality of the kingdom through compassionate ministration.[350] Matthew suggests that the mission of Jesus is also the mission of the disciples to the Jewish community (10:7–8) and then to the church at large (28:19). Bosch refers to 9:35–38 as Matthew's summary of the mission activities of Jesus (4:23–25), and pointedly highlights the word of Jesus about a plentiful harvest, an allusion to a wider mission – a mission for which the disciples are commissioned to spread the good news throughout all Syria.[351] After being baptized, receiving the Spirit, receiving anointing and being tempted, Jesus the Messiah began his public teaching and healing ministry (earthly mission), and through it proclaimed the good news of the kingdom.

2.4.2.1 Teaching and Proclaiming the Good News

Matthew 9:35 rounds off his account of the ministry with a narrative that closely echoes 4:23 and thus frames the larger section dealing with the earthly mission of Jesus. The Greek verb Matthew employs for teaching is διδάσκων (*didaskōn*), which is a present participle active from the original word διδάσκω

---

349. Keil and Delitzsch, *Commentary on the Old Testament*, 496.

350. Allison, *Studies in Matthew*, 138–39; and Davies and Allison, *A Critical and Exegetical*, 411–12.

351. Bosch, *Transforming Mission*, 62.

(*didaskó*) meaning to teach, to direct and to admonish. The term "to proclaim" has been closely analyzed in section 2.4.2.3. To this effect, Blomberg and also Bruce have indicated that Jesus is commissioning the apostles to continue his teaching and proclamation ministry to all people starting from Israel.[352] According to Kapolyo, Matthew's Gospel is a missionary document that resulted from the mission of the twelve in the sense that "it came out of mission and is to be used in mission."[353] Fulfilling the same purpose as Matthew 4:23–25, Alford says this major discourse on Jesus's mission introduces the theme of the Lord's travelling from place to place and the calling, selection, teaching and commissioning of the apostles, who are sent out upon the Lord's mission[354] (10:1; Mark 3:16; Luke 6:13). The teaching and proclamation ministry of Jesus is presented in chapters 5, 6 and 7 of Matthew's Gospel while chapters 8 and 9 demonstrate his healing ministry as he brings light, truth, and hope through the good news of God's kingdom. Lenski has observed that the program Jesus outlined in 4:23 is thus to be continued and completed, fulfilling the themes of the Sermon on the Mount, since chapters 5–9 show what is to be the core of Christ's consistent earthly mission:[355] compassionately focused teaching, preaching, and healing.

2.4.2.2 Healing Diseases and Illnesses

Healing is one of the aspects of the ministry of Jesus that Matthew outlines in 9:35. Matthew uses the word θεραπεύων (*therapeuōn*) to emphasize the healing ministry of Jesus's earthly mission. The original word θεραπεύω (*therapeuó*) means to serve, cure, heal or restore a person who has an illness, infirmity, or disease, thus reversing the physical condition of the sick by serving or caring for him/her. The anointing and authority of Jesus compassionately erased every disease and every sickness (πᾶσαν νόσον καὶ πᾶσαν μαλακίαν – *pasan noson kai pasan malakian*) of the poor and suffering people. Matthew 9:35 shows as Hahn describes,

> The "authority" of Jesus both in teaching and in healing. It is clear in this section that the titles ascribed to Jesus, such as

---

352. Blomberg, *Matthew*, 165; and Bruce, *The Synoptic Gospels*, 156.
353. Kapolyo, "Matthew," 1156.
354. Alford, *Alford's Greek Testament*, 98.
355. Lenski, *The Interpretation*, 382.

"Son of David', 'Son of Man', and even 'Lord' do not provide an adequate insight into his full identity. Only by, as it were, hearing him teach and by experiencing his healing can one realize the genuine identity of Jesus Christ, the Son of God, who ministers to people's needs.[356]

Jesus the anointed-redeemer went around with "healing in his wings"[357] (Acts 10:38), as Jamieson, Fausset, and Brown emphasize. Lawson argues that the people's eagerness to hear Jesus speak, and later, to hear his disciples is equaled by their desperation to receive his healing.[358] After commissioning of the disciples, Wiersbe argues, it did not take long before they in turn became involved in the ministry of proclamation and healing[359] with great compassion.

2.4.2.3 Ministering with Compassion

From the ministry of Jesus, Matthew takes us to the Lord's great compassion that sits behind this whole mission. In 9:36, the verb σπλαγχνίζομαι (*splagchnizomai*) means to feel compassion or have pity on, to have the viscera moved, or to be moved in the inner parts – heart, lungs, kidneys, and liver – which were supposed to be the seat of feelings (e.g. love, sympathy, and pity). Lenski argues that writing 'his heart was stirred,' and of Jesus being 'compassionate' is the strongest way to translate this passage, "for it indicates not only a pained feeling at the sight of suffering, but in addition shows a strong desire to relieve and to remove the suffering."[360] The term συμπάσχω (*sympáschō*) which means to suffer with, to be affected in common with, or to feel the other's pain, expresses the love, sympathy and pity which experiences the other's suffering, and ἐλεεῖν (*eleeín*) means to show kindness or mildness.

The same verb is also used in 14:14; 15:32; 18:27 and 20:34 to express the fact that Jesus was "moved with compassion." Lenski observes that the fact that Scripture has recorded so many instances in which the compassion of Jesus is expressly evidenced shows that his heart was always filled with feelings

---

356. Hahn, *Matthew: A Commentary*, 131.
357. Jamieson, Fausset and Brown, *Critical and Explanatory*, 34.
358. Lawson, *Matthew*, 133.
359. Wiersbe, *The Bible Exposition*, 36.
360. Lenski, *The Interpretation*, 382.

of pity and merciful kindness for the distressed.[361] He further argues that the heart of Jesus was ever moved with compassion whenever and wherever sorrow of soul and suffering of body met his eyes.[362] Campbell echoes this construal, noting that the compassion of Jesus is one of the richest, deepest, and most comforting of all his 'savior qualities.'[363] While conducting his itinerant ministry, Jesus saw the multitudes who were weary, depressed and cast away – ἐσκυλμένοι καὶ ἐρριμμένοι. The verb ἐσκυλμένοι (*eskylmenoi*) means to harass, to distress or to trouble, and ἐρριμμένοι (*errimmenoi*) means to be helpless, to throw down/off, to toss away and to lose spirit. The past tense employed in the text (9:36) denotes the intensity of the people's oppression and its perpetually discouraging and persistent effect on them.

Thus, as Weber writes,

> He felt compassion for their lack of spiritual shepherding and the presence of spiritual abuse. A shepherd feeds, comforts, heals, guides, and protects his sheep . . . Jesus was physically moved by a stomach-wrenching empathy for the plight of his flock. He was literally sickened by the poor leadership of Israel's hypocritical religious leaders[364] (Num 27:17 and Ezek 34:5–23).

As Jesus stated earlier in Matthew 9:13, Weber argues that mercy or compassion is an attitude that grows into an action leading to an effort to meet people's needs.[365] Jesus's fervent plea to the apostles to send out more laborers into the plentiful harvest speaks powerfully of his stomach-wrenching empathy and motivation to meet the people's needs and shows his concern for their spiritual condition.

2.4.2.4 Harvesting Plentifully and Appealing for More Workers

In Matthew 9:37–38 Jesus abruptly introduces a new figure of speech into the narrative, thus passing from that of 'shepherd-less sheep' to that of the

---

361. Lenski, 383.
362. Lenski, 383.
363. Campbell, *Opening up*, 60.
364. Weber, *Holman New Testament*, 130.
365. Weber, 130; see also Blomberg, *Matthew*, 166; Jamieson, Fausset and Brown, 34–35; Hahn, *Matthew: A Commentary*, 131; Robertson, *Word Pictures*.

abundance of the harvest that is ready to be reaped,³⁶⁶ as Bruce, and Lenski assert. This transition in imagery refers to the commissioning of the apostles. The term used for harvest is θερισμὸς (*therismos*) also used for crops and reaping. Bruce highlights the fact that the figure of the people as 'shepherd-less sheep' aptly reflects Jesus's mood of passive sympathy whereas the figure of the abundant harvest ready to be reaped reveals his active purpose: passing from being a mere pitying spectator to being an active missionary of help.³⁶⁷ The verb ἐκβάλλω (*ekballō*) really means to bring forth, to produce, to push out, drive out, to draw out with violence or to send out; an aorist subjunctive active that suggests the determination of the action.

The aorist imperative passive verb δεήθητε (*deēthēte*), which means to beseech, to request fervently, to feel pressing need or to pray earnestly describes the nature of Jesus's plea in 9:38. Scholars suggest that the mission is God's work and ἐκβάλῃ being the urgent necessity existing, moves Jesus, the Lord of the harvest, to thrust forth or to drive forth more laborers, for the field is ripe.³⁶⁸ Following this train of thought, other scholars – Kapolyo, MacArthur, and Marshall and Keough – seem to agree with the fact that Jesus's energetic request for prayer as the remedy to this emergency is a call for a much greater number of ministers of the gospel to extend God's mission.³⁶⁹ Therefore, Bruce explains that "ἐκβάλῃ, is a strong word (see Mark 4:29, ἀποστέλλει), even allowing for the weakened force in later Greek, implying Divine sympathy with an urgent need. Men *must* be raised up who can help at this time."³⁷⁰

Christ had a thorough faith in his father's benign providence. In this sense, Bible Hub notes that "the prayer, expressed in terms of the parabolic figure, really points to the ushering in of a new era of grace and humanity – *Christian* as opposed to Pharisaic, legal, Rabbinical"³⁷¹. Some scholars like Laqueur; Sanders; Lange and Schaff; Long; Weber; Jamieson, Fausset and Brown; and

---

366. Bruce, *The Synoptic Gospels*, 157; and Lenski, *The Interpretation*, 384; see also Eims and Eims, *Laboring in the Harvest*.

367. Bruce, *The Synoptic Gospels*, 157; see also Weiss, *The Four Gospels*, 119.

368. Lange and Schaff, *A Commentary*, 179; Lewis, Crossman and Hoke, *World Mission Manual*, 8; and White, *Listening Carefully*, 13.

369. Kapolyo, "Matthew," 1156; MacArthur, *The MacArthur Bible*, 1140; and Marshall and Keough, *Mind, Heart and Soul*, 100.

370. Bruce, *The Synoptic Gospels*, 157.

371. Bible Hub, "Expository Greek Testament."

Lenski have argued that the statement 'the harvest is great' extends beyond the Jewish field, widening into the vast field of the world crowded with souls needing to be gathered to Christ[372] (Matt 9:37–38; 13:38; Luke 10:2; John 4:35–36; 10:14; see also Jer 8:20 & Rev 14:15). After training the twelve, Jesus speaks of "praying" for "more workers" to carry on his great earthly mission, to work at bringing the "harvest" into the kingdom. In support of this reflection, Lenski argues,

> Our prayers do not save the harvest or even a part of it. Our prayers unite in God's concern for the harvest, make us of one mind, heart, and will with him, partners of Jesus himself. The matter goes much deeper than rationalizing thoughts are able to penetrate. Jesus does not tell the disciples to go out and to get workers. This mistake has often been made, and workers are brought in that God has not called. The harvest is God's, and he must provide the workers, ἐκβάλλειν εἰς, 'throw them out into the harvest,' . . . The wonder will always remain that God, the primal cause, uses us and our prayers, the secondary causes, and does not discard them. The secret of this conjunction lies in the infinite grace of the divine will which unites him and us through Jesus . . . What a blessed relation between the workers in the harvest and the Lord of the harvest!"[373]

Now, let us look at how Jesus's manifesto in Luke 4:18–19 can be exegeted to help our construal of the Lord's earthly holistic mission.

2.4.3 Exegeting Luke 4:18–19

The text of Luke 4:18–19 is traditionally referred to as the manifesto of Jesus's kingdom. It is significant because in the mission theology discussion it has become a key text for the definition of mission. It is one of those New

---

372. Laqueur, *Harvest of a Decade*, 64; Sanders, *Judaism: Practice*, 230; Lange and Schaff,179; Long, *Health, Healing*, 62; Weber, *Holman New Testament*, 130–131; Jamieson, Fausset and Brown, 35; and Lenski, *The Interpretation*, 383–385.

373. In terms of such a theme, Lenski observes: "Verbs of praying are construed with ὅπως, which ἵνα has not crowded out. We cannot argue that the Lord of the harvest, owning it as he does, will naturally see to it that it is brought in. We may be sure that he will do so even without our prayer (as Luther remarks in connection with the Second Petition of the Lord's Prayer)." Lenski, *The Interpretation*, 385–388; see also Weber, *Holman New Testament*, 131.

Testament texts that are central to exegetically understanding the missionary activities of Jesus. There are various interpretations given linking the passage to Jesus's compassionate ministry. Therefore, I want to establish exegetically what the original audience of both Jesus and Luke understood by the text in the context of the prevailing scholarship, as well as its modern applicability to the church's compassion ministry. The study has been taken phrase by phrase.

2.4.3.1 The Political and Socio-Economic Contexts

The Lord Jesus lived in Israel and carried out his earthly ministry within a political and socio-economic context shaped by rebellion, sin, oppression, and exile. The Jewish nation fell into the hands of oppressive and domineering foreign powers from time to time,[374] as Obeng-Amoako states. Jesus was born, grew up and ministered during such an epoch. Uwaegbute notes that "foreign powers like Assyria, Babylon, Persia, Greeks, and Seleucids all ruled the Jews at different times of history. During the time of Jesus, the whole of Judea was colonized by the greatest of all empires that ever existed – Rome."[375] A large number of Israelites were poor, deprived, and broken-hearted during this era, and lived under conditions of total injustice, tyranny, and domineering and imperious leadership, typical of Roman imperialistic rule,[376] as Uwaegbute further notes.

For the Jews, Isaiah 61:1–2 was a messianic passage promising vindication. Therefore, when Jesus began his earthly mission as the promised Messiah in the synagogue by quoting from Isaiah 61:1, "'The Spirit of the Sovereign Lord is on me, because the Lord has anointed me to proclaim. . . .'", he probably meant to shock and stir his audience. In this respect, Wiersbe states that "the Jewish rabbis interpreted this passage to refer to the Messiah, and the people in the synagogue knew it. One can imagine how shocked they were when Jesus boldly said that it was written about him, and that he had come to usher in the acceptable year of the Lord."[377] Even more disconcerting to the listeners was the fact that Jesus's announcement in Luke 4:19 ended on the words

---

374. Obeng-Amoako, "The History," 25.
375. Uwaegbute, "A Challenge of Jesus," 145.
376. Uwaegbute, 147.
377. Wiersbe, *The Wiersbe Bible*, 149.

"the year of the Lord's favour"[378] and did not mention the "day of vengeance of our God" as recorded in Isaiah 61:2, which, significantly, most Israelites were impatiently expecting. Gooding observes that "for many people, particularly those who believed in him, this was a shock and a disappointment, especially when they found out what it would mean."[379] Following this train of thought, scholars argue that instead of the expected military or political leader who had come to deliver them from the Romans' oppressive imperial rule, Jesus was presenting himself as the promised Messiah, but one who comes to deliver his people from slavery, physical hardships and sin, with the jubilee motif applying all of this to his own ministry, in an economic and a political sense, as well as in both a spiritual and physical sense.[380] Moreover, Wiersbe argues, Jesus was certainly anointed to proclaim salvation to bankrupt sinners, deliverance to the blind, healing to the heartbroken, liberation for the oppressed from bondage, demons and diseases.[381] Indeed, Jesus was anointed to proclaim the nation of Israel's spiritual year of Jubilee.

2.4.3.2 Anointing of the Lord's Spirit

The manifesto of Jesus Christ is grounded on his anointing by the Lord's Spirit (Luke 4:18). According to Koech, "'Anointing' in Scripture means to authorize or set apart a person for a particular work or service. Priests, kings, and prophets were anointed. Oil was poured on the head of the person being anointed (Exod 29:7)."[382] The story of Jesus's anointing started in Luke 3 and 4 with his water baptism in the Jordan River, the coming of the Holy Spirit upon him and his temptation by the devil in the desert. Then he returned to Galilee, performing miracles and teaching with a unique authority, for which reasons the crowds followed him in huge numbers (Luke 4:14). He entered the synagogue, took the scroll, and read from the passage that he 'found' there – in Isaiah 61, as later reported by the evangelist Luke in 4:18–19.

---

378. When Jesus spoke of the "year of the LORD's favor" or the "acceptable year of the LORD" (Luke 4:19), he was making reference to Leviticus 25 where the poor and captives were set free on every fiftieth year corresponding to the Jewish Year of Jubilee.

379. Gooding, *According to Luke*, 83.

380. Obeng-Amoako, "The History," 282; Fitzmyer, *The Gospel According to Luke*, 532–533; Green, *The Gospel of Luke*, 210–211; Hopkins, *Introducing Black Theology*, 26; Keener, *The IVP Bible*, 190; and Wiersbe, *The Wiersbe Bible*, 149.

381. Wiersbe, 149.

382. Koech, "The Spirit Motif," 162.

The verb εὗρεν is transliterated *heuren* and translated 'he found'. The verb is employed to suggest that Jesus, being under the power of the anointing, chose the text of prophet Isaiah 61:1–2,[383] as Uwaegbute observes. He further states that the content of Jesus's manifesto (Luke 4:16–21) on earth was divinely predestined to respond directly to the political context of the time, which was characterized by the prevailing oppressive and punitive living conditions of the Jews in their marginalized socio-economic state.[384] Jesus's mission on earth was divinely inspired and not an after-thought instigated by the Jews' political and socio-economic situation. Neither was Jesus's reading of Isaiah 61 a coincidence. However, Jesus was not anointed through the pouring of oil on his head; his anointing was done through the Holy Spirit's power coming down upon him. Obeng-Amoako argues that, in the same way, "followers of Christ can receive the anointing of the Holy Spirit for service in the Lord's vineyard."[385] The original Greek word for "to anoint" used in Luke 4:18 is χρίω (*chrió*) which also means to consecrate by anointing – literally denoting the empowering of the Holy Spirit, and representing Jesus as someone who is divinely authorized and appointed by God to minister as king, prophet and priest.[386] The verb is ἔχρισέν (*echrisen*: aorist indicative active – 3rd person singular), and is translated 'He anointed'. It is similar to χείρ (*cheir*: hand) and χραίνω meaning (*chraínō*) to besmear, or to touch with the hand, to rub with oil akin to consecrating to an office. From the Septuagint, מָשַׁח (*mashach*) means to anoint, similar to smearing the one who received anointing from God from among the Jews, the consecration of Jesus to the messianic office, and "furnishing him with powers necessary for its administration (Luke 4:18 after Isa 61:1), contrary to common usage with an accusative of the thing, ἔλαιον (*elaion*: oil) – like verbs referring to the putting on of clothing, etc,"[387] as Buttmann indicates.

The Spirit of God anointed Jesus and empowered him before he started his holistic earthly ministry. Describing the basis of Jesus's earthly ministry, Stronstad explains (as Luke 4:18 seems to suggest) that "Jesus is not

---

383. Uwaegbute, "Challenge of Jesus' Manifesto," 151.
384. Uwaegbute, 147.
385. Obeng-Amoako, "History of Assemblies," 282.
386. Curtius, *The Greek Verb*, 201; Buttmann, *A Catalogue*, 131; see also Thayer, *Greek-English Lexicon*.
387. Buttmann, *Catalogue of Irregular Greek Verbs*, 131.

only anointed by the Spirit, but He is also Spirit-led, Spirit-filled, and Spirit-empowered."[388] In addition, he argues that Luke intends "the Spirit's anointing, leading, and empowering of Jesus to be programmatic for his entire ministry."[389] Jesus's anointing was intended for his earthly ministry, and Koech suggests that in his public ministry Jesus appears as the bearer of God's Spirit, not for his own gratification but for the satisfaction of the marginalized and poor people in society, and of those needing salvation, liberation and healing: the poor, the oppressed and the sick.[390] Furthermore, Koech points out that the marginalized in our current society also face serious issues, which includes spiritual, social, psychological, political and physical oppression; the liberation coming from the power of the Holy Spirit is therefore crucial.[391] Concerning this, Jesus outlines in Luke 4:18–19 the following items of proclamation as the reasons for his anointing.

2.4.3.3 Proclaiming Good News to the Poor

Most scholars have argued that "proclamation of the gospel to the poor" marked the beginning of the earthly ministry of Jesus.[392] According to Stein, the proclamation of the good news reveals for Luke the purpose of the earthly ministry of Jesus.[393] Moreover, he points out that Jesus himself chose the passage of Isaiah 61:1–2 to describe his ministry,[394] thus, pointing to its fulfilment.

For Stein, Luke upholds the view that "to proclaim the good news" means "to preach or teach the gospel."[395] The term κηρύσσω (*kérussó*) is the original Greek word for to proclaim or to preach. This and the expression εὐαγγελίζω (*euangelizō*) which means to proclaim the good news or preach the gospel, are essentially synonymous. This implies that to proclaim, to preach or herald the message of deliverance or salvation for the people of God speaks of Jesus's vocation and dignity. Also – to Lange and van Oosterzee – as "the servant of

---

388. Stronstad, *The Charismatic Theology*, 45.
389. Stronstad, 45.
390. Koech, "Spirit Motif," 160.
391. Koech, 156.
392. Jamieson, Fausset and Brown, 102; and Stein, *Luke: An Exegetical*, 156.
393. Stein, *Luke, An Exegetical*, 156.
394. See Luke 4:43–44; 8:1; 9:2, 6; Acts 8:4–5; 10:36–37. These passages underline the continuity with the preaching of John the Baptist in Luke 3:18. Stein, 156.
395. Stein, 156.

Jehovah he was, in his work and destiny, the type and image of the Messiah, the perfect servant of the Father . . . the Messiah, who had brought in an eternal redemption."[396] Therefore, Jesus came with the fullest right to begin his earthly ministry,[397] as Lange argues.

In Luke 4:18, the Greek term used is πτωχός (*ptochos*) to translate 'poor', thus designating people in a perpetual state of poverty: materially poor, socially poor, and spiritually poor (Matt 5:3).[398] Several Greek terms are used to describe the concept of poverty in the New Testament. Nida and Louw have itemized the following: πτωχός, πένης, ἐνδεής and πενιχρός.[399] The word πένης describes the situation of a 'poor person' and is transliterated *penes* and found in 2 Corinthians 9:9. The term ἐνδεής is used to translate 'in need, needy or poor', which is found in Acts 4:34 and is transliterated *endees*. The word πενιχρός is found in Luke 21:2 designating the 'poor, needy' with transliteration *penichros*. Ronsen argues that a person who is described as *penes* is possibly less poor than the one who is *ptochos* and the latter is in a similar situation to the person who is *endees* but only due to the fact that the one who is *endees* is in "a serious lack of resources required for living rather than a continuous state of destitution" (like the *ptochos* person). According to Ronsen, "the use of *penichros* describes a person who lacks the essential means of livelihood."[400] This understanding echoes the view upheld by Lange and van Oosterzee.

Therefore, the term πτωχός denotes impoverishment of earthly wealth and literally designates one who is deeply destitute and spiritually poor. According to Vine's understanding of Mathew 5:3, it is one who is destitute of the Christian virtues and everlasting riches.[401] Such a person may be spiritually poor either in an evil sense or in a good way (such as being a humble, hungry, thirsty, and devout person). Unlike Vine, McCrae rejects any attempt to spiritualize the poor. He claims, "A church which is not composed of the

---

396. Lange and van Oosterzee, *A Commentary*, 73.
397. Lange and van Oosterzee, 73.
398. Πτωχός *occurs* 34 times in the Bible.
399. Nida and Louw, *Greek-English Lexicon*, 564.
400. Ronsen, *Mission Drift?* 42–43.
401. Vine, *The Expanded*, 864.

poor or standing in solidarity with the poor is not a church!"[402] The word "'poor' is a strong Lukan concern," says Stein and he further elucidates that for Luke the term "poor" refers to the economic status of a person while also referring to the humble poor whose hope is in God.[403] Green observes that "numerous attempts have been made to find here a referent to the 'spiritually poor' or, more recently – reflecting the concerns of a material-oriented interpretative method – to the economically poor. Both of these definitions of the 'poor' are inadequately grounded in ancient Mediterranean culture and the social world of Luke-Acts."[404] However, he argues that while the notion of "economic poverty" is not to be fully excluded from the definition, the "poor" in Luke's view includes all the disadvantaged and excluded in society, mostly on account of what he terms "diminished status honour."[405] So, it might be fair to assume that the term "poor" carries broader understanding.

Moreover, Hopkins stresses that "no amount of spiritualizing of this passage can remove the divine emphasis on those in poverty and oppression."[406] The Greek term σωτηρία (soteria) means salvation, deliverance, prosperity, welfare, preservation, and safety. Writing from the same perspective, Austin explains that in Greek, salvation carries a broader and more holistic meaning than is often conveyed in English because several concepts are inbuilt in σωτηρία, embracing restoration to a state of soundness, safety, wellbeing and health, as well as protection from risk of destruction.[407] The proclamation of good news to the poor is therefore a message that includes wider holistic concepts of salvation such as granting freedom to the prisoners.

2.4.3.4 Proclaiming Freedom for the Prisoners

The original Greek word for prisoner is δέσμιος (desmios), which also means captive, binding and bound. According to Stein, the proclamation of freedom

---

402. McCrae explains: "Poverty is the unfulfillment of basic human needs required to adequately sustain life free from disease, misery, hunger, pain, suffering, hopelessness and fear, on the one hand, and the condition of defenceless people suffering from structural injustice on the other." McCrae, "Good News," 520.

403. Stein, Luke, *An Exegetical*, 156.

404. Green, *The Gospel of Luke*, 210–211.

405. Green, 211; see also Fitzmyer, *Gospel According to Luke*, 532–533; and Martin, "Luke," 214.

406. Hopkins, *Black Theology*, 26.

407. Austin, *Salvation-Soteria*.

to prisoners is to be understood metaphorically, and that although "it may include healings and exorcisms, freedom always refers to the forgiveness of sins elsewhere in Luke-Acts."[408] The term ἄφεσιν (*aphesin*) is used in Luke 4:18 to signify freedom, deliverance, dismissal, forgiveness, and complete pardon from sin. In this sense, Jesus was not proclaiming freedom to literal captives of war but ἄφεσις (*aphesis*) to people who were captives of guilt (Luke 7:41–50), of money (Luke 19:1–10) and of Satan (Luke 8:26–39), as Butler, Gooding, Green and Hughes fervently argue.[409]

For his part, Uwaegbute points to the fact that Jesus's proclamation of freedom for the captives/prisoners had both literal and spiritual implications, while his audience understood it in terms of the release of Jewish prisoners from Roman prisons.[410] Furthermore, he maintains that this is because the Roman occupiers of Jesus's time had already taken a great number of Jews prisoner. Equally, many Jews had lost their inheritance, property, and lands to Rome's imperialistic rule. And worse still, the whole of the Jewish nation was captive to Rome,[411] says Uwaegbute. Hughes, Reiling and Swellengrebel and Vincent adhering to a literal and spiritual understanding, explain that the terms "captive" or "prisoner" in Isaiah 61:1 and Luke 4:18 refer to people who are in some sort of slavery (bondage to money, debts, guilt, hatred, Satan, sensuality),[412] including that of sin.

2.4.3.5 Proclaiming the Recovery of Sight to the Blind

The proclamation of recovery of sight to the blind is another dimension of Jesus's manifesto in Luke 4:18–19. The term "blind" in Greek is τυφλοῖς (adjective-dative masculine plural, transliteration: *typhlois*), and the original word is τυφλός, meaning physical, mental, or spiritual blindness (4:18; 6:39). Commenting on this, Gooding asserts that "this obviously included the offer of literal sight to the physically blind" (see 7:21–22; 18:35--43), while also

---

408. See Luke 1:77; 3:3; 24:47; Acts 2:38; 5:31; 10:43; 13:38; 26:18. Stein, *Luke, An Exegetical*, 156.

409. Butler, *Holman New Testament*, 63; Gooding, *According to Luke*, 82; Green, *Gospel of Luke*, 212; and Hughes, *Luke*, 142.

410. Uwaegbute, "Challenge of Jesus' Manifesto," 152.

411. Uwaegbute, 152.

412. Hughes, *Luke*, 142; Reiling and Swellengrebel, *A Handbook*, 200; and Vincent, *Word Studies*, 291.

implying the recovery of spiritual sight or eyes of people to enable them to turn from darkness to light (Acts 26:18) that Christ offers.[413] In support of this viewpoint, Reiling and Swellengrebel suggest that τυφλός in the text refers as well to blind people who are personally unhappy and socially weak (see Luke 14:13, 21). Moreover, he adds that those people are among the specific objects of the messianic healing ministry of Jesus and that they are viewed as the πτωχός (*ptóchos*, poor) who receive the good news.[414] Stein argues that the word "blind" here is a metaphorical reference to those who are "spiritually blind" (Luke 1:77–79; 2:30–32; 3:6; Acts 9:8–18; 13:47; 22:11–13; 26:17–18).[415] In Greek, ἀνάβλεψιν (*anablepsin*) is a noun (accusative feminine singular from its original word ἀνάβλεψις) which is translated "recovery of sight" or "restoration of sight." Reiling and Swellengrebel define ἀνάβλεψις as being given physical and spiritual new eyes, implying a shift from the non-concrete to the concrete.[416] In this respect, Russell argues that "Jesus used his divine nature to cure people while simultaneously teaching the gospel. Should we not also seek to impact people holistically,"[417] by setting free the oppressed and the broken-hearted?

2.4.3.6 Proclaiming the Oppressed Free from Brokenheartedness

In Jesus's manifesto as revealed in Luke 4:18–19, he promised to set free the oppressed and broken-hearted. The Greek word Jesus used in the text for "oppressed" is τεθραυσμένους (*tethrausmenous*), an accusative masculine plural and perfect middle or passive participle of the verb θραύω (*thrauó*) which means to break in pieces, to crush, smite or to shatter. Robertson describes the term "the oppressed" in Luke 4:18 as referring to people who were "broken in heart and often in body as well. One loves to think that Jesus felt it to be his mission to mend broken hearts like pieces of broken earthenware, real rescue-mission work. Jesus mends them and sets them free from

---

413. Gooding, *According to Luke*, 82.
414. Reiling and Swellengrebel, *A Handbook*, 200.
415. The latter example shows some interesting parallels in Luke-Acts: the idea of 'sending' in Luke 4:18 and Acts 26:17; of recovery of sight in Luke 4:18 and Acts 26:18; of proclamation of forgiveness, freedom or release in Luke 4:18 and Acts 26:18, see also Isaiah 42:7; 49:6; 58:8, 10. Stein, *Luke, An Exegetical*, 156.
416. Reiling and Swellengrebel, *A Handbook*, 201.
417. Russell, 25.

their limitations."[418] According to Uwaegbute, the Jews underwent different types of heart-breaking injustices and brutalities from the Roman imperialist government and the message Jesus came to proclaim was therefore meant to be a promise of joy and comfort to the oppressed.[419] Moreover, he adds that the people were not only victims of political brutality, but also people whose hearts were broken because of the oppression of Satan and the onslaught of sin.[420] Hopkins argues that "biblical stories provide examples of God siding with oppressed people. At the foundation of the Hebrew Scriptures is a continuous story about how Yahweh heard, saw, and delivered oppressed Hebrew slaves from bondage to liberation"[421] (Exod 3:6–11; Num 24:17; Isa 58:6).

Elucidating on the spiritual-physical meanings in Luke 4:18, Hopkins observes that the effect of Jesus's manifesto was not only the freeing of the invisible spirits of the oppressed, but also their freeing from the real slavery of the imperialistic and oppressive ruling class whose purpose was the accumulation of profit based on forced work, thus oppressing humanity.[422] Stein notes that the 'oppressed' in the text, although the term involves a literal dimension because of the Roman imperialist rule in the days of Jesus's earthly ministry, also includes oppression by evil spirits in the form of diseases, including mental illness, and demonic attacks[423] (Luke 4:31–37; 13:16; Acts 10:38). According to Butler, the oppressed Jewish nation was to be released through the good news Jesus proclaimed of freedom from oppression and renewal of physical, emotional, and spiritual strength.[424] This is a holistic approach to proclaiming the brokenhearted free.

2.4.3.7 Proclaiming the Year of the Lord's Favor

Κηρῦξαι ἐνιαυτὸν Κυρίου δεκτόν (*Kēryxai eniauton Kyriou dekton*) is translated by the phrase to "proclaim the year of the lord's favor." In this phrase the original word δεκτός (*dektos*) is employed to mean acceptable and to describe something that is welcomed and received favorably because it is pleasing.

---

418. Robertson, *Word Pictures*, 64.
419. Uwaegbute, "Challenge of Jesus' Manifesto," 152.
420. Uwaegbute, 152.
421. Hopkins, *Introducing Black Theology*, 23–24.
422. Hopkins, 24; see also Uwaegbute, 153.
423. Stein, *Luke, An Exegetical*, 156.
424. Butler, *Holman New*, 63.

Keener as well as Robertson point out that this is the final promise Jesus proclaimed in his manifesto before handing back the scroll to the attendant, describing the future of the Jewish nation in terms of the year of jubilee and picturing Christ's own conception of his earthly mission[425] (Isa 61:1–2; 49:8–13; 58:6; Lev 25:8–17; 2 Cor 6:2). Jamieson, Fausset and Brown; and Martin maintain the view that Jesus concluded his reading with the words, "to proclaim the year of the lord's favor" without reading the next line about the day of God's vengeance in Isaiah 61:2 in order to deliver a specifically messianic message.[426] Martin argues that "when Jesus added, *today this Scripture is fulfilled in your hearing*, the implication was clear. Jesus was claiming to be the Messiah who could bring the Kingdom of God which had been promised for so long – but his First Advent was not his time for judgment (vengeance);" see John 3:17.[427]

Whereas the jubilee year had never been observed as part of Israel's national existence, some scholars, such as Fitzmyer, Keener, Uwaegbute, and Wiersbe affirm that the earthly ministry of Jesus was meant to demonstrate practically what the jubilee year or the "year of favor" was meant to entail: providing both material and spiritual needs followed by the forgiveness of sin and eternal life.[428] As stated earlier, Wiersbe, in this respect, observes that during this year of favor, "slaves were set free and returned to their families, property that was sold reverted to the original owners, and all debts were cancelled. The land lay fallow as man and beast rested and rejoiced in the Lord."[429] It is from this perspective that Reiling and Swellengrebel argue that it is in this very year of jubilee that the lord will show divine favor on his people through his earthly ministry of comforting all who mourn (see similarity with Luke 1:30).[430] Writing from the same perspective, Butler states: "Today is the day. This is the year God will show favor and grace on his people. A young man from Nazareth can do all this? He can bring in the true Jubilee

---

425. Keener, *IVP Bible Background Commentary: New Testament*, 190; and Robertson, *Word Pictures*, 65.

426. Jamieson, Fausset and Brown, 103; and Martin, "Luke," 214.

427. Martin, "Luke," 214.

428. Fitzmyer, *The Gospel According*, 532–533; Keener, *Bible Backgrounds Commentary*, 190; Uwaegbute, "Challenge to Jesus' Manifesto," 153–154; and Wiersbe, *The Wiersbe Bible*, 149.

429. Wiersbe, 149.

430. Reiling and Swellengrebel, *A Handbook*, 202.

year when we release not only our slaves but also our nation from oppression and captivity (see Lev 25:8–55)?"[431] Along this line, Fitzmyer notes that, "the Isaian description of a period of favour and deliverance for Zion is now used to proclaim the period of Jesus and the new mode of salvation that is to come in him."[432] This interpretation goes in line with Stein's insinuation.

Jesus, therefore, claims that the kingdom of God had come through him, fulfilling the Old Testament promises. Salvation is now and here being offered to all,[433] as Stein writes. Although Jesus deliberately omitted "the reference to the 'day of God's vengeance' from his quotation of Isaiah 61:2 to emphasize the present time and opportunity for salvation, the context of this passage also implies the notion of divine vengeance,"[434] as Tannehill comments.

Basically, Luke 4:18–19 is the fulfilment of Isaiah 61:1–2 and a synonym for the "good news of the kingdom of God," as Luke 4:43 shows. In short, Jesus fulfilled all the promises in Isaiah 61:1–2 through his own earthly ministry, not in an economic or political sense, but in a spiritual and physical sense,[435] as Wiersbe remarks. Empirically speaking, what implications do Matthew 9:35–38 and Luke 4:18–19 have for my examination of parachurch agencies and their practices of mission? An application of these two scriptures to this current study is suggested and presented at the end of the Research Discussion (chapter five – section 5.8) in order to outline my personal convictions in relation to this research. Having reviewed in this chapter the specific literature in relation to the research question, the next chapter begins the research methodology phase by outlining the design and methods used for the study.

---

431. Butler, *Holman New Testament*, 63.
432. Fitzmyer, *The Gospel According*, 533.
433. Stein, *Luke, An Exegetical*, 157.
434. Tannehill, *Narrative Unity*, 68; see also Stein, 157.
435. Wiersbe, *The Wiersbe Bible*, 149.

CHAPTER 3

Research Methodology

In the previous chapter, I reviewed the literature grounding this empirical study. In this chapter, I continue my research procedure with the focus being on the research methodology I need to conduct the investigation. I have chosen qualitative interview methods as being appropriate in designing this empirical research. Why these approaches? Because, I have dealt with a social phenomenon that needed serious investigation and these methods are appropriate in order to explore, explain and to better understand the subject of this research, as well as to collect in-depth information, opinions, experiences, behaviors, contexts and phenomena. For this research study, qualitative multiple case study techniques were important as they address – on the basis of several samples – the 'how' and 'why' questions which enable in-depth understanding of phenomena, and of people's experiences, including their context and real-life conditions.

The concept of mission drift in parachurch agencies, which is the research object of this study, was introduced in detail in section 1.1.4. The main research key question or empirical unknown as it is applied to the research object determines the choice of multiple case techniques as the most appropriate method for this research and is presented in the following section (3.1). The empirical unknown (EU) for this study and the five auxiliary research questions (RQ) are introduced in section 1.4. The overall research design is presented in a simplified form in the following figure.

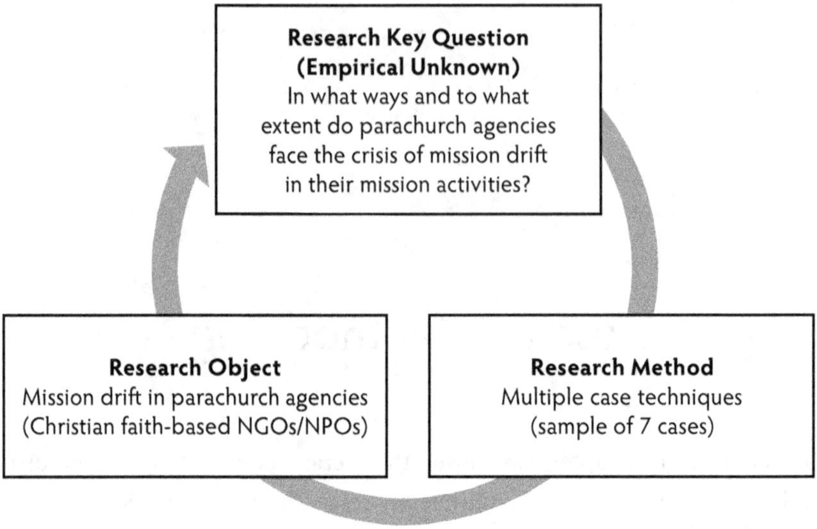

```
        ┌─────────────────────────┐
        │   Research Key Question │
        │   (Empirical Unknown)   │
        │  In what ways and to what│
        │  extent do parachurch   │
        │  agencies face the crisis│
        │  of mission drift in    │
        │  their mission activities?│
        └─────────────────────────┘
```

┌───────────────────────────┐   ┌───────────────────────────┐
│   **Research Object**   │   │   **Research Method**   │
│ Mission drift in parachurch│ │ Multiple case techniques │
│ agencies (Christian faith-│   │   (sample of 7 cases)   │
│ based NGOs/NPOs)   │   │   │
└───────────────────────────┘   └───────────────────────────┘

Figure 3.1: Schematic Overview of the Research Design

This multiple case study is based around seven parachurch agencies delivering holistic church-related missions across the world. Smith implies that the research design uses an empirical approach, focusing on collective or multiple sources of data with a questionnaire type of interview that covers a series of different kinds of written questions (fifteen in total) in order to solicit different types of data,[1] requesting responses from a whole range of interviewees. The questionnaire is written in English, but has been translated[2] into French and German, so as to reach the relevant informants without the problem of a language barrier. Key informants were selected and consulted as the primary data source, supported with a brief historical review of each parachurch organization's commitment in delivering a holistic type of Christian mission, as well as documentary analyses of important organizational documents and field observations.

---

1. Smith, *Writing and Research*, 126.
2. With French as my first language, I have translated the questionnaire myself from English to French with the service of 'Google Translate' and 'Deepl Translate' (https://www.deepl.com/translator) wherever it was needed. The translation from English to German is done by a professional and vice versa. See these translated questionnaires in appendixes 2 and 3. All the texts used in the thesis in languages other than English are translated and the original version put in the footnotes.

This study predominantly used a written questionnaire to conduct empirical research interviews. The research also involved two or three face-to-face interviews to satisfy the wishes and convenience of some interviewees. The research interview questionnaire excluded closed-ended questions (e.g. two-point questions, multiple choice questions and scaled questions) from the investigation because they only give the respondent the possibility to respond with a simple "yes" or "no" to indicate the extent to which he/she agrees or disagrees with features of a real-life situation. Such responses are not relevant to this study. Instead, the questionnaire has included open-ended questions. Sincero argues that open-ended questions fall into the following categories: word associated questions; thematic apperception test questions; completely unstructured questions; and sentence, story or picture completion questions.[3] They allow the interviewees to inform the interviewer by giving free-form answers without a predefined option, thus supplying their own answers. The respondent is expected to answer the questionnaire with examples and stories utilizing new and deeper insights.

3.1 Multiple or Collective Case Design

The research approach that I have selected for dealing with mission drift in parachurch agencies in this thesis focuses on a multiple case study. In general, Yin defines case studies as an "empirical inquiry that investigates a contemporary phenomenon within its real-life context, especially when the boundaries between phenomenon and context are not clearly evident."[4] In this respect, Bryman notes that this format is used in this research because of the space it provides for intense analysis of a real-life situation through the use of several sources of evidence.[5] The method allows an in-depth documentation of the procedures and outcomes across all the selected cases, as well as more powerful explanations and descriptions[6] – Creswell writes – taken to grasp the concept of mission drift; procedures which can be beneficial to other church-related NGOs/NPOs dealing with the phenomenon. The

---

3. Sincero, "Types of Survey Questions," 2–3.
4. Yin, *Case Study Research*, 13.
5. Bryman, *Social Research Methods*, 57.
6. Creswell, *Educational Research*, 45.

collective case study at hand has to do with seven Christian holistic development agencies who have communicated their holistic approach to mission. This is detailed in Table 3.2 under section 3.1.5 (selection of interviewees). These agencies were chosen because they are established NGOs/NPOs within their field, and this qualifies them as representative sample of cases for other Christian faith-based organizations.

Ayres, Kavanagh and Knafl acknowledge that using case study as a research strategy is not without its critics.[7] It has been critiqued, for instance, by Robson and McCartan as "a soft option lacking rigor, often seen as an exploratory precursor to a more established approach."[8] At the same time the case study method, taken from a positivist standpoint – says Yin – is discounted as an unsatisfactory approach because of its deficiency in terms of empirical generalizability, with the in-depth review of multiple cases.[9] He accurately describes case studies as having a focus on developing and generalizing theory rather than enumerating frequencies.[10] Thus, case studies are particularly valuable for studying the organization's internal struggles, as they provide valuable in-depth data about the staff's interpretations of those crises that may result in mission drift.

In the multiple or collective case studies approach, Yin suggests that "six to ten cases are required to satisfy the requirements of the replication strategy," because "there are no hard-and-fast rules about how many cases are sufficient to provide compelling support for the initial set of propositions – if the results turn out as predicted."[11] Moreover, Yin argues that since "the multiple case studies design does not rely on the type of representative sampling logic used in survey research, the typical criteria regarding sample size are irrelevant."[12] Therefore, this research refers to seven instrumental bounded cases (parachurch agencies) selected to provide a more in-depth understanding of the mission drift phenomena. The purpose of a collective or multiple case study is to involve more than one case in order to develop a more in-depth analysis

---

7. Ayres, Kavanaugh and Knafl, "Within-Case and Across-Case," 871–883.
8. Robson and McCartan, *Real World Research*, 137.
9. Yin, *Case Study Research*, 19.
10. Yin, 48.
11. Yin, 46.
12. Yin, 50; see also Patton, *Qualitative Evaluation*, 53.

of the phenomena by examining a number of different missions carried out by Christian faith-based organizations.

Within social science, according to Stake, Eisenhardt and Graebner, the advantage of multiple case study is that it focuses on several agencies of the same type to identify identical characteristics, yielding more testable, generalizable and robust theory, while single case would focus on the issue at the level of a single organization.[13] Nevertheless – to Ragin and Geertz – it should be observed that single case studies are no less inferior in value to multiple cases[14] because the fieldwork of any qualitative research involves in-depth case studies and powerful disciplinary force, which is demanding, coercive and assertive.[15] The research is designed deliberately to follow the pattern of multiple case study, which allows this study to conclude with some empirical generalizations, making comparisons across them, while single case analyses theological inferences,[16] as Cassell and Symon state. It should be noticed that for this research, "empirical generalizations would involve application of data to a wider population,"[17] of parachurch agencies, as Cassell and Symon insinuate. Hartley makes clear that empirical case studies usually embrace multiple case study design because the research phenomenon can be best addressed through this method.[18] Cassell and Symon observe that multiple case studies are valuable, but careful "attention needs to be paid to the quantity of data which must be collected and analysed,"[19] to avoid misconceptions.

Based on this information, I applied a collective case study to test the concept of mission drift[20] to render description and to develop notions about the phenomena or issues.[21] Scholars – Galunic and Eisenhardt; Gilbert; Edmondson, Bohmer and Pisano; and Mintzberg and Waters – argue that the

---

13. Stake, *The Art*, 88–89; Stake, "Qualitative Case Studies," 138; and Eisenhardt and Graebner, "Theory Building," 27.
14. Ragin, "'Casing' and the Process," 225.
15. Geertz, *After the Fact*, 119.
16. Cassell and Symon. *Essential Guide*, 315.
17. Cassell and Symon, 315.
18. Hartley, "Leading and Managing," 324.
19. Cassell and Symon, 326.
20. Anderson, "Decision Making," 201–222; and Pinfield, "A Field Evaluation," 365–388.
21. Mintzberg, "An Emerging Strategy," 582–589; and Eisenhardt, "Building Theories," 532–550; and Eisenhardt and Graebner, "Theory Building," 25–32.

issues can be found within the organizations,[22] at the internal group process[23] and at the strategic level.[24] This qualitative research embraced a collective case or multiple case design to analyze the concept in context-specific settings (mission drift), viewed as a real world setting," asserts Patton, "where the researcher does not attempt to manipulate the phenomenon of interest."[25] Creswell argues that "the case study method explores a real-life, contemporary bounded system (a case) or multiple bounded systems (cases) over time, through detailed, in-depth data collection involving multiple sources of information . . . and reports a case description and case themes."[26] Earlier on, Creswell stated that a case study is "an exploration of a 'bounded system' . . . a program, an event, an activity, or individuals."[27] While a considerable number of case studies focus on single case research, frequently used because of its exclusive characteristics, the multiple or collective case studies method allowed this researcher to investigate the theory under evaluation through the use of a repetition or replication strategy.

In multiple case study design, the repetition strategy is carefully carried out in two stages: (1) a literal replication stage – cases are chosen to predict or obtain similar results, and (2) a theoretical replication stage – cases are chosen to investigate in order to approve or disprove the patterns identified in the literal replication stage,[28] as Eisenhardt alludes. Usually, the theoretical replication is known to predict contrasting results for predictable reasons.[29] Thus, Chambers argues that a collective case research is,

> Similar to experimental research in the laboratory, where a researcher may want to conduct two or three literal replications of a certain result by conducting the same experiment several times and four to six slightly different experiments by

---

22. Galunic and Eisenhardt, "Architectural Innovation," 1229–1249; and Gilbert, "Unbundling the Structure," 741–763.
23. Edmondson, Bohmer and Pisano, "Disrupted Routines," 685–716.
24. Mintzberg and Waters, "Tracking Strategy," 465–499.
25. Patton, *Qualitative Research*, 39.
26. Creswell, *Qualitative Inquiry*, 97; see also Bryman, *Social Research Methods*, 57.
27. Creswell, *Qualitative Inquiry*, 61.
28. Eisenhardt, "Building Theories," 532–550.
29. Yin, *Application of Case*, 33.

manipulating conditions in order to establish if results indeed vary for predictable reasons.[30]

Yin upholds the view that the mode of generalization in a multiple case or collective case design is through "analytic generalizations."[31] Following the same line of interpretation, Patton affirms that these are logical generalizations rather than "statistical generalizations,"[32] in which the empirical results of a particular case study are compared with the concept of mission drift used as a template. According to Yin, replication can be claimed if several samples are shown to support the previously developed concept, and thus the empirical results can be considered if even more "cases support the same theory but do not support an equally plausible, rival theory."[33] It should be observed that collective case study can involve three types of case studies as follows: those that are shared, joint, or independent,[34] as Salmi observes. For this research, the researcher has decided on one independent multiple case study.

3.1.1 Selection of Cases

The research for this case study is drawn from the larger population of Christian faith-based NGOs/NPOs. Consequently, Eisenhardt argues that while it is very important to define from which population the cases are drawn, "A random selection of cases out of this population is neither necessary, nor even preferable."[35] Because, the study relies on theoretical rather than statistical sampling,[36] as Eisenhardt and Graebner write.

The cases in a multiple case study have the potential to enable the researcher to analyze a specific phenomenon[37] – in my case mission drift in parachurch NGOs/NPOs. In choosing the cases for this study, I carefully selected church-related agencies that provided the opportunity to analyze three phenomena, these being isomorphic-holism (hybridity), internal secularization, and the nature of intricate relationships with donors. I am using

---

30. Chambers, "Growing a Hybrid," 54.
31. Yin, *Application of Case*, 33.
32. Patton, *Qualitative Research*, 237.
33. Yin, *Application of Case*, 33.
34. Salmi, "Collective Case Studies".
35. Eisenhardt, "Building Theories," 537.
36. Eisenhardt and Graebner, "Theory Building," 25–32.
37. Stake, "Qualitative Case Studies", 134–164.

a purposive sampling strategy – according to Schwandt – in order to ensure that each agency is relevant to the research question.[38] A purposive sampling strategy (also known as a selective, subjective or judgmental technique) is a sampling method in which the researcher relies on her/his own judgment for the identification and selection of cases and samples related to the phenomenon of interest in order to conduct the study. Cassell and Symon say that "to sample means to select the case or cases for study from the basic unit of study (or population) when it is impossible to cover all instances of that unit."[39] This study finds itself in the same configuration where it is impossible to study all the existing church-related organizations.

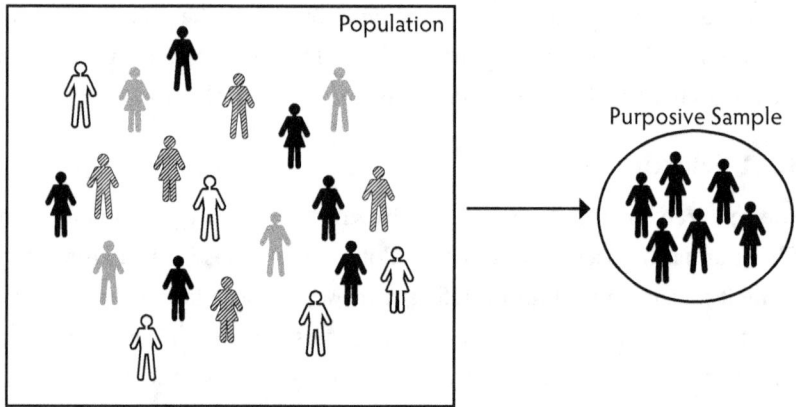

Figure 3.2: Purposive Sampling Technique

The use of purposive sampling of cases helps "to build variety and provide opportunities for intensive study,"[40] as Stake points out. Likewise, scholars like Palinkas, Horwitz, Green, Wisdom, Duan and Hoagwood retain the understanding that using a purposeful sampling for qualitative research enables collection and analysis of data.[41] Unlike Yin, who suggests six to ten cases in

---

38. Schwandt, *Dictionary of Qualitative Inquiry*, 39 and 57.
39. Cassell and Symon, 315; for figure 3.2 and figure 3.3, see also Dudovskiy, *The Ultimate Guide*.
40. Stake, "Qualitative Case Studies," 134–164.
41. Palinkas et al., "Purposeful Sampling," 533–544.

a multiple case study,[42] Eisenhardt recommends four to ten cases in order to conduct convincing and manageable research.[43] He rightly insists that a research project with less than four cases would hardly generate convincing empirical grounding for research, with much complexity to investigate (unless the sample engages several mini-cases within it), and it quickly becomes difficult to handle and analyze the volume and the complexity of the data if the study involves more than ten cases.[44] However, for this research, it sounds logical to involve seven parachurch agencies as a multiple case study. Seven study samples are a reasonable number to provide the opportunity in this research to study the generalizability of the cases. In turn, this can be applied to other parachurch NGOs/NPOs delivering holistic types of Christian service. Nevertheless, I am also interested in spotting particularities and have therefore selected specific cases that have different origins, missions objectives, scope, financial opportunities, and governance structures (the characteristics of the selected cases are shown in Table 3.3).

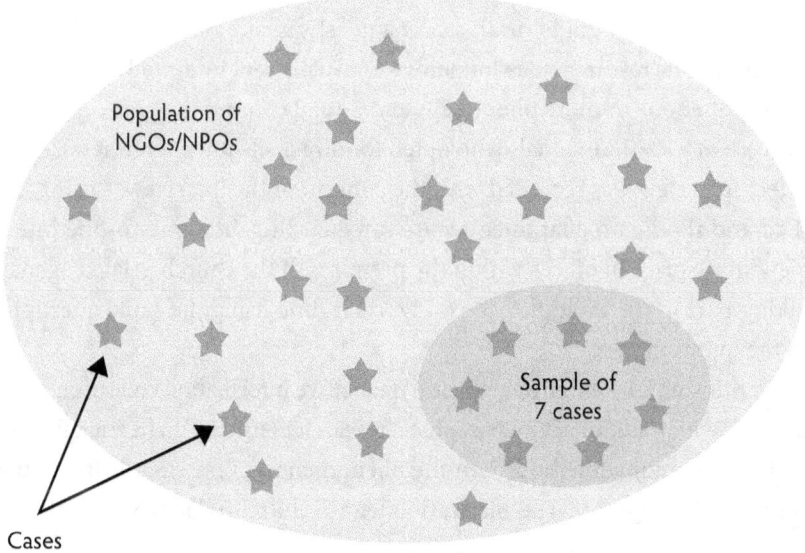

Figure 3.3: Population of Parachurch Agencies – Purposive Sample of Seven Cases of Study

---

42. Yin, *Case Study Research*, 46.
43. Eisenhardt, "Building Theories," 545.
44. Eisenhardt, 545.

3.1.2 Data Collection

A qualitative research interview can be described – according to Kvale's description – as "an interview, whose purpose is to gather descriptions of the life-world of the interviewee with respect to interpretation of the meaning of the described phenomena."[45] During data collection, the researcher needs to see the research topic from the standpoint of the interviewee in order to understand why and how he/she comes to have this individual perspective,[46] as Cassell and Symon suggest. The goal of the qualitative research interview method is to gain an understanding of how each informant articulates the mission of their agency and whether he/she feels that their NGO/NPO is delivering a holistic Christian service or if the organization is dealing with the phenomenon of mission drift.

This research embraces a multiple or collective case study method that focuses on understanding the various dynamics of each selection present within the settings of the study case in order to collect relevant data,[47] a view defended by Eisenhardt. The collection of data for the study is mostly done using an interview guide (in this case a questionnaire) consisting of fifteen questions. The research questionnaire was usually sent by e-mail to the interviewee after one or more phone calls and e-mail communications, except in the case of a few individuals who opted for direct sit-down interviews. Each direct interview was recorded with the consent of the interviewee using my iPad and iPhone to guarantee secure safeguarding. The one-to-one interviews took place in offices within the premises of the church-related agency taking part in the multiple case study: each time using the same questions in the questionnaire.

In this study, I combined empirical qualitative information collection techniques[48] with traditional bibliographical research methods[49] to be triangulated with observational methods[50] on the phenomenon of mission drift and the susceptibility to internal secularization within church-related NGOs/NPOs.

---

45. Kvale, *InterViews*, 174.
46. Cassell and Symon, *Essential Guide*, 11.
47. Eisenhardt, "Building Theories," 534.
48. Such as a research questionnaire for interviews.
49. Such as books, journals, magazines, reports, newspapers, historical facts, electronic data, and online resources.
50. Such as self-assessment validation (direct observations or experience in the field).

Some scholars – Green, Camilli, Elmore, Skukauskaiti and Grace; and Yin – argue that a full triangulation can be attained only when multiple sources of data emerge from the same evidence.[51] Moreover, Yin carefully indicates that

> when you have really triangulated the data, the events or facts of the case study have been supported by more than a single source of evidence; when you have used multiple sources but not actually triangulated the data, you typically have analysed each source of evidence separately and have compared the conclusions from the different analyses – but not triangulated the data.[52]

Therefore, the multiple information sources in this thesis were designed to generate full triangulation and to result in the collection of various complementary evidences and data.

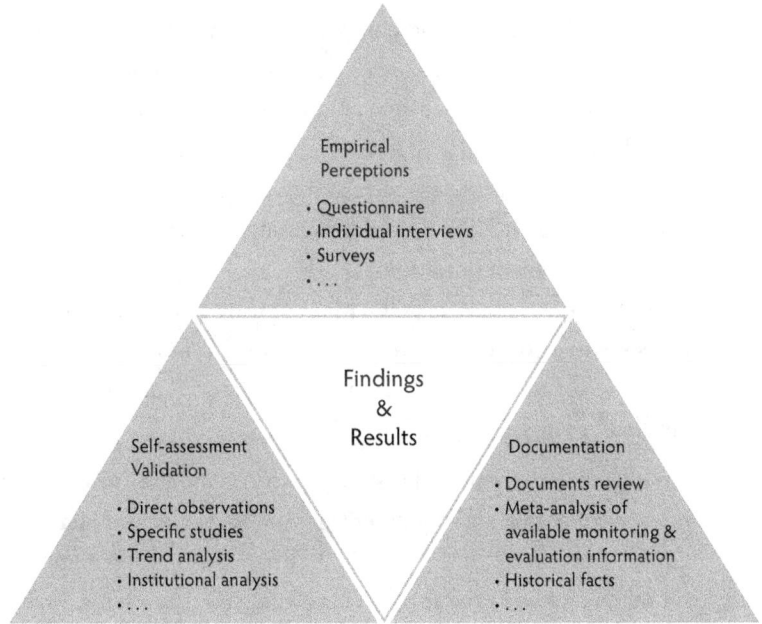

Figure 3.4: Synthesis to Interpret Data and Analysis Through Triangulation

---

51. Green et al., *Handbook*, 115; and Yin, *Case Study*, 18.
52. Yin, *Application of Case Study*, 98-99.

3.1.3 Research Analysis of Data

After data had been collected, I read and re-read the questionnaire feedback, assessing the descriptions of experience shared by the various informants, and listening and re-listening to the voice recordings in order to extract relevant statements for the study. Then, the data collected was itemized into units with related meaning and categorized by themes using codes to create sections. In his argument, Yin suggests that the ideal strategy in analyzing the research data coming from a multiple case study is to "follow the theoretical propositions that led to the case study."[53] The theoretical propositions that led this study's data collection plan are as follows:

1. That tensions may arise in trying to reconcile a parachurch agency's mission (Christian worldview) with the worldview of its unbelieving funders, resulting in mission drift.
2. That delivering Christian faith-based mission and services within a secular environment and competitive social mission has the potential to restrain Christian identity and in the end lead to the internal secularization of the parachurch organization.
3. That the pressures associated with raising funds may result in coercive, intimidating, mimetic and normative isomorphic holism, making it difficult to differentiate parachurch agencies from their secular counterparts.
4. That the pressures associated with operating strategic paradigm shifts – when confronted with an existential crisis – are likely to affect the organization's Christian identity, and that this may in turn lead to mission drift.

I have followed a "content analysis approach" to analyze the qualitative data I have been collecting and documenting. In this respect, Bhatia implies that content analysis provides the possibility of analyzing information collected from interviewees in the form of recordings, written texts, imagery, physical items, or even media.[54] Therefore, for this thesis, content analysis was used as an appropriate tool to analyze the questionnaires, open-ended interviews, communication artefacts and documents, and to focus group

---

53. Yin, *Case Study Research*, 130.
54. Bhatia, "Your Guide."

data,[55] as Krippendorf indicates. Through this method, I was able to analyze collected and documented information in the form of verbal and non-verbal cues from the interviewees (with their permission). Additionaly, I recorded the interview conversations and noted the responses plus feedback from both the distributed questionnaire and face-to-face interviews. Data collection was done in three languages (English, French and German) with quotes translated into English and footnoted in the original language.

The purpose of using open-ended interviews over and above strict standardized or non-directive interviews is – according to Denscombe – "to maintain a clear list of topics that need to be covered but to allow flexibility for the interviewee to elaborate on points of interest."[56] It should be observed that a standardized interview (also called a structured interview or a researcher-administered survey) aims to ensure that each interview is conducted with precisely the same research questions and following exactly the same order,[57] as Lindlof and Taylor argue.[58] Inversely, Thorpe and Holt affirm that a non-directive interview (also called an unstructured interview) aims to ensure that questions are not prearranged but are prepared, much like a normal everyday conversation which tends to be free flowing and informal. Even though empirical qualitative interviews can be time consuming, and data analysis seems to be more complicated due to the non-standard nature of the information given, these interviews provide depth and insight into the phenomenon of mission drift being studied in this research. The data collected is rich in validity, yet I need to be aware that my subjectivity or prejudice as a researcher may influence the reliability and consistency of the research outcomes (see next section: Reliability and Validity of This Empirical Research). Moreover, as Denscombe says, the inhibitions of the participants coupled with "the intrusion into their private thoughts and feelings" may skew the outcomes of the data.[59] However, he also says that "the therapeutic effect of taking part in an interview can be rewarding, particularly set within the Living Theory context,"[60] since the interviewees are given an opportunity to reflect

---

55. Krippendorf, *Content Analysis*, 33.
56. Denscombe, *The Good Research*, 177.
57. Lindlof and Taylor, *Qualitative Communication*, 20.
58. Lindlof and Taylor, *Qualitative Communication*, 20.
59. Denscombe, *The Good Research*, 203.
60. Denscombe, 203.

on and to discuss their ideas, wishes and values without feeling that they are being criticized or interrupted. Bearing this in mind, I was able to analyze verbal and non-verbal cues from those interviewees whose permission had been given, and to record the interview conversations and feedback from the distributed questionnaire.

3.1.4 Reliability and Validity of This Empirical Research

Multiple case studies are usually undertaken in the early stages of the development of a theory. Any problems related to reliability and validity at these early stages might have flow effects, and these flow effects or 'ripple effects' can last "throughout later stages when emerging theoretical relationships are formally tested," says Chambers.[61] As noted by Silverman; Gibbert, Ruigrok and Wicki and Yin, the lack of a rigorous pursuit of reliability and validity in empirical case study research is especially problematic.[62] Therefore, it is particularly essential for this multiple case study research that I take measures to ensure that the reliability and validity of this research is achieved by using content analysis methodology. As displayed in tabulated form below, the social science scholars – Gibbert and Ruigrok; Silverman – categorize research actions or measures under four main criteria: reliability, construct validity, internal validity, and external validity.[63] The following table has been adapted from the studies[64] conducted by Gibbert, Ruigrok and Wicki; and Yin.

---

61. Chambers, "Growing a Hybrid," 80.
62. Silverman, *Doing Qualitative Research*, 211; Gibbert, Ruigrok and Wicki, "What Passes?," 1465–1474; and Yin, *Application of Case Study*, 34.
63. Gibbert and Ruigrok, "The 'What' and 'How'," 8; and Silverman, *Interpreting Qualitative Data*, 225.
64. Gibbert, Ruigrok and Wicki, "What Passes?," 1467 and Yin, 34.

Table 3.1: Reliability and Validity Criteria

Criteria		Description	Tactic	Research phase in which the tactic is ensued
Reliability	Credibility (lack of random fault)	Establishing that the collection and analysis of data can be replicated with the same findings.	Developing a multiple case study procedure. Safeguarding and coding the data twice.	Collection of data Analysis of data
Construct Validity	Truth (lack of systemic or non-random fault)	Demonstrating correct operational measures or actions for the concepts, constructs, or variables of interest.	Collecting data from multiple sources. Forming a clear evidence chain. Keeping track of key respondents for eventual review of the study draft.	Collection and analysis of data Analysis of data Analysis of data
Internal Validity		Demonstrating a fundamental relationship between the constructs of interest and findings.	Pattern matching (comparing empirically observed phenomena with theoretical credible explanations).	Analysis of data (theory building)
External Validity		Demonstrating an area to which the research's results can be generalized and its relevance beyond an academic audience.	Replication logic Providing a clear rationale for the multiple case study sampling (selection of parachurch agencies) Keeping track of key respondents for eventual review of the study draft	Collection of data Collection of data Analysis of data

3.1.4.1 *The Reliability of the Study*

Since the analysis of content deals with written questionnaire texts and interview transcripts, empirical research presents the researcher with the challenge of reliability and validity that may result from multiple readings and interpretations of the same textual information. It should be observed that some scholars like Gibbert, Ruigrok and Wicki have rigorously criticized case study research for lack of objectivity and consistency despite recent academic progress made in creating detailed guidelines on methods and techniques for improving reliability and validity of case research approaches, procedures, and findings.[65] The reliability of this particular research on mission drift in parachurch agencies comes from the trustworthiness of the twice-coded collected data and on the validity of the outcome findings. Reliability guarantees validity, and ensures that the data collected and the process of analysis operated can be repeated with the same outcomes thus demonstrating the absence of random errors.[66] The goal of reliability in this empirical study research was achieved by ensuring that the measurement of errors is fundamentally random, that the study is analyzing what it claims to analyze while fulfilling its predicted hypothesis, and that the results can be used meaningfully, by minimizing any possible unnecessary variables. This theoretical framework helps to ensure that the results of this research study have been accurately measured, and that they are acceptable and usable. It guarantees that this study has reached the level of being correct and the state of being valid.

As Krippendorf states: "Reliability is not concerned with the world outside of the research process. All it can do is to assure researchers that their procedures can be trusted to have responded to real phenomena, without claiming knowledge of what these phenomena 'really' are."[67] With regard to this collective case study research concerning mission drift, the reliability of the data collected to analyze the phenomenon is boosted by replicating research efforts under different scenarios (e.g. by collecting information from multiple sources of data, by involving several informants to work on the same

---

65. Gibbert, Ruigrok and Wicki, "What Passes?" 1465; see also Yin, *Case Study Research*, 41.
66. Gibbert, Ruigrok and Wicki, 1469.
67. Krippendorf, *Content Analysis*, 268.

information independently, and by categorizing and double coding the same data after some time has elapsed to enhance its consistency).

3.1.4.2 The Validity of the Study

Contrary to *reliability*, which "is not concerned with the world outside of the research process"[68] – as Krippendorf argues – *validity* relates to the truth, and so cannot be proven by duplicating analysis of the same information,[69] says Chambers. Why is validity important for this research study? It is important for the purpose of strengthening the reporting of data by ensuring that the findings among the study interviewees represent real results as compared to similar people outside the research study. The theory of validity is important in order to determine research questions and it ensures that the researcher is utilizing questions that accurately measure the phenomenon of importance.

For this research, it is imperative to show the difference between construct validity, internal validity and external validity. It should be noted that construct validity (also known as concept validity) has to do with the establishment of the correct operational actions and measures for the concepts of interest. As described by Gibbert and Ruigrok, construct validity is a procedure that "refers to the extent to which a study investigates what it claims to investigate, i.e., to the extent to which a procedure leads to an accurate observation of reality"[70] – in this case, the concept of mission drift in parachurch NGOs/NPOs. In a typical empirical collective case study, construct validity is normally realized and assessed through the triangulation of data with the establishment of a "clear chain of evidence" and keeping track of feedback on the draft case study report from sample parachurch agencies,[71] as Yin insists. All these procedures have been used in this qualitative empirical research. As mentioned earlier (under section 3.), multiple sources of data such as the interviews questionnaire and organizational documents (both internal and publicly available) are utilized to gather the necessary information for this study of mission drift in CFB-NGOs/NPOs.

---

68. Krippendorf, *Content Analysis*, 268.
69. Chambers, "Growing a Hybrid," 82.
70. Gibbert and Ruigrok, "The 'What' and 'How,'" 8; see also Yin, *Case Study Research*, 41; and Denzin and Lincoln, *Handbook*.
71. Yin, *Case Study Research*, 41.

External validity, also known as social validity or generalizability, has to do with the establishment of a domain (i.e. a population of cases relating to parachurch agencies) from which the research's results can be generalized and through which the relevance of the study can be assessed beyond an academic audience. Gibbert, Ruigrok and Wicki; Yin; and Numagami advocate the view that external validity is grounded in "the intuitive belief that theories must be shown to account for phenomena not only in the setting in which they are studied, but also in other settings."[72] This allows analytical generalization from empirical observation to produce a theory of mission drift in parachurch agencies. Besides, following this train of thought, Gibbert, Ruigrok and Wicki; and Eisenhardt argue that theory development that encompasses four to ten case studies for empirical research can offer a good basis for analytical generalization and suggest an acceptable rationale for cross-case study.[73] In these seven study cases, external validity is realized through the use of replication logic (combining literal and theoretical case replications) and analytic generalization from empirical observations to theory.

Internal validity, also referred to as logical validity has to do with the establishment of a fundamental relationship between the concepts of interest (i.e. constructs/variables of interest) and the outcomes of the study,[74] as Gibbert, Ruigrok and Wicki imply. In a multiple case study research, Yin affirms that the most usual procedure to increase internal validity is "pattern matching."[75] Pattern matching is used in the theory-building phase to refer to scholarly discussions whose aim is to compare empirically observed phenomena with theoretically plausible interpretations – either predicted patterns or previously studied and established patterns in different contexts. Theory triangulation is used as an internal validity measure to verify research results by adopting multiple perspectives. These measures are discussed at length in chapter 4.

As pointed out by Krippendorf, "In the pursuit of high reliability, validity tends to get lost" because of the researcher's "common dilemma of having to choose between interesting but nonreplicable interpretations that intelligent readers of texts may offer each other in conversations, and oversimplified or

---

72. Gibbert, Ruigrok and Wicki, "What Passes?" 1468; Yin, *Case Study Research*, 31; and Numagami, "The Infeasibility," 3.
73. Gibbert, Ruigrok and Wicki, 1468; and Eisenhardt, "Building Theories," 532–550.
74. Gibbert, Ruigrok and Wicki, 1467.
75. Yin, *Case Study Research*, 105.

superficial but reliable text analyses generated through the use of computers or carefully instructed human coders."[76] It is from this perspective that Gibbert, Ruigrok and Wicki emphasize the problems of trade-offs between different validity measures: "Without a clear theoretical and causal logic (internal validity), and without a careful link between theoretical conjecture and empirical observations (construct validity), there can be no external validity in the first place."[77] This ensures the replicability of the research.

In summary, this empirical study was accomplished by using multiple case study research design. It utilized seven specific samples to develop a case study protocol; double coding data to boost the reliability of the process of collection and analysis and used multiple sources of data to establish a clear chain of evidence (to boost construct validity). Key participants were requested to review crucial data from preliminary results (to boost external validity), and I employed pattern matching methods to build theory from study samples (to boost internal validity). Consistent with these recommendations, the seven case agencies in this empirical research (see below Tables 3.2 and 3.3) represent a mix of theoretical and literal replications which the study has identified and have been discussed later in section 4.1 of chapter 4. It should be noted that Yin makes the distinction that "literal replication" refers to similar cases selected for empirical study research based on the assumption that the predicted results will be same, whereas "theoretical replication" refers to cases selected based on the theory that they will produce different outcomes.[78] The multiple case study at hand highlights external validity as the fundamental quality measure, at the expense of construct and internal validities.

3.1.5 Selection of Interviewees

The selection of participants for the interview questionnaire involved a direct approach to leadership for authorization and then to a key informant in each parachurch NGO/NPO, to discuss parameters, communicate the questions, and seek assistance in either setting up interviews or making arrangements to collect answers. With all the agencies, I first approached the management to gain their support for this research. I asked permission to conduct

---

76. Krippendorf, *Content Analysis*, 270.
77. Gibbert, Ruigrok and Wicki, "What Passes?" 1468.
78. Yin, *Application*, 105.

either a direct interview or send the questionnaire by e-mail, interviewing senior managers and frontline staff members from each of the seven parachurch agencies.

Table 3.2: Profile of the Interviewees

Parachurch Agencies	Managerial Staff	Frontline Staff	Number of Interviewees	Countries of Participants	Languages of Interviews
Compassion International	2	3	5	Burkina Faso	English
Latin Link International	3	2	5	Switzerland, Nicaragua, UK	English, French, German
Medair International	2	3	5	Switzerland	English, German
MEOS Interkulturelle Dienste	2	1	3	Switzerland	English, German
Mercy Ships International	3	2	5	Switzerland	English, French, German
Service de Missions et d'Entraide (SME)	2	2	4	France, Switzerland	English, French
Youth With A Mission (YWAM)	1	4	5	USA, Togo, Switzerland, Burkina Faso	English, French
FINAL TOTALS	15	17	32	8	3

The sampling of these seven parachurch agencies is intended to be representative of parachurch organizations in the area of Christian faith-based mission, and to involve their social and spiritual commitments. Higgs, Richardson and Dahlgren; Sarantakos; and Bernard echo this view, noting that to make sure the sampling is representative, a non-probability purposeful sampling is used to achieve a sample of informants that provides data[79] based on how the seven selected church-related organizations dealt or are dealing with the issue of mission drift in delivering Christian faith-based services. The representation of the sample cases also took into account the ethical considerations of this thesis as defined by UNISA.

Table 3.3: Profile of the Parachurch Agencies

Parachurch Agencies & Websites	Founding Date	Localization and Area of Service	# of Staff	Characteristics: Main Mission from the Online Mission Statement
Compassion International	1952	Worldwide	± 2000	Releasing children from spiritual, social, economic, and physical poverty.
Latin Link International	1991	From the West to Latin America	171	Mission mobilization, reducing Bible poverty, church development, evangelism, education, and increasing human dignity in Latin America.
Medair International	1989	From Switzerland to 12 countries in the world	1750	Being inspired by Christian faith to relieve human suffering in the most remote and devastated places of the world – emergency relief and recovery.
MEOS Interkulturelle Dienste	1963	Switzerland	45	Accompanying migrants holistically and passing on God's love across cultural borders, while promoting intercultural skills and activities inside Switzerland.

---

79. Higgs, Richardson and Dahlgren, *Developing Practice*, 14–16; Sarantakos, *Social Research*, 153; and Bernard, *Research Methods*, 189.

Parachurch Agencies & Websites	Founding Date	Localization and Area of Service	# of Staff	Characteristics: Main Mission from the Online Mission Statement
Mercy Ships International	1978	From the USA and 16 other national resource offices in Europe and South Africa to African poor countries	± 2,500	Bringing hope and healing to the forgotten poor by providing a lasting legacy of healthcare and free safe surgeries while following the 2000-year-old model of Jesus.
Service de Missions et d'Entraide (SME)	1976	From Switzerland to some countries in Africa, Asia, and Middle East	74	Providing education and professional training through partnership with churches. Sharing Christian values by bring peace and hope to people in fragile contexts based on the unconditional love of Christ.
Youth With A Mission (YWAM)	1960	Worldwide	± 15,000	Bringing people to know God through Jesus and making him known to others by offering practical training, micro-income generation, social action and mercy ministries, and evangelistic activities.

3.1.6 The Role of Cultural Interpretation in the Research Questions

In considering empirical research, one may ask the following question: Why did cultural interpretation in the analysis of the interview questions not influence the results of the study? While I was aware of the fact that cultural interpretation can influence the outcomes, I opted for a "questionnaire-based approach" to help minimize that influence – an influence which can occur while processing information in a cursory and hasty manner.

I decided that a more thoughtful processing of the questionnaire would help to minimize cultural influence in interpretation. As social psychologists, Briley and Aaker have succeeded in demonstrating: "Culture-based differences in persuasion arise when a person processes information in a cursory, spontaneous manner, but these differences dissipate when a person's intuitions are supplemented by more deliberative processing. . . . Corrections to these default judgements occur when processing is thoughtful."[80] From the standpoint of Briley and Aaker's claim, I have argued that a "questionnaire-based-approach" investigation does significantly minimize the role of cultural interpretations in analysis of the research questions. Therefore, a "questionnaire-based approach" to investigation negates cultural influences on the results.

Being alone, rather than in the presence of the interviewer, the respondents had time to answer the questions – without feeling pressured. This is different from collecting data through a "microphone-based interview" or through individual interviews, where the interviewee can be intimidated by the presence of the interviewer – depending on the culture. Furthermore, the seven selected NGOs/NPOs are all international organizations. Therefore, the respondents are very well acquainted with international (intercultural) exposure and were in a good position to interpret the questions with a minimum (or even zero) cultural interference with the findings of the research.

3.2 Commitment to Research Ethics

Since ethical concerns may arise at various stages while doing a qualitative study, I have complied with UNISA's research ethical guidelines. In an additional development of this understanding, Creswell argues that ethical concerns arise at multiple points in the investigation process, especially "during data collection and in writing and disseminating reports."[81] Moser

---

80. Briley and Aaker, "When does Culture," 395.
81. Creswell, *Educational Research*, 27, see also 553.

appropriately notes that this is especially true for empirical multiple case research, in which the researcher investigates/engages in organizational and interpersonal real-life situations involving the exchange of information, knowledge, thoughts, opinions, feelings and experience.[82] Conducting empirical research on the concept of mission drift in parachurch agencies with and about human respondents required a necessary anticipation that proactively addresses potential ethical issues associated with this research design. McNiff and Whitehead pertinently argue that it is essential for the ethical framework of any empirical qualitative research to consider safeguarding, accessing, and assuring good faith in research approaches.[83] In addition, Yin aptly indicates that conforming to ethical practices will strengthen the integrity, validity, and quality of a research investigation,[84] thus overcoming the usual criticisms of the weakness of empirical case study research.

3.2.1 Informed Consent

Throughout this thesis, I have made certain that participants are not included against their own desire or without their consent. Comprehensive information on details of this empirical study on mission drift was provided to all interviewees and respondents as they received the questionnaire along with a consent letter. This procedure was intended to give them knowledge of the interview questions, and the possibility of opting out of the interview at any time; in a way that avoids misunderstanding. Some organizations and potential individual participants withdrew after discovering the content of the questionnaire. Those who opted to participate signed the consent form they had received, which formally clarified the nature of my inquiry, the terms of participation, the purpose of the interview, and the scope of the research study. Subsequently, I gave the respondents the opportunity to pose any questions they had for further clarification. Afterwards, I proceeded to conduct one-on-one scheduled sit-down interviews and to collect data from the questionnaire's feedback.

---

82. Moser, "Commercial Investments, 134.
83. McNiff and Whitehead. *All You Need*, 77.
84. Yin, *Application*, 242; see also Creswell, *Research Design*.

3.2.2 Permission to Conduct the Interview

The use of qualitative interviews, as the technique of this study dictates, necessitates some ethical observations. First and foremost, I sought permission from the headquarters of the various parachurch agencies, as well as from the leaders of local offices where necessary. In this regard, the people involved in the church-related NGOs/NPOs and individual participants were informed that their contributions were completely on a voluntary basis,[85] as suggested by Babbie. Since every human is entitled to privacy and self-determination, personal and sensitive data obtained from the respondents has been handled with confidentiality. Moreover, no private information or personal story has been divulged without the explicit authorization of the informant. In addition, I undertook to handle the contents of interviews according to the rules of academic confidentiality. Furthermore, I have opted to treat all information as anonymous (including for those who have requested non-anonymity), so that no personal connections could be made with any statement. In this chapter, I have outlined the design and techniques needed to conduct this research study. In the next phase (chapter 4), I will analyze the research findings and then discuss the results (in chapter 5) while making a comparison with previous studies.

---

85. Babbie, *The Basics*, 63.

CHAPTER 4

Empirical Findings

In the previous chapter, I defined the research design and methods chosen to successfully conduct this study. This chapter presents and analyzes the outcomes of this empirical research study on "Dealing with Mission Drift in Parachurch Agencies." The outcomes were derived from looking at seven Christian faith-based NGOs/NPOs serving holistically in mission, using an interview questionnaire that solicited answers from thirty-two participants. The results that emerged from the fifteen questions that composed the questionnaire are precisely equated and interrelated in section 4.1, analyzed and interpreted in section 4.2, triangulated in section 4.3, and then discussed in chapter 5 of this thesis.

In this chapter, no informant's name is used in the reporting of the research outcomes in order to preserve their anonymity. In this way, I am keeping my pledge to use academic principles of ethical observation regarding confidentiality and anonymity. However, the names of authors of published documents, previous empirical research, and publicly available data are given in the chapter dedicated to discussion just as in the other parts of this thesis.

4.1 Case Studies: Holistic Mission Background

This section presents research findings relating to the qualitative content analysis of an in-depth interview questionnaire conducted with the seven case parachurch agencies. I also call these agencies "Christian faith-based NGOs/NPOs" or "church-related organizations" in this study. Firstly, I outline a summary of the collected mission statements and mission objectives of the case agencies (Table 4.1). Secondly, I present the results in section 4.2 on the differences in nature and approaches to holistic mission engagement without naming the parachurch agencies by using anonymous designations, such as NGO one, NGO two, etc. In a similar way, the respondents are designated by interviewee one, interviewee two, etc., also for the sake of anonymity. The verbatim quotes are put in *italic* so that the research participants' voices stand out. Then, the findings regarding the "research unknown" are presented in the next section (4.2.1) and are outlined in relation to the research questions.

To show the data that are related to the concept of holisticalization, the investigation demonstrates that all seven agencies claim to practice a certain kind of holistic service typified by expressions such as the following verbatim quotes. To this effect, interviewee nineteen attests: *Our organization follows "the 2000-year-old model of Jesus," bringing hope and healing to the world's forgotten poor.*[1] With regard to their holistic approach to mission, the following interview participant states: *We are doing what we do in a "holistic transformational way," working from a biblical worldview and offering the transformational development that God expects of us.*[2] In terms of such a theme, interviewee fourteen notes the following: *Our agency was founded 30 years ago, with the desire to be the exact representation of "God's hands and feet"*[3] *in the most difficult places in the world. We want to live out those hands . . . with physical support, speaking into people's lives, praying for people. Everything is done with a holistic approach.*[4] In this respect, interviewee ten declares:

> We believe in "Integral Mission", a concept on mission developed in Latin America, which sees both evangelistic activities and social action or development work as integrated together in following Jesus's example. . . . We support churches and Christian projects in having an impact on social development, transformation, evangelistic outreach, conversion and discipleship in

---

1. Interviewee 19, interviewed by author, e-mail interview, May 20, 2020.
2. Interviewee 9, interviewed by author, e-mail interview, January 30, 2020.
3. The concept of "God's hands and feet", which I call in this study the "two-hands" of the gospel (or the good news) consists of one hand ministering to the spiritual-salvific needs of people, while the other offers the fulfilment of physical, material, social-justice, and socio-economic needs.
4. Interviewee 14, interviewed by author, e-mail interview, January 23, 2020.

their local communities, thus focusing on holistic proclamation of the gospel.[5]

The table 4.1 shows this holistic missional understanding (based on commonalities in their original mission statements) and, I believe, summarizes very well each organization's approach to mission as well as the nature of its work.

The outcome of this research shows that all the agencies investigated are unanimous in their mission statements and mission objectives, with little difference in their approach to mission and their understanding of the nature of mission. This table clearly illustrates the results of the research regarding the seven case agencies, and the characteristics of their mission statements and objectives with respect to the holistic mission ideal reflected in Jesus's approach to his earthly mission. This research outcome supports the understanding that all seven CFB-NGOs/NPOs were originally founded to be engaged in Jesus's holisticalization of mission (as schematized later in Figure 4.2 under section 4.2).

Reflecting the results, the next figure summarizes the process of moving away from the original mission statement and mission objectives of the organization as mission drift. As depicted in Figure 4.1, the 'drift' may occur at the point when the agency begins to trade its Christian identity (called 'drifting point' in this study) and gradually moves away from a 'previously' stated holistic mission course or objectives towards secularization, and to eventually become a merely secular humanitarian organization – completely disregarding its original spiritual values (see section 1.1.4 and 2.1.5). Mission drift can also occur in the other direction: mission organizations theoretically committed to holistic mission but actually ending up investing only in evangelism. Mission drift can therefore happen in one or the other direction. However, as the following graphic illustrates, the results of this research indicate that in some of the seven agencies there is a complete redirection from Christian holistic mission to the position of offering secular humanitarian developmental works or services.

---

5. Interviewee 10, interviewed by author, e-mail interview, March 9, 2020.

Table 4.1: Overview of the Seven Cases' Mission Statements and Objectives

Commonalities in Original Mission Statements
Providing holistic transformation (development) and being or providing a Christian benchmark for freeing people from spiritual, physical, cognitive, social-justice, socio-economic and socio-emotional poverty. This implies winning souls for Christ and offering physical and material development. Helping people to become Christ-like in character and behavior as well as in dignity and self-possession. Releasing people from the bondage of poverty and enabling them to become fulfilled Christians in order to be involved in the advancement of Jesus's mission (the extension of the kingdom of God).

Approaches to Mission & Nature of each Agency's Mission						
Quote 5:	*Quote 6:*	*Quote 7:*	*Quote 8:*	*Quote 9:*	*Quote 10:*	*Quote 11:*
Delivering people from spiritual and material poverty in Jesus's name making them Christian believers (NGO seven).	Supporting people in their personal development while meeting the needs of society all-inclusively through the mission of Christ (NGO three).	Proclaiming the good news of Jesus by strategically reducing Bible poverty and increasing human dignity (NGO six).	Being an agency inspired by Christian faith to save lives and relieve human suffering by empowering communities (NGO five).	Passing God's love across cultural borders by ministering to migrants holistically and promoting intercultural skills in church's mission (NGO one).	Bringing hope and healing while following Jesus' model of mission by loving and serving the poor (NGO four).	Improving heath ad promoting food security through education based on Jesus' model to reduce poverty (NGO two).

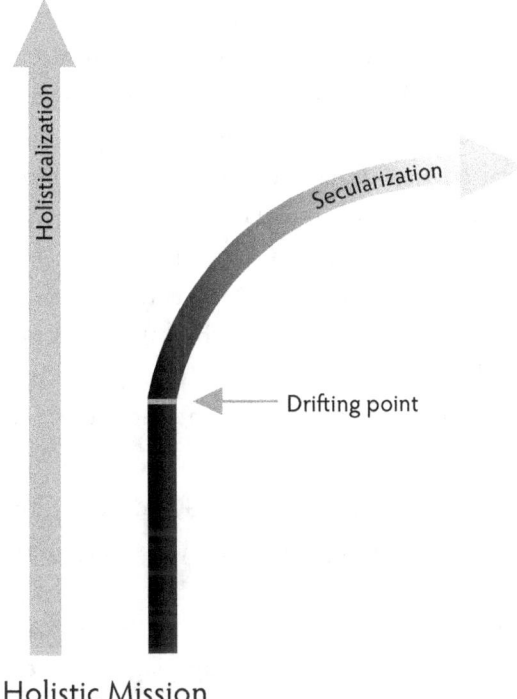

Figure 4.1: Schematic Overview of the Concept of Mission Drift

4.2 Research Outcomes from the Analysis of Seven Case Studies

The data collected is displayed according to the order of the five research questions in this study. Based on the investigation's outcomes, I can analyze the results using percentages; which helps to situate the three main findings from the perspective of the thirty-two respondents. Finally, I summed up the findings with an illustrative graphic (Figure 4.2) and drew some conclusions.

4.2.1 Findings in Relation to EU: Parachurch Agencies and Mission Drift

This study addresses the research unknown (EU), which is the key research question concerning the ways and extent to which parachurch agencies are faced with the crisis of mission drift in their mission activities. The question asks: *In what ways do parachurch agencies face the crisis of mission drift in their mission activities?* This section therefore provides an answer to the research's 'empirical unknown' while presenting the issue of mission drift as being real, even though the outcome shows that only about 28 percent of interviewees say they have experienced it. Based on these findings, nine people out of thirty-two interviewees from four of the seven agencies[6] participating in the research study considered that their Christian faith-based or church-related organizations are facing mission drift. Data analysis has revealed significant differences in the ways and the extent to which the phenomenon of mission drift occurs and how it affects each parachurch agency. With reference to the occurrence of mission drift, the following participants of this empirical research interview state:

- Unfortunately, we can see many NGOs drifting from their first mission and partnering with institutions and governments all over the world.[7]
- Yes, we have experienced mission drift. Between 2015 and 2019, we considered the possibility of engaging in partnering with humanitarian mission agencies in training farmers. . . . It caused mission drift significantly as it involved significant time and finance in staff training, etc.[8]
- We recognized that we had drifted from our original purpose as a Christian mission agency and from the Christian identity and faith values God gave us, with a lot of frustration among staff and key partners who finally left. We have realized that the bigger, the richer and the better known our NGO become [sic], the higher the risk also become [sic] to drift away.[9]

This data suggests the existence of serious deviation from the original or founding mission objectives and statements, causing a significant denial of Christian identity and faith values. In turn, this has caused frustration and the ultimate departure of key partners and staff, as experienced by NGO three. In an extreme development of this view as relates to finances, interviewee

---

6. NGO one, NGO four, NGO five, and NGO seven.
7. Interviewee 5, e-mail interview by author, April 25, 2020.
8. Interviewee 6, e-mail interview by author, January 19, 2020.
9. Interviewee 27, e-mail interview by author, March 31, 2020.

twenty-four testifies without any ambiguity: *Yes, I think finances have at times the tendency to steer Christian organizations towards mission drift.*[10] It is from this perspective that interviewee sixteen notes the following:

> We tried to hide a little bit our Christian identity on our websites. Our partners were very much against the terms "evangelize," etc. . . . If people would hear that we want to convert people then they will stop supporting. So, the agency was writing certain proposals to secular agencies. We, and especially myself, were very much concerned that we were compromising our core values and our calling in order not to offend those organizations and to release the money. . . . People came to me and said: "It seems like we are drifting". The social aspects like helping people and being accepted by the secular world is more important than the fact that people find Christ and are being transformed by him.[11]

The content of the above statements supports the observation that, for the purpose of fundraising, some church-related agencies act to appear like secular NGOs – trying to hide evidence of their Christian faith identity to the point of banning some Christian terms such as 'evangelize' from their publicly communicated documents, from responses to interviews by investigative journalists or government officials, and from their websites. The findings of this study suggest that, according to its extent, mission drift can result in compromising the core values and calling of parachurch agencies in order not to offend potential funders, which would jeopardize the release of money. Further, the previous interviewee puts it this way: *So, it looks like the money becomes more important than the calling. And this concern has very much confused our colleagues.*[12] To this effect, one respondent notes that: *If the NGO prioritizes financial support for a project to the detriment of Christian ethics applied right from the creation of the organization, this can become a*

---

10. Interviewee 24, e-mail interview by author, April 13, 2020.
11. Interviewee 16, e-mail interview by author, May 23, 2020.
12. Interviewee 16.

risk to drifting.[13] Moreover, another informant, following the same train of thought regarding Christian faith-based mission agencies and their funding modalities, quotes a statement by George Verwer, the founder of Operation Mobilization, who has stated that we should, *"Be aware: not all money comes from God."*[14] This is a very pertinent observation and a forewarning to parachurch agencies.

This study reveals how for some agencies, social aspects such as attending to people physically, materially and financially and being accepted by the secular world, can become more important than helping people come to Christ in order for them to be transformed holistically. However, it is sometimes a matter of efficiency and quantifiable outputs. In holistic discipleship, it can be noticed that is easy to report on physical and social impacts of the organizations in a short span of time than it is on spiritual-salvific impact, especially concerning meaningful conversions to Christ. Another significant piece of data that this study reveals regarding mission drift concerns an unhealthy mission practice that occurred in one agency. In that particular Christian faith-based NPO, the staff has the habit of using social acts to attract people to them in order to share the gospel with them, hoping that there will be conversions. The response is documented as follows by interviewee sixteen:

> I was involved to start a German class with our agency, a very successful project in Bern. The person who was leading the group in the beginning made a statement which really alerted me. He said: 'You know, we used the German classes as a "Mittel zum Zweck"[15] to attract people to come to us, but in order to make them do what we actually want, which is to share the gospel and hope that there will be conversions. I totally disagree with that. I believe that teaching German, helping people to integrate here, listening to their struggles concerning job, housing, listening to their hurts about the past, is as much part of our calling in our holistic ministry approach.[16]

---

13. Si l'ONG met en priorité le soutien financier à un projet au détriment de l'éthique chrétienne appliquée dès la création l'organisation cela peut devenir un risque à la dérive. Interviewee 21, e-mail interview by author, June 20, 2020.

14. Interviewee 17, e-mail interview by author, April 29, 2020.

15. A means to get to the objective.

16. Interviewee 16.

This informant argued that for him, assisting people with their social needs is as much part of Christian agencies' vocational mission – it is not just a *Mittel zum Zweck*. That way of doing holistic mission is seriously endangering the concept of staying "mission true". The study also pinpoints the concept of "reverse mission" and the following participant suggests,

> Missions can be subject to following missiological trends, for example, the concept of 'reverse mission' – which in this case consists of people going from the Global South to the West with the gospel – which is good but which can be very complex and can make organizations prone to mission drift in the sense that those people do come to the West in the name of 'mission work' but ending up working for their own interest and material needs.[17]

The findings of the research show that mission drift also occurs because of the changing face of missions, such as "mission mobilization"[18] and "life-time commitment to mission"[19], as the following respondents write:

- And the whole idea of 'mission mobilization' has become trendy. In my view, the latter in particular has distracted the mission from looking more carefully at the real needs in the continent, that we could help to address in conjunction with local agencies.[20]
- With the changing face of missions, candidates for mission no longer commit to life-time service – since long term service is now being viewed as a maximum of 5 years. There are therefore potential risks of "drifting" simply from the higher turnover of mission term members.[21]

Thus, it can be construed that CFB-NGOs/NPOs can also suffer mission drift due to lack of candidates for mission, as well as the presence of "trendy" short-term missionaries and/or the issue of "reserve mission." Moreover, the

---

17. Interviewee 8, e-mail interview by author, February 14, 2020.
18. Mobilizing people as volunteers for *Missio Dei*.
19. Devoting one's life to respond to God's call as a missionary until retirement or death occurs.
20. Interviewee 8.
21. Interviewee 9, e-mail interview by author, January 30, 2020.

idea of weak "mission spirituality" in CFB-NGOs/NPOs is viewed by the study as a triggering fact in mission drift:

- Expressing my concern that there were areas where we as a holistic mission agency were "adrift" from our founding values and this drift could lead to our demise. It was certainly due to some spiritual weakness, which I call "weak mission spirituality" that led us to almost losing our holistic DNA.[22]
- Parachurch organizations that have lost sight of their spiritual dependency on God would inevitably drift at one point.[23]
- If missionaries do not work enough on their spiritual health and their fellowship with the Lord, there is reason to see their missionary work stray from their primary mission. This is probably what happened to our NGO – which initially had this integral vocation.[24]

The outcomes of this investigation show the ways in which "classic mission" works, and how church-related ministries are changing and adapting to societal changes while also being influenced by postmodern trends. The wide acceptance of changing values in society as well as in the church leave their mark on the way parachurch agencies operate today. In a time and season when there exists a postmodern worldview that does not really accept absolutes or simple truth, "drift" is an important factor to be reckoned with, as this study shows. In the next section, I present the results of the study relating to RQ1. The data is discussed in chapter 5.

---

22. Interviewee 27.

23. Paraekklesiale Organisationen, die ihre geistige Abhängigkeit von Gott aus den Augen verloren haben, würden unweigerlich irgendwann abdriften. Interviewee 13, e-mail interview by author, January 28, 2020.

24. Si les missionnaires ne travaillent pas suffisamment sur leur santé spirituelle et leur communion avec le Seigneur, il y a de quoi voir leur œuvre missionnaire s'éloigner de la mission première qui était la leur. C'est ce qui sans doute est arrivé à notre ONG – qui au départ avait cette vocation intégrale. Interviewee 29, e-mail interview by author on March 13, 2020.

Table 4.2: Overview of Mission Drift Occurrences

Ways and Extent of Mission Drift	Adapting mission to societal changes: postmodern trends
	Deviation from original mission objectives
	Mittel zum Zweck (Means to an end)
	Reverse mission
	Fundraising and growth ambition to the expense of Christian identity and core values
	Socializing needs to the expense of spiritual needs
	Turnover of mission term
	Hiring unbelieving professionals
	Weak mission spirituality

4.2.2 Findings in Relation to RQ1: Holisticalization

The first question of this research is designed to investigate the implementation of holisticalization among international parachurch agencies: how they reconcile their evangelistic-missionary and socio-humanitarian works among the poor. The question (RQ1) is framed as follows: *Do Christian faith-based international mission organizations believe in biblical holism, and implement and practise holistic-incarnational mission?*

The assumed answer to this question is that the statement is true because these parachurch agencies are Christ-centred organizations confessing that Jesus Christ is the lord of their personal lives and the ministries of their agencies (NGOs/NPOs). The empirical analyses reveal that 63 percent of the respondents interviewed (see Figure 4.3) are working with a holistic understanding of their mission. Some of the interviewees have formulated this holisticalization concept in this way:

- Our organization is really driven by a 'holistic child development concept' which finds its source in Matthew 9:35 and Luke 4:18–19 where compassion is being demonstrated and biblical holism revealed. . . . We bring nutritional support, health care, sustain churches and communities with toilets, solar energy, playgrounds, classrooms, school fees, school supplies. . . . Every week the beneficiaries receive the curriculum teachings based on four aspects: spiritual, physical, socio-emotional and cognitive. These

- curricula enable us to talk about Jesus to beneficiaries and many of them give their lives to Jesus.[25]
- Our organization works in five areas: social engagement, education, biblical values, media and business.[26]
- We identify with various elements in the texts of Matthew 9:35–38 and Luke 4:18–19. For example, we teach the lordship of Jesus and are moved by compassion to meet the needs of people (poverty and illiteracy) in the communities where we serve.[27]

The results of this study indicate that the majority of the seven agencies have a teaching curriculum based on two main aspects: the spiritual – covering all the needs of the human soul and spirit on the one hand, and the physical – covering socio-economic, cognitive, social justice, and other aspects. Moreover, the investigation showed that these agencies partner with local churches (see the applicable guide of the theoretical framework in section 5.9 under point 7) as an opportunity to develop and foster a "discipleship curriculum." This is done in order to reinforce their holistic engagement in church mission, thus acting in harmony with both the words and the actions of Jesus as seen in Matthew 9:35–38 and Luke 4:18–19. One outcome of this study is to demonstrate the interviewees' identification with the elements in these two texts from the two evangelists, Matthew and Luke, which display the teaching and preaching of the lordship of Jesus and outline his socio-humanitarian preoccupations. interviewee fourteen advocates strongly for the inseparability of Jesus's message and Jesus's deeds; that what he did and what he said cannot be separated, and that this should be mirrored by church-related NGOs/NPOs. Highlighting this theological/missiological reflection that underpins their agency's holistic concern, he asserts:

> We believe that we cannot separate Jesus' message and Jesus' deeds. What he did and what he said. So, preaching the gospel is also doing and living out the gospel. And that's what Jesus did. I think the problem in churches and Christian organizations is

---

25. Interviewee 5.

26. Unsere Organisation arbeitet in fünf Bereichen: Soziales Engagement, Ausbildung, Biblische Werte, Medien und Business. Interviewee 7, e-mail interview by author on June 7, 2020.

27. Interviewee 6.

that we separate the two. Certain organizations claim that "we are preaching the gospel" and others say "we are not preaching we are doing the gospel." But Jesus shows that you cannot separate them.[28]

In addressing this missiological theme (holistic approach to mission) in a different way, interviewee sixteen suggests the following reflections:

> Mathew 9:35–39 and Luke 4:18–19 are very important texts for me and for us as a church-related organization. I believe we had a time as an organization where we were quite one-sided: only caring about the spiritual needs of the people. We wanted that they are saved.... These two Bible statements speak about a holistic approach (body, soul and spirit) and this is something that I have pushed forth in our mission.[29]

Preaching the gospel also means doing and living out the gospel, and that is what Jesus did (Matthew 4:23–25). This study's findings also bring to light an ancient debate regarding holistic mission. They reveal that some organizations claim that they are "preaching" the gospel, and others say they are not preaching but "doing" the gospel. Jesus, however, shows that you cannot separate the two. When Jesus met people, he would always ask them, "What can I do for you?" He never just started by doing what he thought was right. Of course, he was God; he knew, but he still asked people, "What can I do for you?" In many cases, it was physical help: healing. In other cases, it was through telling a story, a parable or asking very pertinent questions. Based on these data, it can be concluded that this is the kind of the example parachurch agencies need to follow. In this sense, interviewee sixteen emphasized his missiological understanding with the following example: *In a parachurch NPO (not a secular NGO), if a doctor is only operating and caring for the medical-physical needs of the sick, then he/she is not being holistic in his/her approach – since the spiritual part is not there . . . At the very least he/she should collaborate with others who care for the spiritual needs.*[30] For this respondent, the concept of holisticalization in CFB-NGOs/NPOs is to be promoted.

---

28. Interviewee 14.
29. Interviewee 16.
30. Interviewee 16.

Following these arguments, if the spiritual part is missing, then Christian NGOs have not fulfilled the holistic mission envisioned in Matthew 9:35–38 and Luke 4:18–19. This research reveals that the application of these texts is what makes the difference between church-related NGOs/NPOs and secular humanitarian organizations. With the effect of globalization, a missionary organization is no longer a Christian humanitarian organization; the latter is based on Christian values but does not have a vocation to do spiritual ministries. It is from this perspective that the following participant – interviewee eighteen – tries to communicate, as follows:

> Our NGO is not (or no longer) a missionary organization, but a humanitarian organization based on Christian values. In this sense, those of our volunteers who are Christians are called to reflect the Love of God in their words and deeds, but not necessarily to "evangelize". I believe, like many in the organization, that concrete actions can touch people more than words. And I believe that a Christian faith-based medical (health care) humanitarian organization that tries to have the scalpel in one hand and the Bible in the other will not be effective with either.[31]

Having said this, the synopsis of the research findings emphasizes the fact that "holistic" means a combination of the social and the spiritual. Therefore, I conclude this section with a plea for a holistic emphasis on social engagement and spiritual-biblical values and the concern to always work in partnership with national churches and local parishes in a rounded manner. According to this research, parachurch agencies do support churches in their countries of assignment, and through Christian projects have an impact in terms of holistic transformation in social development and evangelistic outreach (conversion and discipleship) in their local communities. The respondents suggest that, in order for Christian NGO/NPO's to be seen as constituting God's hands by making a contribution to his earthly mission, the proclamation of the word

---

31. Notre ONG n'est pas (ou plus) une organisation à visée missionnaire, mais une organisation humanitaire basée sur des valeurs chrétiennes. En ce sens, ceux de nos bénévoles qui sont chrétiens sont appelés à refléter l'Amour de Dieu dans leurs paroles et leurs actes, mais à ne pas nécessairement « évangéliser ». Je crois, comme beaucoup dans l'organisation, que des actes concrets touchent davantage que des paroles. Et je crois qu'une organisation chrétienne médicale humanitaire qui tente d'avoir le scalpel dans une main et la Bible dans l'autre ne sera efficace avec aucun des deux. Interviewee 18, e-mail interview by author on May 20, 2020.

of God must have the same status as social engagement. What if, however, in the organization holisticalization is not the case? Would this mean that it is an indication that the agency is going through an internal secularization issue?

4.2.3 Findings in Relation to RQ2: From Internal Secularization to Humanitarization

The theory of internal secularization and/or humanitarization in Christian organizations needs, I believe, to be investigated as it is of particular interest. Therefore, this second research question is purposed to evaluate the concept by finding answers to the following (RQ2): *Have Christian organizations lost their Christian faith-based identity, compromised on their mission objectives, and become humanitarian agencies?* The purpose here is to find out if there is an issue of internal secularization in parachurch agencies. The analysis looked at Christian NGOs/NPOs' struggles with mission drift issues in relation to their original mission statements. According to the findings of this research, only 9 percent of the research participants spoke about the problem of internal secularization. This outcome seems minimal, and yet very significant. To this effect, participants attest:

- The distinctive character of Christian NGOs should be the message of the cross. Jesus should be at the heart of all our relief and development actions because if we do good for people without telling them about Jesus or without being motivated by Jesus's love for them, then we become a humanitarian agency or philanthropists, and in this case, we are no different from the Rotary Club, Lions Club, UNHCR, Red Cross and Red Crescent or UN agencies which operate on a secular and humanitarian basis. It's sad, but that's what has become of some of our so-called Christian organizations that have lost their Christian identity and values.[32]

---

32. *Le caractère distinctif des ONGs chrétiennes devrait être le message de la Croix. Jésus devrait être au cœur de toutes nos actions de secour et de développement car si nous faisons du bien aux gens sans leur parler de Jésus ou sans être motivés par l'amour de Jésus pour eux, alors nous devenons une agence humanitaire ou des philanthropes, et dans ce cas, nous ne sommes en rien différents de Rotary Club, de Lions club, du HCR, de la Coix-Rouge et du Croissant-Rouge ou des agences onusiennes qui fonctionnent sur des bases séculières et humanitaires. C'est triste mais c'est qu'est devenues certaines de nos organisations dites chrétiennes.* Interviewee 26, e-mail interview by author on May 8, 2020.

- Yes, the effects of secularization within our agency is [sic] one of the issues that have brought us down the road of prioritizing humanitarian activities. This is certainly due to what our main donors require of us because now we can no longer show the 'Jesus film' or have worship with the patients. We have moved from being a small church-related agency to an international humanitarian NGO.[33]

The findings of this research indicate that some international Christian NGOs have developed from Christian missionary organizations to becoming faith-based humanitarian agencies with or without Christian values. Many famous Christian organizations are at risk of solving social problems such as poverty using money, irrespective of their Christian-spiritual values and of their original mission objectives. This research indicates that those particular agencies do not collaborate with local churches. Instead, they partner with local governments and financial institutions for favorable treatment, and also to be able to be placed on the frontline of the work of visible humanitarian agencies, as interviewee thirty-one denounces:

> Relationship with the church is not really a necessity. It used to be the case in the past. Now, the focus is on the governments for visibility and fund donors for financial reasons. Money for more humanitarian activities and fame for acceptability and growth. The management is now made of high professionals who have proven their performance in business sectors and who hire staff for our NGO with no consideration of their spiritual background. In my view, the organization totally dechristianized and secularized.[34]

This data also highlights the fact that internal secularization begins with the high level of professionalism needed regarding the processes of management: seeking of capable employees to be placed in leadership positions irrespective of their beliefs (part of the recruitment and hiring processes), the ambitious desire for growth and the pursuit of ever higher levels of performance. Therefore, because of these attitudes, as the data displays, there

---

33. Interviewee 32, e-mail interview by author on June 25, 2020.
34. Interviewee 31, e-mail interview by author on May 5, 2020.

is no room for God or for prayer in the decision-making process – only full adherence to core humanitarian principles regardless of their unfriendliness to Christian faith. In terms of such a theme, another informer argues against management's view of professionalization. Taking an opposing position, interviewee thirty-two writes: *Humanitarization took place because the board of directors and the management have decided to become more and more humanitarian, and therefore, have hired non-religionists for strategic positions in the name of "professionalism."*[35]

This is a decision that may gradually lead to the "drifting" of the agency's missional mandate, vision, and objectives. This would then introduce internal secularization, which would lead the NGO/NPO on the road to humanitarization. Seen from this perspective, the empirical results of the effect of "high professional standards" show that very high-quality humanitarian programs require a vast amount of public exposure to maximize levels of funding. This compromises God's calling according to the original mandate, and instead, operates to the benefit of high-quality humanitarian programs. The outcome derived from RQ2 illustrates that, among some of the CFB-NGO/NPO workers interviewed, once the biblical and spiritual values are viewed as secondary, then there is an issue involving the temptation of internal secularization, which will sooner or later give birth to a purely humanitarian organization. Now, let us see how church-related organizations can put in place constructive and stable paradigmatic changes in their mission programs.

4.2.4 Findings in Relation to RQ3: Paradigm Shifts

The question is: Are these Christian faith-based NGOs/NPOs constrained to undergo the challenge, which involves the risk of mission drift, or are they happy to accept it as a paradigm shift in their mission objectives? This study, in addressing this research question, aims to examine various paradigmatic changes relating to NGO/NPOs. It also examines the prospects, opportunities, constraints and challenges that Christian relief and development workers may face, and asks for their analysis of the concept of mission drift. The findings of this study show that paradigmatic changes occur when the board of directors and management decide there is a need to amend the organization's mission. These paradigm shifts are then put in place to adequately address the needs of

---

35. Interviewee 32.

beneficiaries and to maximize the number of those benefiting. In addressing the issue of paradigm shift in their CFB-NGOs/NPOs, the following research interview participants attest:

- High quality and God's calling. We have achieved this paradigm shift in our NGO and we have stayed very faithful to our original mandate.[36]
- The biggest paradigm shift we have undergone like a number of other agencies is that mission is now multidirectional, and we followed that way for the benefit of the people we diligently serve.[37]
- Since the existence of our ministry, the organization went through some paradigm shifts in order to be able to address adequately the needs of beneficiaries and reach out to the maximum. . . . Policy is born from a combination of foresight and history. Some of it comes from a desire to seize new opportunities, some of it from painful experiences.[38]

According to the study's results, some "shifts" come from a desire to seize opportunities as articulated by interviewees five and twenty-two (see also interviewee nine), or to overcome painful experiences, challenges and constraints as rightly emphasized by interviewees five and thirty-two. However, some paradigm shifts appear to have been divinely directed, resulting in sizeable opportunities, and yielding paradigmatic growth and visionary stability for the agency. Interviewee six acknowledges:

> Yes, we have experienced a few paradigm shifts. A recent paradigm shift has to do with boldly but humbly rejecting mission opportunities that do not fall within our areas of calling and strength. That has helped us remain true to God's mandate on our mission while prayerfully supporting other kingdom efforts as much as we can. We have regular seasons of prayer and reviewing the mandate of our mission. Unless we experience revival, there could be very serious mission drift.[39]

---

36. Interviewee 14.
37. Interviewee 9.
38. Interviewee 5.
39. Interviewee 6.

This data reveals that some church-related agencies have courageously rejected mission opportunities that do not fall within the organization's areas of calling; thus, remaining true to God's mandate concerning their mission. On the other hand, the result of the study also points to the fact that working conditions are going to become even harder for parachurch agencies, and some of them have already changed their statutes, as the following respondents indicate:

- In order to benefit from the funds of the government's Directorate for Development and Co-operation, our agency, like others, has modified its statutes to orient itself a little more towards the context of Swiss/international development in order to meet institutional requirements.[40]
- Overall, Western Christian NGOs/NPOS that operate under a pyramid leadership model are structured and directed to meet institutional requirements . . . Many Christian agencies may close their doors in the future, and a certain number may gradually put aside their Christian identity in order to continue to exist, or face the advent of incoming anti-Christian persecution. The increasingly severe demands of donors, as well as the closure of certain countries to the gospel, puts pressure on Christian faith-based organizations. These agencies may find it increasingly difficult to work in some countries without "shifting the paradigm" to meet international requirements, thus, losing the heart of their Christian faith-based mission . . . Faith is no longer a pillar in the life of the majority of the population. Humanism and humanity – yes; Individual freedom too, but not faith in God. In fact, governments tend to establish rules that favour non-religious (or non-faith) organizations.[41]

---

40. Afin de bénéficier des fonds de la Direction (gouvernementale) du développement et de la coopération, notre agence, comme d'autres, a modifié ses statuts pour s'orienter un peu plus vers le contexte du développement suisse/international afin de répondre aux exigences institutionnelles. Interviewee 22.

41. Globalement, les ONGs/OBNLs chrétiennes occidentales qui fonctionnent selon un modèle de leadership pyramidal . . . Elles sont profondément pensées, structurées et dirigées pour répondre aux exigences institutionnelles . . . De nombreuses agences chrétiennes vont fermer leurs portes à l'avenir, et qu'un certain nombre vont progressivement mettre de côté leur identité chrétienne afin de continuer à exister, ou faire face à l'avènement de la persécution

Consequently, as this investigation reveals, for some CFB-NGOs/NPOs, there is almost no place to welcome divine direction. It has therefore become difficult to be recognized and heard as a confessing NGO/NPO without the reorientation of its original vocational mandate and objectives. The following table takes into account the number of respondents per theme under the motive.

Table 4.3: Overview of the Paradigm Shift Motive

Motive for a paradigm shift (theme)	NGO 1	NGO 2	NGO 3	NGO 4	NGO 5	NGO 6	NGO 7
Opportunities	50%	0	0	80%	0	34%	20%
Constraints	25%	0	0	0	20%	0	20%
Prospects	0	40%	20%	0	20%	66%	40%
Challenge	0	0	0	0	0	0	0
God-driven	0	60%	40%	0	40%	0	20%
Number of interviewees	4	5	5	5	5	3	5

In conclusion, it can be observed that none of the interviewees saw the paradigm shift operated by the management of their agency as a challenge. At the same time, 80 percent (four respondents out of five) from NGO 4 suggested that the shift in their agency was done out of an opportunity to be financed and become well known. Up to 66 percent from NGO 6 saw the shift as a prospect – a projection into future stability. The results showed 60 percent of the people interviewed from NGO 2 consider the paradigm shift as God-driven. The following section outlines potential causes of mission drift and their consequences on Christian agencies.

---

anti-chrétienne. Les demandes de plus en plus sévères des donateurs, ainsi que la fermeture de certains pays à l'Évangile, exercent une pression sur les organisations chrétiennes. Ces agences peuvent trouver cela de plus en plus difficile de travailler dans certains pays sans «changer de paradigme» pour répondre aux exigences internationales, perdant ainsi le cœur de leur mission chrétienne... La foi n'est plus un pilier pour la vie dans la majorité de la population. Humanisme et humanité – oui: la liberté individuelle aussi, mais pas la foi en Dieu. En fait, les gouvernements ont tendance à établir des règles qui favorisent les organisations non religieuses (ou sans la foi). Interviewee 25, e-mail interview by author on May 25, 2020.

4.2.5 Findings in Relation to RQ4: Causes and Consequences of Drifting

Using RQ4, this research also addressed the issue of the identification of potential causes and consequences of mission drift for a Christian faith-based organization's holistic missional values, Christian identity, and original mission objectives. The question is framed as follows: *Do Christian missionary NGOs/NPOs identify potential causes and consequences of mission drift on the organization's holistic missional values, Christian identity and original mission objectives?* The empirical results of the study support the assumption that fundraising and 'out-boundary' ambition for growth are the basis for the occurrence of 'drift' in mission. This issue was mentioned by seven people out of the nine who have recognized the issue of mission drift in their institutions. The study showed that receiving funds from governments, non-Christian donors and international stakeholders has the potential to cause mission drift – with the loss of Christian identity and values as the irreversible consequence. To this effect, interviewee five indicates:

> The potential chance that can gradually slide our NGO to becoming a secular humanitarian organization can be when the funds will become a problem in order to pursue the program or if the leadership decide to partner with governments and local institutions to face some financial issues. Those governments and institutions will come with their rules and visions before funding our programs and these will lead us to becoming a secular humanitarian organization.[42]

Other significant data mentioned in the report of this research study highlights the issue of employing workers from outside the body of co-religionists, such as atheists, Muslims, or people adhering to religious beliefs other than Christianity, as the two following participants to the interview point out.

- One agency was entrusted by the State with caring for the refugees. They were also paid by the State and accountable to the State. And that has led to a move which has really made me sad, but also a lot of people within the agency are confused. So, the NGO had to employ people irrespective of their background:

---

42. Interviewee 5.

some of them Atheists, some Muslims or Non-religious. As a consequence, some of them even opposed the gospel – hindering the activities and the sharing of the gospel. This hurts many of our staff who still hold on to the founding holistic ministry of the NPO. . . . There was a big outcry: why? Because if the NPO becomes a purely social agency, fully agreeing with everything including the restrictions the government puts on them, since you are 100 percent funded by them – then you are not fulfilling the holistic Christian mission the NGO was established for.[43]

- In general, it is a big trap (risk) to venture towards non-Christian donors, because they very quickly impose their vision of the humanist world, and this can bring us into compromise with regard to our Christian values.[44]

The table 4.4 summarizes the related causes of mission drift and their levels of consequences.

As has been already mentioned (section 4.2.1), communication with journalists can be critical, challenging and even provocative, but Christian workers should not be intimidated or ashamed of the gospel. This can hinder the work of a church-related organization. Moreover, interviewee seven addresses this issue as a concern that has multi-faceted consequences on the organization's management. He highlights the fact that in their parachurch agency:

> The management was afraid of being accused of trying to evangelize people by the journalists whenever they came and they said things which I found very compromising. Things like: "No, we are strictly only teaching German. We are not talking about faith or religion. We are not evangelizing. We will not try to convert anybody. Church is church and this is strictly teaching German. We are having a social approach." I felt like this is

---

43. Interviewee 16.

44. En général, c'est un grand piège (risque) de s'aventurer vers de bailleurs non-Chrétiens, car ils imposent très rapidement leur vision du monde humaniste, et cela peut nous amener dans le compromis vis à vis de nos valeurs chrétiennes. Interviewee 26.

Table 4.4: Overview of Mission Drift's Causes and Consequences

Mission Drift Causes	Consequences
Partnership with governments	Rules controlling the NGO/NPO Accountability to the state Restrictions on evangelism
Partnership with financial institutions	Imposition of their vision of humanistic NGOs/NPOs Confusion among the staff Demand for implementation of anti-biblical activities and values Betrayal and denial of the organization's Christian identity
Employment of non-Christian professionals	Opposition to the gospel Hinderance to the spiritual activities Compromising on holisticalization
Loss of contact with the church	Cessation of spiritual activities Internal secularization End result: humanitarization

betraying our call and denying our Christian mission identity and being ashamed of the gospel.[45]

In general, the study as summed up in the table, suggests that hiring or partnering with non-Christians or approaching such donors is a big trap that involves a considerable risk because they can very quickly impose their non-Christian and/or humanist vision. This can cause a CFB-NGO/NPO to compromise its Christian values. Unbelieving or non-Christian donors present a danger to the pursuit of the spiritual goals of CFB-NGOs/NPOs because they may end up demanding the implementation of anti-biblical or anti-spiritual activities as a condition of their funding of the project. The next section of the study presents what has been called "holistic contextualization"

---

45. Das Management hatte Angst, von Journalisten, die kamen, beschuldigt zu werden, Menschen zu evangelisieren und sie sagten Dinge, die ich als sehr kompromittierend empfand. Dinge wie: „Nein, wir unterrichten ausschließlich Deutsch. Wir sprechen nicht über Glauben oder Religion. Wir evangelisieren nicht. Wir werden nicht versuchen, jemanden zu konvertieren. Kirche ist Kirche und hier wird ausschließlich Deutsch gelehrt. Wir haben einen sozialen Ansatz." Ich hatte das Gefühl, dass dies unsere Berufung verrät, unsere christliche Missionsidentität leugnet und sie sich für das Evangelium schämten. Interviewee 7.

as a strategic way for CFB-NGOs/NPOs to remain faithful to their original mission objectives.

4.2.6 Findings in Relation to RQ5: Holistic Contextualization

Finally, the research investigated the concern for, and necessity of contextualization in addressing the fifth research question (RQ5). *How do these CFB-NGOs/NPOs contextualize their mission objectives and praxis in relation to making decisions about possible paradigm shifts, and how do they integrate Jesus's holistic mission concept (which is evangelistic and socio-humanitarian) into their Christian mission identity in order to avoid the crisis of mission drift?* Contextualization is realized by collaborating with the poor in order to identify the needs of the beneficiaries and then to respond holistically to insure long-lasting missional effects, as this study clearly demonstrates. It is from this perspective that interviewee eleven attests: *Our organization is church-related – that means we focus on local churches which are close to the communities and know the beneficiaries well, as well as how to meet their needs in order to attain their holistic transformation. Partnership with the local churches is strategic.*[46] Following this holistic contextualization train of thought, interviewee twenty-four states:

> Inspired by God's love, we advocate, build capacity and work with local churches and communities to apply language expertise that advances meaningful contextualized and transformational development: education, health and engagement with Scripture for instance. Sometimes, there is a need for a survey to be conducted locally to determine the needs of the community and how it can be contextualized holistically.[47]

The empirical outcomes of this study point out that for better contextualization, parachurch agencies engaged in holistic transformation should partner with churches that are close to their communities and who know them well, so as to determine how to better contextualize their programs. In this respect, interviewee ten observes:

---

46. Interviewee 11, interviewed by author, e-mail interview on May 31, 2020.
47. Interviewee 24.

> Depending on the community, instances of possible contextualization might be the adaptation of aids, programs, language, or using biblical terms to local cultural settings. All of these can have strategic value. Then, the local church takes control of the program under the direction of the NGO, and hires staff based on the agency's values and selects beneficiaries for whom the program is going to be implemented.[48]

These participants see contextualization as being planned at two levels: first, on a level that is Christ-centred, through collaboration with local churches; and second, on a level that adapts communication to fit into a traditional context. This is because each community has its own way of understanding, and finding the appropriate way to contextualize is key to impacting lives holistically. The research showed that identifying and honoring elements of local cultures (such as the local control or management systems and the adaptation of languages, programs and aids while using biblical terms to local cultural settings) that align with the agency's objectives, teaching Scripture with culturally relevant applications, and developing a relevant mission praxis that meets the day-to-day needs of the people is much more transformational in a holistic way.

As CFB-NGOs/NPOs work in a reciprocal 'valued-partnership' with the local church leadership, there is an ongoing process of the adaptation of programs, and of the holistic contextualization of the objectives of the agency according to the local population and their needs, without trading the God-given values that communicate the Christian character of the organization. The outcome of this empirical research shows that sometimes it takes a survey to determine whether a community needs the program the agency is offering to them and, if it does, how this can be contextualized in an all-inclusive Christian mission setting. To better illustrate the idea of holistic contextualization, the following informant – interviewee thirty-two – used the image of 'the bridge':

> A parachurch agency, which is holistic like ours, which connects two aspects of each Christian holistic mission, offers a meeting point of contextualized spiritual and social exchange space – the

---

48. Interviewee 10.

bridge. On this bridge, the beneficiaries move in both directions and benefit from each contribution for the improvement of their social and spiritual conditions.[49]

In this way, the findings of this study uncover the fact that the challenge of contextualization has two dimensions: firstly, to connect people in a meaningful way for the increase of their welfare and, secondly, to come alongside them in their cultural settings so that they can adapt to their new environment of Christian faith (see section 5.9). Contextualization is powerless if one is working without God, whereas placing less emphasis on activism and more on relying on God would help to see that God's purpose is achieved through the agency's loyalty to God's calling. The empirical results of this research study are triangulated with two previous studies in the following section as a summary of this study's findings.

4.2.7 Summary of the Key Findings

As indicated earlier (section 4.), the general report overview for this empirical research study relates to seven church-related NGOs/NPOs with the participation of thirty-two people in total. This study has shown that in terms of levels of participation there has been an average of four persons per agency. In terms of participation in the research questionnaire, 47 percent of the respondents hold managerial positions and 53 percent are frontline staff.

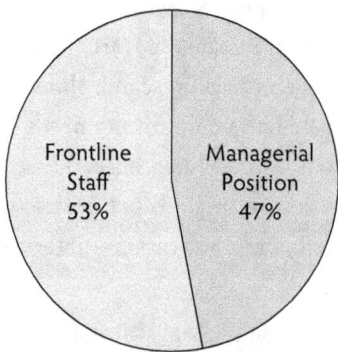

Figure 4.2: Schematic Overview of Participation

---

49. Interviewee 32.

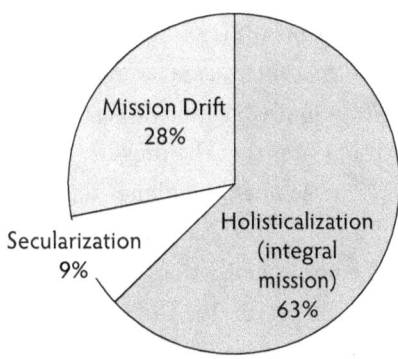

Figure 4.3: Schematic Overview of the Research Findings

The findings of the research also show that out of the total number of thirty-two participations in the interview, 28 percent of the interviewees (nine out of thirty-two) recognized that they were to some degree facing the experience of mission drift (a state in which Christian activities are gradually becoming weakened) in their mission work, while only 9 percent (three people out of thirty-two) admitted that their organization was on the road to humanitarization[50] and possibly to becoming a secular humanitarian international organization. Based on these results, if one adds up the outcomes of mission drift and humanitarization, we arrive at 37 percent. Now, after seeing what this percentage represents proportionally, one can understand how substantial 'drifting' is and how this is a real threat to church-related agencies and their practice of biblical holism. There is, therefore, a certain progress towards insubstantiality within parachurch NGOs/NPOs with regard to their commitment to holistic mission. The results of the study essentially reveal

---

50. *Humanitarization*: If one refers to David Johnson's analysis of present-day Russian society, Humanitarization is "a curricular shift towards the humanities and social sciences, and away from the natural sciences;" Johnson, *Politics, Modernization and Educational Reform*, 153. If this understanding of Johnson is correct, then it is equally true that Humanitarization in Christian NGOs/NPOs is a curricular shift towards the humanities and social welfare of the good news of Jesus, and totally drifted away from the spiritual mission and biblical salvific message. Humanitarization equals internal secularization – meaning the NGO drifted long time ago and come to a point of absence of Christian activities. In this study, humanitarization is to be understood differently from 'humanization,' the first being the disproportionate preferment of the 'social works' aspect of the gospel (the socialization of the gospel) to the detriment of its salvific message (the spiritualization of the gospel), whereas the second has to do with humanizing life with courtesy. 'Humanization' is an act of imbuing human beings with dignity in our unethical and fraudulent society where lower-class people are constantly debased to make profit.

that about 63 percent of the people (twenty out of thirty-two) who took part in the research affirmed that their agencies are committed to holisticalization – following the 'Jesus model' of holistic earthly mission.

The research also indicates that the bigger, the better known, and the richer a CFB-NGO/NPO becomes, the higher the probability of it 'drifting' and becoming a secular institution. Another very important outcome of the investigation is that the more the agency employs unbelieving co-workers to managerial positions, the greater the chances of drifting from its original mission. Further analyses of the results, the following empirical unknown (EU), and research questions (RQs) introduced in section 1.4 elaborate the findings of the study analysis.

Consequently, as a result of mission drift, the organization abandons its Christian mission distinctiveness and thus, can qualify for assistance from governments and international financial institutions. In contrast, a Christian faith-based organization that keeps its mission inclusive and 'intact' will follow the 'mission model' of Jesus as shown in Matthew 9:35–38 and Luke 4:18–19, and therefore, will reflect and replicate the holisticalization,[51] that defines Jesus's approach to mission. The following chapter sketches a general overview of the research outcomes relating to the phenomenon of mission drift.

4.3 Triangulating the Study Results: Avoiding Mission Drift

This study's research results have shown (in section 4.2.3) how gradual internal secularization ultimately leads to the humanitarization of Christian agencies, thus causing the forfeiture of their Christian faith identify. According to this research, the mission of Christian faith-based agencies has two main components: first, Christian values and faith culture and, second, the Christian mission itself, which is a holistic mission. The findings of this research indicate that mission drift occurs when either (or even both) of these components are lacking in the mission of a CFB-NGO/NPO. This report, which relates to the triangulation of these research findings on how to prevent mission drift,

---

51. *Holisticalization*: The dual nature context of the ministry of Jesus on earth. It involves biblical holism and the all-inclusive character of the gospels.

agrees with the views expressed in the publication by Greer and Horst,[52] and the research by Pellowe.[53] To provide evidence of the internal validity of this study's results, data has been cross verified by looking at the available documents, internet sources and mission and/or vision statements of the various organizations investigated (see illustration in Figure 3.4).

In order to avoid the occurrence of mission drift, on the basis of this research, one would agree with Greer and Horst, and with Pellowe's publications that Christian faith and God-given mission must be the central concern of and the reason for the existence and work of CFB-NGOs/NPOs.[54] Leaders of parachurch agencies must integrate and preserve Christian identity in all aspects of their organization's existence and mission. This implies the passing on of biblical holism and spiritual distinctiveness from one generation of leadership (team and staff) to the next. The transmission of Christian faith values within a parachurch agency and the passing on of the holistic heritage of the organization from one generation to the next is generally based on the leadership's commitment to God's mission (*missio Dei*). This is defined by the vision and mission statements of the NGO/NPO. Greer and Horst, and Pellowe discovered that all too often one generation's passion for God becomes the preference of the second, then becomes irrelevant to the third and then unknown to the next in the same way that the Israelites lost their faith in God, as reported in Judges 2:10–14.[55] In this way the Israelites totally drifted from God-given views to a secular worldview.

The indication of this present research, in accord with Pellowe's investigation, is that management must make the question of faith a crucial factor in any major decisions regarding shifting the paradigm on which the organization is based. This process (of shifting the paradigm) must include trusting

---

52. Greer and Horst, *Mission Drift*.
53. Pellowe, "Mission Drift."
54. Greer and Horst, *Mission Drift*; and Pellowe, "Mission Drift".
55. The failure of the Israelites to pass on their beliefs to the younger generations: "After that whole generation had been gathered to their ancestors, another generation grew up who knew neither the Lord nor what he had done for Israel. Then the Israelites did evil in the eyes of the Lord and served the Baals. They forsook the Lord, the God of their ancestors, who had brought them out of Egypt. They followed and worshiped various gods of the peoples around them. They aroused the Lord's anger because they forsook him and served Baal and the Ashtoreths. In his anger against Israel the Lord gave them into the hands of raiders who plundered them. He sold them into the hands of their enemies all around, whom they were no longer able to resist" (Judges 2:10–14 NIV).

God for provision and having a grounded theological discussion in relation to reframing the NGO/NPO's mission, in the belief that faith remains indispensable and that it must saturate every aspect of the continuing mission work. Human resource practices, programs and designs must be based on a Christian worldview and be permeated by a faith culture that defines relationships with funding partners.

Seen in the same perspective, the results of this study are in accord with Greer and Horst's publication, where they define the qualities of healthy executive management.[56] They outline the necessity of being prayerful and careful in the recruitment of co-workers, especially in hiring co-religionists for leadership positions. They also stress not bending on core values in terms of the mission, and creating policies that safeguard the organization in terms of the distinctiveness of its Christian faith, and that keep to the history, original mission statement, founding purpose and central objectives of the organization.[57] In short, in relation to mission drift, these scholars show, as does this empirical study, that loss of Christian identify and poor leadership recruitment are driving forces that lie behind "drifting".

Both this research and the authors I have mentioned conclude that the pressure on a CFB-NGO/NPO to secularize comes primarily from the forces exerted within the agency (from board, management, and staff) as compared to external forces (donors, governments, and the influence of other NGOs). Pellowe states that it is often the case that the board members and the decision-making panel are professional executives who do not necessarily have the theological resources and missionary experience to protect the NGO/NPO against 'drift' from its original mission.[58] In spite of working in a CFB-NGO/NPO, the lack of a solid theological education might lead to the overlooking of biblical ethics and principles, theological norms/standards, spiritual traditions/history, Christian identity, and the missional conventions, expectations, assumptions or inconsistencies embedded in the choices that management faces.

After thoroughly presenting the empirical results of this case study research and triangulating with two other empirical research (book print

---

56. Greer and Horst, *Mission Drift*, 87.
57. Greer and Horst, 87.
58. Pellowe, 1.

and online publications), I moved on to discuss the findings laid out in the fifth chapter of this research. The discussion in chapter 5 pivoted around the main areas of these findings. It also aimed to connect them with previous empirical studies and other scholarly publications.

CHAPTER 5

Research Discussion

This chapter discusses the results of the research study, presenting a theory that accounts for mission drift in parachurch agencies, which has emerged from this study and other empirical research. The outcome is to be viewed as a set of concepts discussed as a 'conceptual model.' In a further development of this understanding, scholars like Tatomir, McDermott, Bensabat, Class, Edlmann, Taherdangkoo, and Sauter explain that a conceptual model in social scientific research is a set of concepts or a depiction of a phenomenon, a system and generalization of things in the sphere of reality (the real-life), made through the conformation of concepts, which can then be used to bring knowledge to people and help them understand or simulate an issue and/or subject, which the model denotes.[1] Creating a conceptual model, also seen as 'concept building,' is a decisive step in any social-scientific undertaking of things existing in reality (real-life situations). As mentioned by Colquitt and Zapata-Phelan, it "allows scientists to understand and predict outcomes of interest, even if only probabilistically . . . prevents scholars from being dazzled by the complexity of the empirical world by providing a linguistic tool for organizing it . . . [and] acts as an educational device that can raise consciousness about a specific set of concepts."[2] In this case this would refer to mission drift in CFB-NGOs/NPOs. This study has shown that there are a number of pieces of data, which I call 'factual determinants', that consolidate

---

1. Tatomir et al., "Conceptual Model Development," 185; see also "Conceptual Model," in Merriam Webster, *Collegiate Dictionary*.
2. Colquitt and Zapata-Phelan, "Trends in Theory Building," 1281.

the concept of 'mission drift in parachurch agencies' as outlined in the following graphic (Figure 5.1).

The strength of a multiple case-based investigation, as conducted in this study, lies in its ability to yield empirically valid, thought-provoking, and testable concepts/theories. Seeing things from the same perspective, Eisenhardt and Graebner argue that "papers that build theory from cases are often regarded as the 'most interesting' research."[3] It should be reckoned that collective or multiple case-based theories have the weak point of running the risk of being either too narrow, personal, eccentric, characteristic and idiosyncratic or excessively complex.[4] With this in mind, I have endeavored to produce an empirically valid but also testable, tight and reasonably coherent conceptual framework for mission drift in church-related NGOs/NPOs discussed in detail in the following sections.

In summary, the outcomes of this case study research at hand indicate that about 28 percent of the informants recognized to some degree that they faced the experience of mission drift in their mission work, while only 9 percent admitted that their organization was heading towards humanitarization (internal secularization). As a result, the discovery of 'internal secularization' and of mission drift in some CFB-NGOs/NPOs constitute the main findings of this investigation. The results of the study essentially reveal that about 63 percent of the interviewees affirmed that they were committed to holistic mission work; that is, they were following the holistic model of Jesus's earthly ministry. The investigation also shows that the larger, better known, and richer a Christian agency becomes, the higher the likelihood of the occurrence of mission drift and subsequently the incorporation of internal secularization within the NGO/NPO. Equally significant is the fact that the enquiry reveals that the more the organization hires unbelieving professionals for managerial positions, the greater the chances of "drifting" from its original mission. After presenting the research findings in the previous chapter, I discuss in section 5.1 the conceptual framework and contributions of this study to the theory and practice of parachurch agencies. This discussion covers all the major issues highlighted by the results of the study. The purpose is to interpret the

---

3. Eisenhardt and Graebner, "Theory Building," 25.
4. Eisenhardt, "Building Theories," 536–537.

significance of the results and describe them in the light of previous studies in order to explain any new insights and refresh understanding about the issue.

5.1 CFB-NGOs/NPOs Facing the Crisis of Mission Drift in Their Identities

Based on the data collected from RQ2 (Research Question 2), the loss of Christian identity in parachurch agencies is a gradual process that leads to a "drift" away from the organization's founding mission statement. Similar investigation carried out in 2014 by Greer and Horst showed that silently, slowly and with little fanfare, church-related NGOs/NPOs "routinely drift from their original founding purpose, and most will never return to their original intent."[5] A year after this investigation, another piece of research done by Pellowe reported that "most formerly Christian organizations did not intend to lose their identity, but they just drifted quietly, gradually, and slowly."[6] These theses agree with this research's findings, and therefore depict the reality of the concept of the phenomenon of mission drift. As a tangible example, the research by Greer and Horst entitled *Mission Drift: The Unspoken Crisis Facing Leaders, Charities, and Churches* traces how, originally parachurch institutions such as Harvard University, Yale University and the Young Men's Christian Association (YMCA) lost their Christian identities while others, such as Inter-Varsity Christian Fellowship (IVF) and Compassion International have retained theirs.[7] Greer and Horst's argument leads to the conclusion that mission drift in church-related NGOs/NPOs unfolds quietly like a current, and without them being conscious of it, carries the agencies away from their founding identity and core purpose. These institutions do not voluntarily choose to change their mission direction and soften their Christian identity and distinctiveness, and yet one day, what once were Christian faith-based agencies will scarcely resemble the NGOs/NPOs that their founders intended.

---

5. Greer and Horst, *Mission Drift*, 15.

6. Pellowe, *Mission Drift*, 1.

7. Greer and Horst, *Mission Drift*, 17 and 20; see also Edwards, "Faithfull Innovation," 7; and Scheitle, *Beyond the Congregation*, 40.

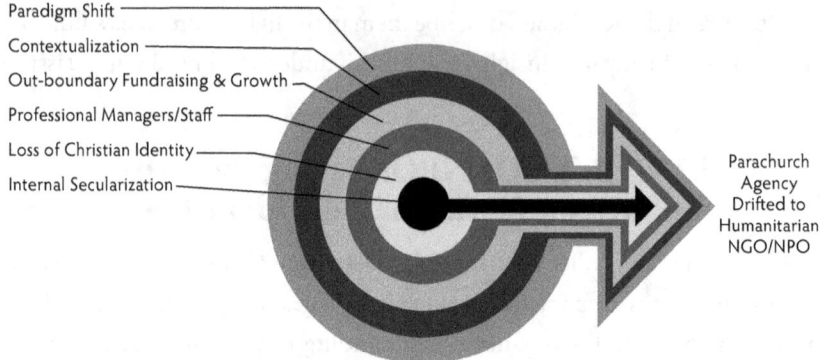

Figure 5.1: Causative-Determinants Conceptual Framework

This graphic emerged from the analysis of the empirical results of this research study. It shows how the concept of mission drift can evolve in a parachurch agency. Mission drift occurs when the leadership sees a legitimate need to engage in a paradigm shift. However, while changing the paradigm contextualization becomes indispensable. This process can become the entry to a trap – starting from the 'drifting point' – if the leadership does not take time to seek divine guidance in order to confirm that the new direction opted for is inspired and directed by God, or relates to his sovereign and providential will for the future of that holistic CFB-NGO/NPO. The process from that point onward would be as follows: the officials of the organization develop an ambition for growth, and then hire professional managers and frontline staff (often non-Christian) to maximize fundraising in order to quickly meet the ambition for growth (see sections 5.7.1 and 5.7.2). In the busy routine of wanting to grow big by all means, and raising funds in an out-boundary manner, the agency would begin to sacrifice its Christian faith-based identity, compromising its original mission statement and squandering its God-given holistic mission. The spiritual preoccupation of the NGO/NPO would then become auxiliary to its socio-humanitarian and secular objectives.

The board members would be focused on professionalizing the organization. Its Christian identity would be diluted and, subsequently, the organization would be gradually infiltrated and debased by internal secularization. As a result, secularization within the parachurch agency would unconsciously, steadily but irreversibly lead to the 'drift' of what was a CFB-NGO/NPO towards becoming a humanitarian organization with few, or no Christian values and God-given vision. Mission drift would have definitely occurred, and the organization's founding mission objectives would have been totally reversed from being that of a Christian holistic mission agency to being a solely humanitarian 'good works organization' without Christ or the gospel as its reference or grounded constituent.

This study, as well as that of Greer and Horst, have shown an overall picture of the prevalence of mission drift and the necessity of Christian identity distinctiveness in preventing it. This contrasts with the very different conclusions of the research by Setran, and Edwards, which seem to equate Christian identity with evangelistic outreach and conversion, saying little about discipleship and transformation.[8] However, a closer analysis of Setran and Edwards' views would suggest that they limit Christian holistic mission to evangelism and social action. This study understood holisticalization to be broader than that, involving on the one hand the various spiritual ministries and on the other the socio-humanitarian activities of Christian mission. According to Wittberg, a parachurch agency's Christian identity should express those holistic features that are fundamental and distinctive in character in order to avoid an NGO's "identity to become confused and result in identity drift."[9] Wittberg continues by saying that "when religious organisations take on multiple, potentially conflicting roles . . . the religious identity is likely to be attenuated."[10] This is a pertinent assessment to be reinforced among Christian faith-based agencies that seek to work holistically in alignment with its mission statement.

Following the same train of thought, Edwards argues that the ultimate way for a church-related organization to communicate its clear Christian identity is in "the very simple words of its mission statement."[11] CFB-NGOs/NPOs can become diverted from their primary Christian identities and mission objectives because of financial reverses, opportunity, or crisis. However, there is a need when considering mission drift, to consider all church-related NGOs/NPOs who do not adhere to a strict understanding of what it means to be a Christian faith-based organization. The conclusions of this case research study suggest that parachurch agencies can be taken over by a new professional

---

8. Setran, *The College "Y"*, 177; and Edwards, "Faithfull Innovation," 23 and 138.
9. Wittberg, *From Piety to Professionalism*, 59.
10. Wittberg, 59; see also Hendrickson, "Charismatic Leadership," 28.
11. Edwards, "Faithfull Innovation," 23; see also Ford, *Christian Wisdom*, 354–356; and Rice, "Toward a Framework," 106.

management agenda, and that this may compromise their ability to deliver their exclusive mission, which will result in the secularization of the core identity and mission objectives of the organization.

5.2 Secularization and Humanitarization: From Christian Agency to Humanitarian NGO/NPO

In this section, I talk about how the attenuation of Christian identity and holistic mission focus in parachurch NGOs/NPOs plays a significant role in the secularization debate, chiefly pertaining to the effect of internal secularization. The following figure illustrates how an organization can become internally secularized. This case study research shows how, once settled within the organization, secularization can mitigate the holistic mission agenda of a church-related agency, promote the implementation of a social gospel (socialization of the gospel) and ultimately create a favorable context for mission drift and the humanitarization of the organization.

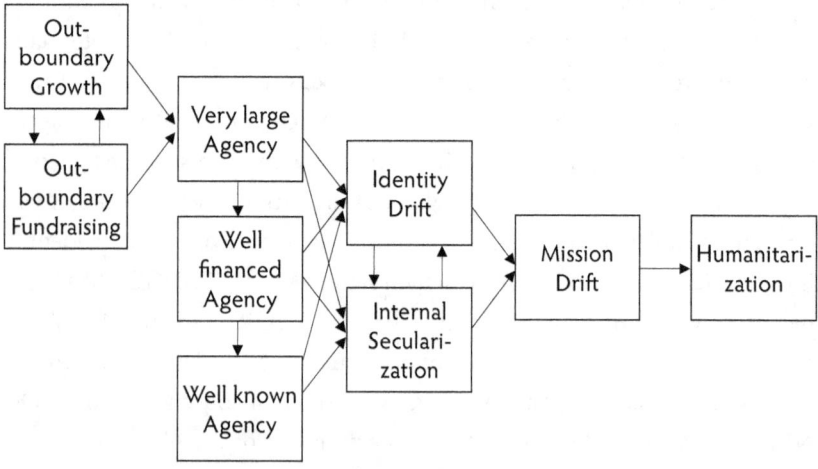

Figure 5.2: Sequential Progression Schematic Framework

An investigation conducted by Gallet supports this research's outcome by stating that when church-related agencies are directly managed by professional administrators and not by co-religionists, it appears to indicate the 'sensed-presence effect' of secularization.[12] Whether this statement connects to internal secularization within a CFB-NGO/NPO needs further analysis, especially in light of the argument posed by Grant, O'Neil and Stephens, that co-religionists and senior managerial replacement might include chaplains and staff rooted in the Christian faith, who endeavor to maintain a holistic mission focus.[13] Moreover, Gallet asserts that senior managers are entrusted with a critical role in keeping Christian identities and ideals.[14] The strength of Gallet's precautionary position, and that of Grant, O'Neil and Stephens, can be found in Guinness's poignant explication: "Compared with the past, faith today influences culture less. Compared with the past, culture today influences faith more."[15] Berger, Dyrness and Kärkäinen, Mashau, and Ireland aptly describe secularization as a worldview, a process in which theory and practice deny the presence of God, faith diminishes in prominence and mission drops in significance, both in society and in the consciousness of the people working in religious missions.[16] This description answers the concern about internal secularization. Parachurch agencies should function as the embodiment of biblical holism, yet may also be seen as providing one of the paths through which secularism may take hold of Christian missions; even those that have long been known for their devotion to holistic mission.

For the purpose of this research investigation and taking all of these insights into account, I defined internal secularization as the presence of certain ideological forces inside a CFB-NGO/NPO that consequently cause the agency's mission to 'drift' to the periphery of its existential objectives, thus bringing in humanitarization. Secularization accomplishes this move by making spiritual mission progressively irrelevant. As Mashau further expounds, "Secularization is the process through which everything considered to be secular is detached from the church. When this process takes place, humans rely mainly on their own knowledge and findings, considering God

---

12. Gallet, "Christian Mission, 124.
13. Grant, O'Neil and Stephens, "Neosecularization and Craft,": 479–487.
14. Gallet, 124.
15. Guinness, *Dining with the Devil*, 16; see also Campbell, "Releasing the Gospel," 168.
16. Berger, "Secularization and De-Secularization," 384; Dyrness, and Kärkäinen, *Global Dictionary*, 803; Mashau, "A Reformed Missional Perspective," 112 and 120; and Ireland, "The Secularizing," 40.

to be redundant."[17] According to Dowsett, Phiri, Birdsall, Terfassa, Yung, and Jørgensen, the process of secularization is believed to have led to the privatization of both Christian faith and church-related organizations,[18] including the initial mission purposes of the latter.

Regarding the problem of internal secularization, Prudhomme puts forward the argument that in most CFB-NGOs/NPOs it has become impossible to discern the ongoing influence of the missionary heritage in a commitment that displays secular motives, even if it does not necessarily exclude all religious references.[19] This lends support to the outcomes of this study. Moreover, to make his point, Prudhomme affirms that if some mission workers choose to join an association of humanitarian aid to the Global South, and contribute largely to its development, they are generally in favor of a deconfessionalization (meaning secularization, humanitarization or socialization) of the organization.[20] This is evidenced by the evolution of "Frères des Hommes" (Brothers of Men), which presented itself very early on as non-confessional and apolitical, erasing the very strong religious commitment of its founder Armand Marquiset.[21] Prudhomme remarks that certainly, those humanitarian workers still use missionary networks, but it is because they are often the only possible conduit in countries whose administration has collapsed, or stalled. The majority of them do not bind themselves definitively and existentially to

---

17. Mashau, "A Reformed Missional Perspective," 110–111.

18. Dowsett et al., *Evangelism and Diakonia*, 302.

19. Prudhomme's view: ". . . dans la plupart des cas il est devenu impossible de discerner la part de l'héritage missionnaire dans un engagement qui affiche des mobiles séculiers, même s'il n'a pas forcément exclu toute référence religieuse." Prudhomme, "Mission religieuse," 27.

20. Prudhomme affirms that "Si un certain nombre de ces coopérants choisissent à leur retour en France de s'engager dans une association d'aide au Tiers Monde, et contribuent largement à leur essor, ils sont le plus souvent partisans d'une déconfessionnalisation des mouvements comme en témoigne l'évolution de 'Frères des Hommes', se présentant très tôt comme apolitique et aconfessionnelle, gommant le très fort engagement religieux de son fondateur Armand Marquiset." Prudhomme, 27.

21. Prudhomme affirms that, "Si un certain nombre de ces coopérants choisissent à leur retour en France de s'engager dans une association d'aide au Tiers Monde, et contribuent largement à leur essor, ils sont le plus souvent partisans d'une déconfessionnalisation des mouvements comme en témoigne l'évolution de 'Frères des Hommes', se présentant très tôt comme apolitique et aconfessionnelle, gommant le très fort engagement religieux de son fondateur Armand Marquiset." Prudhomee, 27.

a church or a missionary agency,[22] as Prudhomme says. Obviously, there is a drift from being a Christian agency to becoming a humanitarian NGO/NPO.

If the original mission of an organization has been so distorted, neglected, and finally forgotten, then its mission can no longer be described as Christian faith-based mission work. It has reached the stage of becoming purely humanitarian work. This is because its holistic mission has been eroded by internal secularization. This means that the resources of Christian faith and tradition, such as the word and the Spirit have been rejected and discarded in favor of the secularistic worldview, which has totally shifted the focus to humanitarianism. In addressing this issue, interviewee sixteen asserts that the leadership of their agency fully agreed with the restrictions of the government totally disregarding the traditional holistic mission that their NGO was founded for.[23] In an extreme development of this view, interviewee twenty-six argues that non-Christian funders quickly impose their humanistic worldview, which leads to compromising the very heart of Christian mission,[24] such as word proclamation and salvific discipleship. In the following section, I discuss how paradigm shift may create mission drift depending on the choices the leadership makes.

5.3 Paradigm Shift Versus Mission Drift

When the leadership of a Christian faith-based agency moves in favor of a paradigm shift (see definition at section 1.1.6), it may have a number of effects in one way or the other on the NGO/NPO's initial mission concept. The outcome of this study brings to light the fact that mission drift can occur due to threats to the agency's existential survival; leading, for instance, the board members to consider hiring non-Christian professional managers and frontline staff in an attempt to implement a paradigm shift to save the organization (see section 4.2.5, interviewee five and interviewee sixteen). However, Ronsen notes that "no Christian movement can survive on the

---

22. He states that, "certes ils utilisent encore les réseaux missionnaires, mais parce qu'ils sont souvent les seuls relais possibles dans les pays où la construction d'un État échoue ou tarde. La majorité d'entre eux ne se lient pas de manière définitive et existentielle à une Église ou une société missionnaire." Prudhomee, 27.

23. Interviewee 16.

24. Interviewee 26.

achievements of the past."²⁵ Thus, it requires a great deal of commitment to core values and discipline in the organization's behavior to ensure that the original holistic mission mandate will still be honored by the new generation of volunteers who have enthusiastically inherited the concept and become involved in the integrated programs. This view, however, raises the question of whether paradigm shift is needed in CFB-NGOs/NPOs.

In an attempt to answer this question, Sommerville argues that organizational mission drift might be gradual and gradational, possibly coinciding with important "paradigmatic changes",²⁶ both in terms of staff mentality and mission activities.²⁷ Moreover, he stresses that "the compounding effects of small changes have the potential to contribute to the ultimate transformation and secularization of the organization."²⁸ Obviously, Sommerville's assessment suggests the negative effect that paradigmatic changes/shifts can have on a parachurch agency. However, Edwards tackles the issue differently, suggesting that

> if an organization resists all changes and moves forward stubbornly steadfast in all of its activities and mentalities, it might forego the opportunity to innovate for the sake of reaching and empowering more *people* with the gospel. For this reason, it is crucial to understand the possibility of faithful innovation or traditioned innovation.²⁹

If one follows this way of thinking, the expected result would be that paradigm shift is required as an opportunity to reach out to the poor and empower them with the gospel. However, though I would agree with Edwards on the fact that change is crucial, the problem here is that his argument does not propose a holistic approach to paradigm shift.

In this discussion, there is a conflict between Sommerville and Edwards's argument. The crucial aspect that divides them is the extent to which the

---

25. Ronsen, *Mission Drift?* 32.

26. Paradigmatic changes are significant imperative adjustments that happen when the usual way of doing Christian mission or thinking about a holistic mission in a CFB-NGOs/NPOs is replaced by a new and unusual way.

27. Sommerville, "Secular Society," 252.

28. Sommerville, 252.

29. Edwards, "Faithfull Innovation," 8.

changes taking place will ensure that the original mandate to provide holistic mission will continue to be honored by the next generation of Christian workers in the parachurch agency. While attempting to nuance these different views, Katz observes that "the difficulty with paradigms is that sometimes they focus on the task of the parachurch agency, sometimes on the activity of God, and other times on the context of ministry."[30]

There is a fourth significant voice in this debate that I would support: that of proposing "faithful innovation", also called "traditioned innovation". This approach is put forward by Greg Jones. In advocating for the importance of "faithful innovation" in church-related NGOs/NPOs, Jones describes how this is accomplished:

> They adapt the old system, create innovation, in order to stay true to their calling. Traditioned innovation is a way of thinking and living that holds the past and future together in creative tension . . . requiring both a deep fidelity to the patterns of the past that have borne us to the present and a radical openness to the changes that carry us forward. Our feet are firmly on the ground with our hands open to the future.[31]

The adaptability of faithfully traditioned innovations to support healthy and visionary paradigm shifts would challenge parachurch agencies to remain committed to their original calling, God-given vision and ultimate mission while being attentive to newly innovated mission activities, which would carry the organization forward while valuing the mission statements and achievements of the past. What unites Jones's view with this research's findings is the idea that church-related agencies would gain freedom to shift paradigmatically while seeking new ways – together with God – to explore new opportunities and to improvise innovative ways to serve the poor holistically. Then, paradigm shift would become an opportunity and not a constraint created by threats facing the agency's existential survival.

Leadership would be able to contextually adapt to new mission realities and needs while being faithful to the heartfelt compassion that motivates them. It would lead them to embrace paradigmatic change and with it a

---

30. Katz, "Apostolic Service," 216.
31. Jones, *Christian Social Innovation*, 51.

greater motivation to move forward, grasping new opportunities and meeting the challenge of new mission realities. Paradigm shift done in this way would lead to faithful or traditioned innovations that are needed, but which are also faithful to past achievements. This research study has additionally explored contextualization as a solution to parachurch agencies' mission challenges in order to see how a CFB-NGO/NPO could balance embracing traditioned innovation while also resisting the kind of mission drift that might arise due to threats to the organization's existential survival.

5.4 Praxis of Parachurch Agencies' Contextualized Holistic Mission

Having previously discussed the necessity of faithful innovation (also called 'traditioned innovation'), viewed as essential to any changes of paradigm needed to reach out to the poor without drifting from the organization's mission statement, I can now turn my attention to the praxis of contextualization in parachurch agencies. Contextualization of the gospel and of Christian holistic mission through words and deeds by church-related NGOs/NPOs is needed to meet the needs of the poor. Myung argues that, in a cross-cultural church-related mission situation where contextualization is paramount, the gospel (the mission of parachurch agencies) has to be renewed theologically and reinterpreted missionally to meet the needs of those people who are served by parachurch agencies.[32] Whiteman is in agreement with this empirical research study findings (according to interviewee ten, interviewee twenty-four, and interviewee thirty-two) since he demonstrates that "there still remains an enormous gulf between the models of contextualization . . . and the practice of contextualized mission"[33] by Christian faith-based missionary organizations. As Hiebert puts it, contextualized practice is an ongoing process that needs to be biblically based, but with cultural perspectives,[34] like contextualized theologies themselves.

In addressing the issue of contextualization, Bosch suggests, "All theologies are contextual theologies, but we should not confuse the essential and

---

32. Myung, "Spiritual Dimension," 236.
33. Whiteman, "Contextualization: The Theory," 5.
34. Hiebert, "Critical Contextualization," 110–111.

universal aspects of the Christian message from its local, contextual ones."[35] I believe that a contextualized holistic mission by Christian faith-based NGOs/NPOs, rather than being theologically theorized, must be ritually, liturgically, experientially and practically acted out to meet people's daily needs. Viewed from this perspective, Gilliland aptly states,

> The goal of contextualization is to enable, insofar as it is humanly possible, an understanding of what it means that Jesus Christ, the Word, is authentically experienced in each and every human situation. The Christian message must be proclaimed in the framework of the worldview of the particular people to whom it is addressed, it must emphasize those parts of the message that answer the questions and needs of those people, and it must be expressed through the medium of the cultural gifts of those people.[36]

Parachurch agencies must develop a contextualized holistic mission praxis and theology that speaks to suffering people: a faithfully innovated "good news"; a genuinely contextualized and yet Bible-based theology of hope for the poor and a gospel in which God inclusively meets people's physical healing, spiritual salvation, and material needs. As church-related NGOs/NPOs become more related and relevant to the cultural, spiritual, and social contexts of the people, they will work to serve in the light of Jesus's earthly contextual ministry, and they will become better able to minister holistically to the wider society. The idea of Jesus's own ministry as a model helps to cast a light on what true contextualization is. In this sense, Newbigin describes how "true contextualization accords to the gospel, its rightful primacy, its power to penetrate every culture and to speak within each culture, in its own speech and symbol, the word which is both No and Yes, both judgment and grace."[37] This is a plausible and supportable argument.

Following Newbigin's description, it should be argued that where the contextual holistic innovations and praxis of a mission agency are not divinely inspired, biblically rooted, and holistically challenged, the organization will

---

35. Bosch, 423.
36. Gilliland, "Contextualization," 225.
37. Newbigin, *The Gospel*, 152.

quickly end up in activism, pragmatism, relativism, philosophical humanism, religious pluralism, syncretism, legalism, religious-ecumenism,[38] and/or socio-humanitarianism, and finally be seen as totally irrelevant and unrelated. Following a similar train of thought, Dowsett and his co-writers argue that bringing biblical text and missional context together appropriately in contact with each new culture, will prove the "diakonia" and evangelistic ministry of parachurch agencies to be "true" and "relevant".[39] In assessing contextual theology in Christian mission, Anderson agrees with Dowsett and his co-writers' argument, stating that in a discussion of contextualization, the culture and worldview of poor people must be included, and that in a religious-pluralistic society,[40] these aspects need to be addressed holistically, contextually and pertinently. So, it is reasonable to advocate the case that holistic missional contextualization must assume the fact that the mission of church-related agencies needs to be dynamically shaped by its particular context in order to appear meaningful and relevant. It must allow for, and adapt to constant change, thus relating the gospel message to all cultures and social contexts.

In this respect, Newbigin argues in a balanced way that "every communication of the gospel is already culturally conditioned." However, he cautions that the gospel "is not an empty form into which everyone is free to pour his or her own content", and finally reminds us that the content of the gospel is "Jesus Christ in the fullness of his ministry, death, and resurrection."[41] Campbell also warns that when the message of the gospel becomes "over-contextualized" and "too enculturated", it becomes something else – nothing more than a mere projection of Jesus's earthly holistic ministry and thus less than the "good news."[42] Newbigin's argument places emphasis on contextual transformation enacted through divine direction and the Holy Spirit's empowerment. The praxis of contextualized holistic mission by parachurch agencies assumes confirmation with the theory of contextual theology adapted to the cultural

---

38. I define 'religious-ecumenism' as being the religious and/or philosophical post-Christendom understanding that wants to promote the equality of all religions and that people are free to choose the belief that best suits them, thus ignoring the sacrificial and salvific message of the cross of Calvary.

39. Dowsett et al., *Evangelism and Diakonia*, 32; see also Ukpong, "What is Contextualization," 179.

40. Anderson, "The Contribution," 88.

41. Newbigin, *Gospel in a Pluralist Society*, 142, and 152–153.

42. Campbell, "Releasing the Gospel," 168.

environment of the poor. This can then transform their religious environment by the Spirit's secret working; which alone brings the gospel's message to life. The purpose here is therefore to propose a new parachurch organizational/holistic mission approach, as suggested by Anderson who states that the message and deeds of Christ through the power of the Holy Spirit reflect the present contextual message that gives salvation and hope to suffering poor people and destitute communities.[43] The praxis of Christian faith-based NGOs/NPOs' holistic mission must be appropriately contextualized to meet the felt needs of poor people and to strive to serve them, always taking into account fast-growing postmodern trends.

5.5 Postmodern Trends and 'Critical-Holistic' Contextualization: A Societal Challenge to CFB-NGOs/NPOs' Mission

The question of contextualization, according to Newbigin, is about "how the gospel comes alive in particular contexts."[44] How does this relate to societal changes such as those following rapid appearance and influence of postmodern trends? The findings of this research led me to advance the following as a tentative response, one suggested by one of the informants:

> Expect it to cross your path. It is a reality in our current world that is undergoing so much radical change in access to news and fake news (with nobody knowing the difference), to communication, the limitless availability of information and therefore also philosophical influences of a magnitude as never known before. All this in a time and season of a postmodern worldview that does not really accept absolutes, simple truth, drift is to be reckoned with. The best response? Holistic contextualization: to accept it as a constant challenge to our belief system, to our life practice, and to how much we can remain humble learners. These are also times in which it is important to listen to the still small voice of the Holy Spirit, of staying connected with him and

---

43. Anderson, "The Contribution," 98.
44. Newbigin, *Gospel in a Pluralist Society*, 152.

expecting God himself to allow us to see the truth and radically be able to walk in it.[45]

Inevitably, as Tennent, and Hurley acknowledge, the realities of postmodern times are going to force faithful church-related agencies to become even more articulate about what constitutes their indisputable Christian faith-based identity.[46] According to Burtness, "Contextualisation is a passionate cry for the recognition of the significance of this time and this place . . . without which the Word is dead word and the Christ a non-living lord."[47] Währisch-Oblau and Mwombeki suggest that to neglect the 'here and now' of Scripture in our society would make our mission non-contextual.[48] Mangayi, and Vähäkangas suggest that contextualizing missiology and mission praxis should begin by stimulating reflexive commitment to potential change, enhancing perspectives on mission praxis, and "addressing historical, philosophical and methodological challenges"[49] as far as mission reorientation is concerned.

The process of 'critical-holistic' contextualization[50] is suggested by Hiebert, Shaw and Tiénou. They propose four approaches towards critical-holistic ways of contextualizing the mission of parachurch agencies: (1) to examine people's response to societal trends and their phenomenological convictions, traditional beliefs and cultural practices, in order to see them through their eyes; (2) to analyze their beliefs and cultural practices in the light of biblical truth, (3) to evaluate the adaptability of their old beliefs and cultural practices in the light of biblical values based on the gospel, and then (4) to finally implement ministries and projects that would holistically transform poor people and their communities.[51] Taking this perspective, I believe CFB-NGOs/NPOs need to understand people's phenomenological convictions, traditional beliefs and cultural practices in order to offer better Bible-based answers to the existential, societal and spiritual questions they face, and to better contextualize the gospel according to the local setting. Währisch-Oblau

---

45. Interviewee 19.
46. Tennent, "Paradigm Shifts," 342 and Hurley, "The U.S. Workplace," 138.
47. Burtness, "Innovation as the Search," 13.
48. Währisch-Oblau and Mwombeki, *Mission Continues*, 22.
49. Mangayi, "The Baptist Union," 2, and 8; and Vähäkangas, "Comments," 531.
50. Hiebert, Shaw and Tiénou, "Responding to Split-Level," 166–182.
51. Hiebert, Shaw and Tiénou, "Responding to Split-Level," 173–174, and 180.

and Mwombeki echo this view, noting that "good contextualization requires wise judgments, not an uncritical acceptance or a rejection of old ways. Wise judgments, however, require a deep knowledge of local realities. Without such understanding, missionaries often jump to false or premature judgments."[52] Moreover, Währisch-Oblau and Mwombeki have reached a similar conclusion on the issue of 'critical-holistic' contextualization.[53] They have drawn attention to the fact that parachurch mission has to prove itself relevant in the postmodern context, by bringing the good news to modern people in the context of a post-Christendom society, taking into account local cultures and traditional beliefs, and thus, connecting the gospel with the lives of the poor.

Considering the view Ma and Ross advocate, mission by parachurch agencies must be inclusively contextualized and concretized as part of their commitment to spiritual salvation and needs, social justice and peace, and physical and material well-being.[54] Mangayi argues that it must promote "the welfare of humanity but also the greater world community, and will function in a holistic and integrated, incarnational, intentional, contextual, empowering and sustainable manner."[55] A helpful way forward has been presented by Woolnough and Ma, who have drawn attention to the fact that 'critical-holistic' contextualization assumes the reality that the "love of God was expressed quite naturally in addressing people's physical and emotional needs in the context of their spiritual needs."[56] If one follows these ways of reasoning, the expected result would be that each postmodern society has its culture, with a different set of questions needing to be addressed biblically, theologically, holistically and contextually. This is because many of the key issues facing church-related agencies usually emerge out of particular societal contexts and real-life situations.

In addressing the pluralistic and relativistic climate of postmodernity, Campbell advances the view that "there must always be a divine standard by which contextualization is evaluated,"[57] in order to unleash the gospel through

---

52. Währisch-Oblau and Mwombeki, *Mission Continues*, 23.
53. Währisch-Oblau and Mwombeki, 23.
54. Ma and Ross, *Mission Spirituality*, 133.
55. Mangayi, "Mission," 25.
56. Woolnough and Ma, *Holistic Mission*, 4; see also Backues, "Interfaith Development Efforts," 71; and Mangayi, "Township Churches," 11.
57. Campbell, "Releasing the Gospel," 169.

the holistic mission of CFB-NGOs/NPOs in present-day cultural contexts. He then poses the critical question: "... by what (or whose) authority do we make decisions regarding contextualization?"[58] The following table suggests a sphere of authority to be considered by parachurch agencies when implementing critical-holistic contextualization.

Table 5.1: Domains of Authority in Contextualizing CFB-NGO/NPO's Mission[59]

Domain of authority	Description	Contextualizable praxis (adaptability & translatability)
The core values: Christian faith-based identity, mission statements and holistic approaches as originally directed by God (Jesus Christ and the Holy Spirit)	Jesus Christ is our supreme authority in mission; therefore, *divine commands and guidelines* must be non-negotiable. Parachurch NGOs/NPOs' first priority is to faithfully and holistically fulfil God's purposes (Matt 28:19–20; John 14:15, 21; and 1 John 5:2–3.	Can be fully translatable but not adapted (non-negotiable core values)
The substance of the founding mission objectives (based on biblical principles and Jesus's model)	*Mission principles* must be drawn from biblical teachings that reveal the works and words of Jesus (Matt 9:35–38 and Luke 4:18–19) and apostolic teachings (Acts 2:42; Rom 16:17; 2 Thess 3:6; 2 Tim 3:16). Only these teachings are to be translated and enculturated following postmodern trends.	The essence is unchanging; to be translated locally and culturally to maintain the dynamic equivalent.

---

58. Campbell, 169; see also Dowsett et al., *Evangelism and Diakonia in Context*, 47 and 53.
59. Table adapted from Campbell, "Releasing the Gospel," 169.

Domain of authority	Description	Contextualizable praxis (adaptability & translatability)
The application of holistic missional methods and patterns	*Patterns and methods* are values and principles in action, expressed in specific cultural contexts (behavior, lifestyles, dress code, religious settings, methods, forms, trends, ideologies and practices) that are normative to first-century Christians (1 Cor 4:16–17; Phil 3:16–17; 1 Thess 1:7–8; 2 Thess 3:9).	To be contextualized and translated to respond to the specific cultural trends or societal changes (faithfully innovated to fit the NGO/NPO's holistic mission objectives)
The expression of parachurch agencies' mission traditions and practices	Mission traditions and practices are established ways of thinking, doing, interpreting and feeling that are culturally inherited. They must be tested according to divine commands, biblical principles, Jesus's earthly ministry and then applied to the cultural relevance (Matt 15:3, 6; Rom 12:1, 2; Col 2:8).	To be contextualized and adapted to the specific local cultural settings (faithfully traditioned innovations)

This table exemplifies four spheres of authority that offer a standard for implementing 'critical-holistic' contextualization in Christian faith-based mission, and the degree of its subsequent contextualizable praxis to be lived in the framework of today's postmodern and post-Christendom trends. Campbell, commenting on the table, writes that "this chart distils the essentials from the non-essentials, it helps filter out anything that may hinder the natural and supernatural movement of the gospel across cultures."[60] Furthermore, Campbell strongly argues that the response to postmodernity

---

60. Campbell, 169; see also Dowsett et al., 39.

calls on Christian faith-based institutions to embrace "the paradoxical tension of being authoritative and contextualized in order to continually evaluate mission strategies for their cultural sensitivity and biblical integrity."[61] He maintains that this paradoxical tension requires CFB-NGOs/NPOs to cultivate an acute discernment between exotic modernity and/or culturally-specific contexts, and between trans-modern essentials and/or culturally-translatable real-life situations[62] or settings.

A helpful way forward towards understanding Campbell's argument has been developed by Sanneh, who has advanced the idea that 'critical-holistic' contextualization is to be built on the supposition that the gospel is timeless and changeless and can therefore be translated into any postmodern culture.[63] The gospel of the kingdom as defined in Scripture is totally relevant to man in the totality of his need. This argument is based on the understanding that the gospel was designed and provided by the same God who made the human heart and who knows the depth of man's alienation from him and from his fellows. Therefore, the revelation of Jesus Christ in Scripture is unchangeable and is always translatable, regardless of the epoch and its cultural contexts or belief settings. Dowsett and his co-writers contend that church-related organizations are to develop a contextualized practice-based missiology that can address postmodern societal needs and also be relevant to post-Christendom multireligious societal contexts.[64] They further argue that although the concept of contextualization seems to be recent, the term is not modern since God in the Bible is portrayed as having always operated in a context, and Christian faith has always functioned within contextual variations.[65] The message of the gospel knows no cultural boundaries, and its teachings and praxis are susceptible to being enculturated,[66] says Campbell, while setting up each contextualizable boundary within its domain of authority.

Nowadays a more humble and participative model of contextualization is required; this is what Newbigin proposes (coming from a different angle)

---

61. Campbell, 169.
62. Campbell, 169.
63. Sanneh, *Translating the Message*, 37.
64. Dowsett et al., *Evangelism and Diakonia in Context*, 48.
65. Dowsett et al., 32.
66. Campbell, 168; see also Kärkkäinen, "Pentecostal Missiology," 17; and Kaoma, "Post Edinburgh," 113.

in his book, *The Gospel in a Pluralistic Society*. He advances the view that the contextualization process begins by attending to the primacy of the Bible as the starting point, and that the gospel is culturally conditioned and should be humbly communicated in terms of the language and custom of the hearers.[67] For Newbigin, a 'humble' way of contextualizing takes into account the fact that there is no pure or superior culture or even a culture-free gospel.[68] To do mission participatively would therefore mean avoiding the 'Western traditional model of "top-down" contextualization', as well as previous approaches that consider that Western missionaries to have the truth and that they bring this truth to other parts of the world. The message of the gospel is thus 'westernized', ignoring local contexts, yet hoping that those people can understand it. Moreover, he asserts that the gospel is, as such, equated with a Western culture – an inadequate way of thinking that assumes that there is such a thing as a culture-free gospel – as part of this pure and superior Westernculture.[69] Newbigin poignantly lays emphasis on "the colonial yoke of the synthesis of nationalism and Christianity inherent in indigenization, adaptation, and accommodation" to the 'Majority World' and the alarming paradox of their "synthesis of nationalism and Christianity" in the name of "local theologies."[70] As 'local theologies', Newbigin refers to 'Liberation Theology', 'Black Theology', 'Dalit Theology', and 'Feminist Theology' as examples which do not involve the crossing of cross-cultural boundaries,[71] as Prince explains. Rather, Newbigin suggests that contextualization must be directed towards the need to communicate God's word so that it speaks the good news of the gospel to the whole context in which the audience is presently living and through which people make their decisions for Christ.[72] In view of the present collapse of Christianity in the "Big West," one can say that CFB-NGOs cannot do God's work without cultural contextualization just like one cannot do mission without exegetical theologization.

In this respect, Newbigin goes to state that Christian missiological theology is "a form of rational discourse developed within the community,"

---

67. Newbigin, *Gospel in a Pluralist Society*, 151.
68. Newbigin, 141–145.
69. Newbigin, 142.
70. Newbigin, *Gospel in a Pluralist Society*, 143 and 148.
71. Prince, *Contextualization*, 54.
72. Newbigin, *Gospel in a Pluralist Society*, 142.

which participatively accepts the authority of Scripture,[73] with the aim of appealing to the hearts, minds and conscience of the listeners. Participative contextualization does not dictate the terms and issues of meeting with the community, but rather challenges the context in depth, so that the gospel is absorbed and domesticated by the listeners,[74] as Newbigin writes. Keeping in mind what has previously been said concerning the issue of "critical-holistic" contextualization in the postmodern world, this line of thought provides a valuable addition to the defense of what is considered here the main argument: that church-related agencies must humbly consider "faithful innovations" that are contextualized, holistic, and participatory, when confronted with societal changes. Therefore, parachurch agencies need to be committed to serving God through their 'diakonia' and evangelistic activities, even as they adapt – without compromising on their holistic mission – to new trends in the contemporary world.

5.6 Mission True Agencies: The Pursuit of Holisticalization and Biblical Holism

The objective in this section is to motivate each parachurch agency that pursues holisticalization to stay 'mission true' in accord with its Christian mission statement and in terms of its mission objectives, identities, and values, both in the present and in the future. This is the target. According to Greer and Horst, "Mission true organizations believe that the gospel is our most precious asset, and that Christian faith is essential to our mission work."[75] Mission true agencies develop a 'mission spirituality', which enables them to pursue the holistic proclamation of the gospel by reflecting on those things that Jesus declared in both word and performed deed through his holistic earthly ministry. What does it mean to stay mission true? Should the fact of staying mission true be the concern of parachurch agencies? And what is then to be understood by the concept of mission spirituality? The following sections discuss matters raised by these questions.

---

73. Newbigin, 142.
74. Newbigin, 152.
75. Greer and Horst, *Mission Drift*, 33.

5.6.1 Staying 'Mission True': The Challenge of the Holistic God-given Missionary Vision

In attempting to answer these questions, I have argued in this discussion, that focussing Christian faith-based NGOs/NPOs' mission statements and field-services on Jesus's earthly ministry as a holistic model would certainly contribute to providing a remedy for the issue of mission drift. This argument was centred on the fact that holism is incarnated in the person of Jesus, not in his programme of activities, based on the gospel (e.g. Matt 9:35–38 and Luke 4:18–19) and framed by a Christian worldview. Woolnough notes that, at a time when the majority of the ecumenical and liberal branches of the church had gone into reverse, drifting from a holistic gospel, emphasizing the social gospel alone, and leaving the personal salvation aspect of the gospel to the more evangelical branch of the church, and the Evangelicals withdrew to the mission of 'evangelism only', individual believers solved the need to stay mission true by founding parachurch NGOs/NPOs.[76] The objective was to tackle development and relief problems holistically around the globe. It is from this perspective that Kaoma emphasizes that a Christian NGO/NPO's mission is expected to emanate from the triune God, and that the church is unambiguously invited to participate on these terms.[77] To this, Bosch argues that to be a Christian institution is "to participate in the movement of God's love toward people, since God is a fountain of sending love."[78] Bosch further asserts that mission exists because God loves people.[79] He showed it through his son Jesus.

Staying mission true, according to Brown, means to be true to the original mission of the institution and also to remain "true to the core values of the past, while incorporating new approaches,"[80] using improved methods and a "people friendly" design. He describes how a church-related organization must have "a clear identity and vision when making programmatic changes and functional shifts that accommodate the realities of a sharply

---

76. Woolnough, "Christian NGOs," 195.

77. Kaoma, "Post Edinburgh 2010," 116.

78. Bosch, *Transforming Mission,* 400; see also Hesselgrave and Stetzer, *Mission Shift,* 22; Finn and Whitfield, *Spirituality for the Sent,* 169; Lord, *Spirit Shaped Mission,* 20; and Harris, *Mission in the Gospels,* 192.

79. Bosch, 402.

80. Brown, *Staying the Course,* 50.

changing world" without changing its core Christian faith-based mission values.[81] Concurring with Brown's way of describing this, I would add that being a mission true parachurch agency requires that it holds fast to its founding mission and makes that mission even more distinctive today than it was in the past. Staying mission true consists of serving God in mission while adapting to postmodern trends and post-Christendom cultural contexts, thus growing holistically without drifting from the mission values, vision, and identity that God has given.

In addressing this issue, Greer and Horst state that "in its simplest form, Mission True organizations know why they exist, and protect their core at all costs. They remain faithful to what they believe God has entrusted them to do. They define what is immutable – their values and purposes, their DNA, their heart and soul."[82] The DNA of biblical holism keeps the heart and soul of the organization in line with God's purposes for God's people. The study conducted by Gallet has shown that in order for Christian faith-based NGOs/NPOs to remain true to their God-given identity, they must not neglect the following facts:

1. The NGO/NPO's name must refer to its Christian faith-based identity and orientation in what it does,[83] and not hide its holistic God-given missionary vision and values;
2. Delivering Christian holistic services within a secular and post-Christendom environment has the potential to weaken Christian identity, sabotage God-given values and limit the expression of biblical holism within parachurch NGOs/NPOs.[84] This may in turn lead to internal secularization and ultimately to mission drift with the consequent fatal loss of 'mission trueness';
3. The intrusion of neo-secularisation into the organization creates potential for the drifting of the NGO/NPO's Christian faith-based identity.[85] In particular, this could end with the abandonment

---

81. Brown, 50.
82. Greer and Horst, *Mission Drift*, 27.
83. Gallet, "Christian Mission," 111.
84. Gallet, 117.
85. Gallet, 118.

of the organization's original mission, rather than its remaining 'mission true';
4. The matter of the diminishment of parachurch agencies' holistic God-given vision and focus on Christian identity plays a vital role in the internal secularisation debate,[86] particularly in relation to the challenge of staying mission true and the risk of mission drift. Where the mission remains true, there is a true holistic proclamation of the gospel.

Table 5.2: Comparative Chart: Mission True vs. Mission Drift

Mission True	Mission Drift
Agencies that show a clear and steady holistic functioning – with spiritual and social aspects at the core of its Christian DNA (holistic God-given vision).	Agencies that used to embrace holistic functioning but now consider that the two aspects (socio-humanitarian and spiritual) are not essential to its Christian identity.
Central and clearly stated Bible-based mission and Christian identity	Agencies that have a vague or peripheral spiritual mission, which is not viewed as a pressing need in society.
Agencies that rely mostly on uncompromised fundraising in order to be financially sustainable.	Agencies that mostly rely on unbelieving donors to run their activities.
Agencies that had have a clear Christian worldview stated in the organization's online mission statement as part of the original vision, with the accent on holistic proclamation.	Agencies with an unclear Christian worldview stated in the organization's online mission statement as part of the original vision. Holistic proclamation of the gospel is seen as unnecessary.

5.6.2 A Holistic Proclamation of the Gospel

This research outcome has brought to light the significance of the holistic proclamation of the gospel in CFB-NGOs/NPOs. In this section, a brief

---

86. Gallet, 122.

exegesis that is biblically based, and intersects with the data[87] is required, to introduce the discussion relating to the instructions of the resurrected Jesus – the Great Commission – to his followers. In Matthew 28:18–20, two terms are essential to the understanding of Jesus's intention pertaining to ministry. Firstly, μαθητεύσατε (Matt 28:19) is from the verb μαθητεύω (*mathéteuó*), which signifies "to make a disciple" or "to be a disciple"; the second is διδάσκοντες from the verb διδάσκω[88] denoting "to teach." Ott sees Matthew 28:16–20 as a 'programmatic text' where the risen Lord commissions his followers throughout all centuries,[89] and Bosch calls it a 'famous dictum'[90] which is witnessed by "proclamation, fellowship and service,"[91] something that must obviously have been understood earlier by the church.

The terms "to make a disciple" and "to teach" are hybrid expressions that reflect the isomorphic-holism of the gospel embodying the nature of the ministry/mission into which Jesus commissioned his followers. None of these words presupposes verbal proclamation or evangelism alone, which is the fundamentalists' idea, but rather a notion of "making" and "teaching" with the purpose of producing holistic transformation in order for people to become disciples. So, it might be fair to infer that the goal of preaching the good news of God's kingdom is to offer the possibility of accepting the grace of God to attain spiritual salvation through Jesus Christ's sacrifice and, as well, receiving grace for physical, social, material, and social wellbeing. And so, the goal of evangelism is to transform lives vertically through salvation in Christ and horizontally through social actions in the name of Jesus. Gustafson pertinently sums up this idea, saying that "evangelism is transformation, transformation is development, and development is evangelism in a very real sense."[92] In short, there is a necessity for all the followers of Christ to enlarge their perceptions of evangelism to something beyond traditional boundaries, yet involving the verbal proclamation of the good news (evangelism for personal salvation of the soul) and the practical proclamation of the gospel

---

87. Interviewee 10.
88. The same verb is utilized in the following passages in Matthew 4:23; 5:2; 7:29; 9:35; 15:9; 22:16, among others.
89. Ott, "Matthew 28:16–20," 3.
90. Bosch, *A Spirituality*, 372.
91. Bosch, *Transforming Mission*, 523; see also Margull, *Hope in Action*, 175.
92. Gustafson, "The Church and Holistic Ministry," 84–85.

(socio-humanitarian concern for people's wellbeing). For both evangelistic and social ministries involve the actual proclamation of the gospel, and we see this in Jesus's earthly ministry. This is holisticalization. This is holistic *Missio Dei*. This is the holism of the good news. And this is holistic proclamation of the gospel – the actual expression of the "two-hands of the gospel" concept defined earlier in section 4.1.

The events recorded in passages such as Matthew 9:35–38; 11:4–6; Luke 4:16–21; and Acts 3:1–26; 10:38 regarding holistic ministry show two main areas of application. On the one hand, they relate to the holistic nature of Jesus's mission in particular (and by extension his followers), and on the other, they tell us about the practitioners engaged in the mission. In this sense, Gallagher and Hertig suggest, "Holistic ministry must be truly holistic" in the sense that the holistic proclamation reveals the gospel-as-word, the deeds following the proclamation reveal the gospel-as-deed, and the powerful presence of the Spirit that transforms people reveals the gospel-as-sign and wonder.[93] Here, one can observe three manners in which the triune God operates: through word, deed, and sign. Observably, though the gospel demonstrates this operation to be a whole (a unity), embracing the evidenced aspects of the gospel as deed, as word, and as sign, in the past century the three expressions have been respectively emphasized by liberals, evangelicals, and Pentecostals,[94] as Gallagher and Hertig, and Olson conclude. Moreover, it is a fact that all three are necessary to make the gospel real in people's lives. It is with this in mind that Tizon and Myers suggest that preaching of the word is needed to clarify deeds; deeds are needed to verify the connotation of the words proclaimed; and power, signs and wonders are needed to reveal the source of all that the good deeds have accomplished.[95] The strength of this argument is found in the interpretation of Steward, who, in expounding on holism in the Bible and the Christian missionary mandate, makes a judicious argument that those people lacking knowledge may first be attracted to the gospel through words, those who are sick and needy may respond to gospel-as-deeds, and the demon-possessed may respond to the gospel's

---

93. Gallagher and Hertig, *Mission in Acts*, 43.
94. Gallagher and Hertig, 43; and Olson, *The Westminster Handbook*, 177.
95. Tizon, *Whole and Reconciled*, 155–156; and Myers, "Modernity and Holistic Ministry," 179–180, see also 183.

powerful signs and wonders.[96] Gallagher and Hertig appropriately assert that a comprehensive announcement of the good news, desiring that those who accept come under the lordship of Jesus Christ, is fundamental, as are compassionate ministry and humanitarian deeds[97] carried out through the power of God's Spirit.

Following these persuasive arguments, it might be fair to add that holistic missionaries or practitioners have a vital role to play in fulfilling the commitments of their agency's holistic mission. Holistic missionaries or practitioners are those who see the nature of poor people's needs, act to contextualize their mission for the envisioned audience, and call out for God's divine intervention in relation to that context and purpose. They are the hands that touch and channels of God that reach out personally to those who do not yet have the knowledge of Jesus,[98] as Gallagher and Hertig state. Verwer notes that the work of holistic practitioners is to some degree an ambitious expression of the doctrine of God and man, which is why it is necessary for there to be the implementation of the "two hands of the gospel" in mission, thus reflecting the holistic nature of Jesus's earthly ministry.[99] Vieira encourages practitioners to acquire some basic training before stepping into the mission field so that they can see the need for a holistic ministry that values both the spiritual and social aspects of the gospel.[100] Holistic practitioners must be made aware of the fact that the people are helplessly lost without Jesus.

In relation to the truth of that last poignant statement, Lewis declares that,

> if the lost are often poor, then a holistic ministry – one in which compassion, social transformation, and proclamation are inseparably related – would seem to be the strategy for this time in the history of that individual: to encounter Jesus Christ, and to experience his transformative power in all levels – spiritual, physical, emotional and social.[101]

---

96. Steward, *Biblical Holism*, 170.
97. Gallagher and Hertig, *Mission in Acts*, 43.
98. Gallagher and Hertig, 43.
99. Verwer, *Sortir de la Zone*, 120–122.
100. Vieira, *La Religion Africaine*, 178.
101. Lewis, *World Mission*, 16.

What is Lewis suggesting? In this respect, Lewis is, in practical terms, urging that "if the 'Incarnation' is the model used to minister to such as these, then holistic missionaries, people whose lives eloquently express the values and the worth of the gospel, would seem to be the messengers of the hour."[102] This is the true sense of the incarnational mission.

I appreciate the way in which Woodward articulates what a holistic practitioner's attitude should be. He concludes by saying that acquiring a concrete understanding of the holistic nature of God's salvific grace in Jesus Christ should inform the holistic practitioner on how to share the gospel.[103] Additionally, Woodward argues that when a missionary understands that the spiritual person, the physical person and the social person are interlinked, the good news he/she shares will sound much more like that of Jesus than the shortened and one-sided versions that mislead believers today.[104] It makes sense that when Christians study, learn, understand, and acquire the art of sharing the good news well, it will become obvious that it is the power of God that holistically and profoundly transforms lives. This way of doing ministry speaks of the transformational power that deeds have as part of the all-inclusive gospel message, which also integrates the aspect of signs and wonders that the good news carries. The emphasis of the Holy Bible is indeed on holism, which is not a formulation of modern humanistic thought but a recurrent topic of Scripture itself. As God's children, we also are called to grow holistically, as shown in the account of the young Samuel in 1 Samuel 2:26. This is analogous to the description of Jesus Christ in Luke 2:52, which models holisticalization in the life and mission of those who are named Christians.

However, the issue of power in the mission of Christian agencies, which is associated with Western superiority and/or advantage, needs to be highlighted here. This aspect of power is not always trivial because: "Knowledge is power. Money is power. 'Helping' is the execution of power,"[105] affirms Ott. Following this view, Harries challenges the superiority of Western Christian mission that consists in their being the donors who possess the "know-how" of mission and exercise their "money-power" and "knowledge-power" over communities;

---

102. Lewis, 16.
103. Woodward, "A Holistic Gospel," 20.
104. Woodward, 20.
105. Bernhard Ott, e-mail message, 18 December, 2020.

instead, he promotes the concept of "vulnerable mission",[106] which consists of using local resources and languages in mission. The Alliance for Vulnerable Mission (AVM), as Harries introduces it,

> Seeks to encourage wider use of mission and development strategies that depend on locally available resources and local languages. These strategies are "vulnerable" in the sense that they do not have fringe benefits built into them, deliberately or otherwise. They will therefore fail unless or until there is strong local confidence in their spiritual or developmental value. The missionary or development worker will allow them to fail rather than prop them up with outside money.[107]

Moreover, "empowerment" in Christian mission is not just the execution of divine power, but also "the process of gaining freedom and power to do what you want or to control what happens to you. Ott contends that especially in "the area of Christian relief work and humanitarian aid, it is important to address this issue because 'empowerment' has become a key term in development work."[108] On the other hand, the money-power and the knowledge-power of the Western "Church is enormous . . . It is not only an impressive monument to the power of Christian missions, but an earnest of the vast fruitage which may be expected within our generation"[109] – says Thomas – even though often, it takes away dependence on God. Evoking holistic empowerment, Durbin, Katoski, Kelley, Simler and Stolfa argue that power in Christian developmental mission enables a comprehensive effort that covers action, advocacy, education, service, and spiritual empowerment.[110]

---

106. For Harries, the concept of the 'vulnerable mission' "may be seen as part of the movement toward contextualization of the gospel of Jesus, which we regard as 'the theory of many and the practice of few.' We would like to see more people take the risks of contextualization and vulnerability in order to reap the rewards that only come to those who value local resources and invest in local languages. If local tools seem slow or weak by comparison with foreign money and English (Spanish etc. – European language), then we say with a wise missionary of long ago, when I am weak, then I am strong (2 Cor 12:10). While vulnerable mission may not be the only biblical approach to mission, it deserves much more attention than it has been getting." Harries, "Encouraging Western People."

107. Harris, "Encouraging Western People."

108. Ott, e-mail message, 2020.

109. Thomas, *Classic Texts*, 76.

110. Durbin et al., *The Empowerment Process*, 1.

The efficacy of the mission of parachurch agencies is intrinsically dependent on their spiritual, monetary, and knowledge-based empowerment. Their own empowerment in these three areas will bestow on them power which can impact the people and communities that they serve in a holistic manner. Money as power, knowledge as power and God's Spirit as power, are all equally important. The acquisition of knowledge and the possession of money are to be viewed as a means of responding to Matthew 28:16–20, because money is power in the hands of the followers of Christ, and knowledge guides them in the use of 'mission consecrated money'.

While giving credence to the notion of holistic mission, Earley and Wheeler challenge the objective interpretation of holistic proclamation, basing their argument on the difference between the "proclamation" and the "affirmation" of the gospel.[111] According to them, "Proclamation describes the giving of a clear explanation of the gospel to a non-Christian as an event (Mark 16:15). Affirmation describes living the character of Christ (John 20:21). Proclamation is preaching the gospel with our lips. Affirmation is being. Proclamation is telling the truth. Affirmation is living the truth."[112] Earley and Wheeler's view undermines the prevailing understanding that the holistic proclamation of the good news involves the gospel-as-word, gospel-as-deed and gospel-as-power; seeking to meet people's needs all-inclusively. There is a lot to be discussed about this claim. However, the limitations set in this case study research means that I can only concentrate on the "holistic proclamation" character of the gospel.

The verbal proclamation-oriented approach to evangelism creates the supposition that "'hearing' the gospel is the equivalent to 'being reached' by the gospel," and Gustafson obviously rejects this construal. A correct understanding of the word evangelism is based on the construal that evangelism is about imparting the good news of God's grace through Jesus Christ in a holistic way, so that it gives birth to a transformation of people's lives, in all cultures, and in various societies, Christian organizations, and human traditions,[113] as Gustafson maintains. The standpoint Gustafson maintains is supported biblically when one carefully reflects on the terms used in Matthew

---

111. Earley and Wheeler, *Evangelism is*, 183.
112. Earley and Wheeler, 183.
113. Gustafson, "Church and Holistic Ministry," 84.

28:18–20 to launch the 'Great Commission.' Gustafson notes that the common exposition of the Great Commission is that Jesus called the church to go out and evangelize by committing to make disciples as Christ did.[114] Moreover, he puts forward the following idea,

> It is ironic to me that the term evangelism is used for the phrase "make disciples" and then is defined as a "verbal proclamation" of salvation in Christ. If to "make disciples" refers to evangelism, then surely, we need to expand our understanding of evangelism from being simply a verbal proclamation of the gospel. To be a disciple is to be transformed. It does not mean to turn over a *part* of one's life to Christ, rather one's *entire* life.[115]

Socio-humanitarian involvement and spiritual-missiological evangelism are both part of Christian responsibility. Holistic proclamation refers to evangelism and social action, both of which are required expressions of the Christian wholistic/holistic mission doctrines of God and man, Christian obedience to the gospel of Jesus and Christian love of neighbor. Nevertheless, ultra-social activism and theological liberalism seem to have the tendency to lead church-related NGOs/NPOs away from the gospel's scriptural and spiritual authority as well as its basic evangelistic concern. It should be observed that the Bible – viewed as the authoritative word of God – was established to give prominence to the holistic nature of the ministry of Jesus, emphasizing the necessity of evangelism and encouraging believers to take action on social issues.

However, a more detailed analysis on this view would reveal that Christian organizations need to construct patterns that reflect the difficulties of our time and the inclusiveness of the *Missio Dei*. Subsequently, a new community begins to form, living in a way that reveals the visible socio-humanitarian model of the messianic message of Jesus as God intended. Furthermore, there must be an extensive fresh horizontal reconciliation between God and the sinful-fallen human race, the church (parachurch agencies) and the world, the believer and the unbeliever, the rich and the underprivileged, even between

---

114. Gustafson, 84.
115. Gustafson, 84.

husband and wife. This is possible in the name of Christ. This seems to be the way 'true mission spirituality' is built.

5.6.3 Holistic Mission Spirituality of CFB-NGOs/NPOs: A Solution to Mission Drifting?

The results of this investigation revealed that all seven parachurch agencies studied in this research began with very Christ-centered mission statements and objectives focused on sharing the gospel holistically. Edwards argues that "while strategies might change and adjustments to culture are made,"[116] the desertion of the spiritual aspect of mission or 'mission spirituality' and its related rapport with mission would be seen as a significant sign of 'mission drift.' A Christ-centered parachurch agency pursues a holistic 'mission spirituality', which is viewed as the animating force and the springboard that inspires and energizes the God-given vision and objectives of the organization. The person of Christ remains the ultimate end, and his earthly ministry remains the ultimate example to follow.

Ver Beek defines holistic mission spirituality "as a relationship with the supernatural or spiritual which provides meaning and a basis for personal and communal reflection, decisions and actions"[117] in Christian development work. Seeing things from a perspective very close to that of Ver Beek, Lonsdale sees Christian holistic mission spirituality as a spirituality that "concerns the whole of human life, viewed in terms of a conscious relationship with God, in Jesus Christ, through the indwelling of the Holy Spirit and within a community of believers."[118] In popular usage, such a definition regains ownership of a word – spirituality – which is subject to a host of misrepresentations. In common usage, Währisch-Oblau and Mwombeki formulate a persuasive statement arguing that,

> Spirituality is seen as pertaining to the inner life, as opposed to life in the world. It points to "being", as opposed to "doing". Since mission is clearly about doing, the juxtaposition of "mission" with "spirituality" immediately sets up the expectation of

---

116. Edwards, "Faithfull Innovation," 21.
117. Ver Beek, "Spirituality: A Development Taboo," 32.
118. Lonsdale, *Eyes to See*, 10; see also Kaoma, "Post Edinburgh 2010," 121; and Franklin, "Mission Spirituality" 22.

a long list of dualities: spirit vs. body; soul vs. flesh; spiritual vs. physical; abstract vs. concrete; imagination vs. reality; faith vs. politics. Behind these oppositions lies another set which is even more insidious: prayer vs. action; Mary vs. Martha; sacred vs. profane; pure vs. defiled; eternal vs. temporal; heaven vs. earth.[119]

The above-mentioned distortions highlight the fact that "holistic mission spirituality" is a controversial issue, and yet it is important and crucial for a deeper understanding of mission and of world Christianity. Ma and Ross pertinently suggest that spirituality is the beating heart of Christian faith-based mission,[120] bridging one generation of missionaries and the next.[121] Mission spirituality is a term that describes that area where the Spirit of God 'initiates', 'guides' and 'empowers the mission of the follower of Christ. He upholds the view that the "Spirit becomes the catalyst, the guiding and driving force of mission."[122] Bosch then defines mission spirituality as a "spirituality of the road," a fully engaged spirituality that is lived out in Christian mission through the charging of the spiritual batteries; mission, therefore, takes place by the impulse of God's Spirit.[123] It is for this reason that mission work needs to follow an understanding of holistic mission spirituality that recognizes the lordship of Jesus Christ both over the Christian Faith-Based NGOs/NPOs themselves, and over the recipients the agencies seek to serve,[124] as Woolnough and Ma observe.

Following the same train of thought, Young, pondering on what he justifiably regards as "spiritual decline" within church-related organizations in general and the Salvation Army in particular, suggests that "this is largely attributable to an intensified focus on social service activities as opposed to an evangelical focus."[125] In his response to this controversial issue, Gittins argues that "saving is a holistic process that involves making sure material

---

119. Währisch-Oblau and Mwombeki, *Mission Continues*, 73–74.
120. Ma and Ross, 225; see also Kärkkäinen, 216; and Martikainen, "Changes in the Religious," 373.
121. Bosch, *Transforming Mission*, 238.
122. Bosch, 113–114.
123. Bosch, *Witness to the World*, 12–13.
124. Woolnough and Ma, *Holistic Mission*, 152.
125. Young, "Army Walking," 6.

needs are met – and that this is done through welfare work,"[126] carried out by parachurch NGO/NPO's. Undoubtedly, a clearly structured spirituality pushes a parachurch agency forward towards its God-centered and God-given objectives, in terms of its values and vision of transformational holistic development. This allows a 'space for grace' – where God can act in and through that organization.

5.7 Mission Drift Exposures

This research study, as illustrated in Figures 1.1, 5.1 and 5.2 and outlined in the findings, sequentially presents the overlapping domains that exemplify how various interrelated concepts can lead to 'drifting' in a church-related agency. The results of this study have shown that an out-boundary pursuit of funds coupled with an obsessive ambition for growth constitute the main factors accelerating mission drift. Another significant domain revealed by this study concerns the hiring of non-Christian professionals as staff members. In these circumstances it is difficult to stay true to the agency's original mission and not to drift. These factors are discussed in detail in the next two sections for the purpose of understanding exposure to mission drift.

5.7.1 Fundraising and Ambition for Growth: Susceptibility to Drifting?

As previously mentioned in describing the causal/determinant conceptual framework for mission drift's evolution (Figure 5.1), fundraising and growth ambition are both central to the development of an organization, but also to its missional downfall. Dempsey argues that mission drift is liable to occur when agencies mature;[127] therefore, older, and larger parachurch organizations are more liable to show signs of drifting away from their original mission statements and objectives. In addressing this issue, Rothschild supports the following view:

> Maintaining the integrity of your mission can be quite a challenge when funders are providing funds for initiatives that are

---

126. Gittins, "The Nature of Mission," 4; see also Davies, "A Missional Miss," 4; and Amalraj, Hahn and Taylor, *Spirituality in Mission*.

127. Dempsey, "Microfinance Mission Drift," 34.

related to your mission but really don't support it. Some "nonprofits" chase such monetary support because they believe it's the only way they can survive. That's a bad idea, but it's tempting.[128]

In this respect, prior research by Chambers that focused on mission drift indicated that in most cases, mission drift relates to "growth strategy decision-making"[129] and therefore conflicts with the original mission of the agency.

This equally is the position of Austin, Stevenson and Wei-Skillem, who make a helpful analogy with hybrid ventures, noting that hybrid organizations or holistic mission agencies "are often pulled into rapid growth by pressure from funders, demand for their products or services, and are pushed by the demands of their social mission to meet those needs."[130] In this way, they further suggest, such NGOs face a major challenge "to resist the powerful demand-pull for growth, and to be more deliberate about planning a long-term impact strategy."[131] In contrast, NGOs that have decided on a slower growth strategy while laying greater emphasis on organizational mission objectives can better resist 'growth-first strategy'[132] and out-boundary fundraising.[133] Growth must be strategically planned in order to be line with God.

The concept of 'growth-first strategy' consists of putting greater emphasis on the agency's ambitious desire to grow large and to grow fast. In some cases, as Austin, Stevenson and Wei-Skillem note, "Growth may not be the best approach to achieve the organization's goals or to have the greatest social impact. Growth for the sake of growth has the potential to squander organizational resources and can actually detract from the organization's overall impact."[134] The following illustrations (in Figures 5.3 and 5.4) picture the obsession with growth that can compromise an agency's mission objectives, jeopardize its founding vision, and detract from its missional impact. The first figure illustrates an active and desperate search for growth described as a "growth-first strategy", which consists of investing in professional board

---

128. Rothschild, *The Non-Nonprofit*, 38.
129. Chambers, "Growing a Hybrid Venture," 37.
130. Austin, Stevenson, and Wei-Skillern, "Social and Commercial," 7.
131. Austin, Stevenson and Wei-Skillern, 7.
132. Copestake, "Mainstreaming Microfinance," 22.
133. Ronsen, *Mission Drift?* 89–90.
134. Austin, Stevenson and Wei-Skillem, 7–8.

members and co-workers in managerial positions to achieve the newly constructed vision. The second illustration clarifies and visually represents the reality of mission drift – leaving the primary boat, the original mission and God-given vision – to settle for a larger vessel with all the risks of "drifting". Both figures are taken from my children's drawings.[135]

Figure 5.3: Schematized "Growth-first Strategy"

---

135. Anaëlle, Johëlle and Raphaël Kombaté.

Figure 5.4: Schematized "Powerful Demand-Pull" for Growth

Many of the scholars such as Bennett and Savani, Hughes, Ramia and Carney, who discuss the challenges related to the existential survival of such agencies also point out the propensity of NGOs/NPOs to slowly shift their mission focus and adapt their approach to meet the demands of their funders.[136] As time goes by, these organizations can become inattentive and confused in relation to their original holistic mission objectives and thus, mission drift occurs,[137] as Saunders writes. According to Young, due to the complexity of running a holistic mission NGO/NPO as it should be run, the presence of these investors and unbelieving professional co-workers would "challenge

---

136. Bennett and Savani, "Surviving Mission Drift," 217–231; Hughes, "The Third Sector,"; and Ramia and Carney, "New Public Management," 253–275.

137. Saunders, "Supping with the Devil," 7.

the effectiveness of its governance structures."[138] Moreover, financiers of all stripes may request influence in the management of a hybrid/holistic agency via seats on the board in order to advance their own agenda,[139] as Billis argues. Young recognizes this, and further cautions that key funders will expect compliance with their own criteria before they fund an NGO/NPO. In fact, he further asserts that hybrid/holistic organizations can be "tempted by financial pressures to shift their activities toward goals favoured by various sources of income."[140] However, Young concludes that "while funding is a cause of mission drift, it is not the 'sole determinant' of whether mission drift occurs"[141] (in hybrid/holistic agencies). Hiring non-Christian co-workers for key positions – even though they are professionals – as if they were co-religionists may be one of the determining causes of mission drift.

5.7.2 Hiring Unbelieving Professionals as Co-Staff: A Christian Identity Drift?

After outlining the degree to which out-boundary fundraising and growth can become a determining factor in causing mission drift, I now discuss the implications of hiring non-Christian professionals. The outcome of this study shows that hiring unbelieving professionals as co-workers, especially at leadership level, may influence the mission objectives of Christian faith-based organizations – something which would probably not have been the case if they were co-religionists in Christ. It is from this perspective that Rabi effectively argues that a holistic approach to leadership involving different professional co-workers with different competencies and motivations may lead to unnecessary influence, which may in turn distract from the primary goal – redirecting the agency's management in a way that prioritizes growth and which may end up causing detriment to its holistic mission objectives.[142] Thus, the holistic organizational mission's purposes may change over time and drift from their original Christian faith-based orientation.

---

138. Young, "The State of Theory," 27.
139. Billis, *Hybrid Organizations*, 50–54.
140. Billis, 33.
141. Young, "The State of Theory," 30.
142. Rabi, "How Social Enterprises," 16; see also Wittberg, *From Piety*, 59; and Gregg, "Playing with Fire," 1–8.

For this reason, some scholars – Canda, Furman and Canda; Vanderwoerd; and Smith and Sosin – have suggested that parachurch agencies must clearly communicate their Christian identity and holistic mission approach, and ensure that they are able to hire persons who share their Christian faith and all-inclusive mission convictions.[143] Cleary echoes this view, arguing that "an unintended consequence of employing 'professionals who lack an informed faith position' has resulted in welfare services drifting away from the religious influences of the church and becoming more secularised."[144] If one follows Cleary's clear-cut position, the expected conclusion would be that employing unbelieving professionals as opposed to co-religionists would reorient the faith-based NGO/NPO's mission and lead to the organization's Christian identity drifting as a consequence. A closer detailed analysis on this view is suggested by Bouma, Cahill, Dellal and Zwartz, who advance the view that in order to deliver holistic Christian mission and protect their ethos, church-related agencies must hire workers who share their Christian beliefs and who can promote that faith.[145] However, this position is not supported by all governmental bodies. One example is the SBA, which argues that there should be no exemptions on the basis of belief, where social welfare or socio-humanitarian service is provided.[146] From this point of view, O'Halloran, and Davis assert that church-related agencies discriminate against non-Christian candidates for employment by asking what they see as inappropriate questions pertaining to participation in church activities and experience in Christian faith-based community organizations.[147] Consequently, these two views undermine the prevailing understanding that parachurch agencies need to employ those who share Christian values because it would be difficult for non-Christian co-workers to affirm these specific values and mission objectives.

Several scholars – Oslington; Ebaugh, Chafetz and Pipes; and Swain – argue that the professionalization of parachurch NGOs/NPOs' welfare

---

143. Canda, Furman and Canda, *Spiritual Diversity*; Vanderwoerd, "Religious Characteristics," 258–286; Smith and Sosin, "The Varieties," 651–670.

144. Cleary, *Reclaiming Welfare*, 27.

145. Bouma et al., *Freedom of Religion*.

146. SBA stands for 'Small Business Administration' which is a US government agency that seeks to assist small businesses and entrepreneurs in order to strengthen and maintain the economy of the nation. Small Business Administration, "Faith-Based Organizations," 2.

147. O'Halloran, *Religion, Charity*, 217; Davis, *Centers for Faith-Based*, 118.

services has led to a decline in the holistic mission focus of Christian faith-based services.[148] A strong objection to the SBA's position and to Callaghan's oppositional views comes from scholars such as Hughes, Cleary, Pallant and Campbell, who uphold the view that professional staff hired by parachurch holistic agencies often object to interference with their spiritual and faith values in matters relating to welfare services or humanitarian activities.[149] Rejection of the view held by the SBA and Callaghan must be supported because drifting is even more likely to occur because of the fact that these professional co-workers view themselves as the agents of major donors, inevitable stakeholders and/or government funding bodies.

CFB-NGOs/NPOs' frontrunners who have fully embraced their God-given vision and their agency's holistic identity will be well positioned to inculcate similar values in their staff. They will also be best positioned to remove explicit reference to non-Christian philosophical ideology, and by using Christian principles, construct, reinforce and establish routines that affirm Christian holistic mission ideology without explicitly needing to make overt reference to it. This type of governance, as Battilana and Lee, and Rabi have claimed, ". . . would also remove internal conflicts – depending on whether the organisation has integrated, differentiated, or selectively coupled corporate design"[150] – with unbelieving members of the professional workforce.[151] It is therefore particularly vital that people who are leading CFB-NGOs/NPOs are clearly aware of the God-given mission of their agency and the complexities of running a holistic Christian faith-based mission. This is central not only to the organization's primary mission objectives but also for the rest of its personnel. As announced in the Literature Review, I have suggested in the following section an application of Matthew 9:35–38 and Luke 4:18–19 to this research study.

---

148. Oslington, "Guest Blog," 1; Ebaugh, Chafetz and Pipes, "Faith-Based Social," 273–292; and Swain, "Do you Want," 78.1–78.8.

149. Hughes, "Theology and Welfare," 1–20; Cleary, Reclaiming Welfare; Pallant, Keeping Faith; Campbell, "Church and Civil Society,".

150. Battilana and Lee, "Advancing Research," 416.

151. Rabi, "How Social Enterprises," 51.

5.8 Applying Matthew 9:35–38 and Luke 4:18–19 to the Present Study

As outlined in sections 1, 1.3.1 and 2.4, Matthew 9:35–39 and Luke 4:18–19 are the two passages I have selected as the biblical platform on which this study finds its scriptural foundations. In this regard, after having exegeted them in chapter two (in sections 2.4.2 and 2.4.3), I now wish to present my strongly held conclusions in the context of holistic mission and to propose relevant and valuable applications for today's Christian mission practitioners. In order to complete the process I started in exegesis, I must move "from interpretation to application, from the past to the present, from the there-and-then to the here-and-now,"[152] as borrowed from Smith. This has highlighted the practical significance of the two texts mentioned above for contemporary parachurch mission agencies. My conclusions strongly underlie my practical approach to the application of the two passages in relation to holistic mission.

The issue of spiritual power and mission needs to be carefully articulated around Jesus's own doctrine of mission dynamics (Matt 9:35–38 and Luke 4:18–19; see also Matt 10:1, 7–8; Mark 6:7–13; Luke 9:1–6; Acts 10:38). Jesus calls his disciples, gives them power and authority, and sends them out to proclaim the message of the kingdom and to heal the sick. He gives them both spiritual δύναμις and ἐξουσία for the mission ahead of them. Christian mission is spiritual warfare, but Jesus supplies us with the necessary divine equipment. Divine power is always needed for attainment of the mission. During his earthly ministry, as the apostle Matthew tells us, Jesus preached the gospel and called for repentance (3:2; 4:17; 9:35–38; 10:7), forgave sins (6:14–15; 9:1–8), fed the multitudes (14:13–21), healed the sick, and drove out impure spirits (9:35b; 10:1, 8).[153] The context (Matt 9:35–10:1, 8) makes it clear that the kind of workers Jesus desires in his kingdom are those who: (1) preach and teach the gospel of the kingdom, (2) heal diseases and (3) drive out evil spirits,[154] as Stamps, Adams, Gerbore and d'Orazio Berkley assert.

---

152. Smith, *Writing and Research*, 132.

153. For further Scripture reading: preaching and calling for repentance (Mark 8:34–38; Luke 5:32; 1 Cor 3:18–23), forgiveness of sin (Luke 7:48; Col 3:13; Eph 4:31–32; 1 John 1:9), showing the true way that leads to life (John 14:6), feeding of thousands of people (Mark 8:1–13, John 6:1–15), healing the sick and driving out evil spirits (Mark 10:46–52, Luke 13:10–17).

154. Translated from: "le contexte (9.35 à 10.1, 8) indique clairement que le genre d'ouvriers que Jésus désire dans son royaume sont ceux qui (1) enseignent et prêchent l'Évangile

This marks the source of the conclusions I have drawn, which underlie the application of Jesus's message revealed by this study.

Coming from this perspective, Sunquist balances diaconal service and kerygmatic/word ministry in the following pertinent way: "Jesus responded to situations with a touch of the hand, a word of encouragement, or a word of judgement; in each case there was power . . . We, however, tend to be reductionist, promoting verbal evangelism alone, or promoting works of mercy alone. Jesus does not recognize this dichotomy."[155] This is "kerygmatic"[156] in the sense that he proclaimed the message of the gospel verbally, and yet "diaconal" in the sense that he attended to the social, economic, material, psychological, physical, political, and spiritual needs of the people,[157] as Koech writes. Moreover, his earthly mission was also "programmatic" in the sense that the Spirit revealed the God-given vision, and "paradigmatic" in the sense that the Spirit set the pattern to follow in relation to the holistic mission, which is also the mission of parachurch agencies. Therefore, the mission of church-related agencies must also be characterized by the leading and activity of God's spirit. To play both kerygmatic and diaconal roles in modern situations, CFB-NGOs/NPOs need the anointing, empowerment, inspiration, and guidance of the Spirit just as Jesus needed it during his earthly ministry/mission.

The holism or the holistic nature of Jesus's earthly mission was not just seen in his programmatic activities. It was notably founded in the holistic person of Jesus. Holism was in the person of Jesus. Newbigin states that Jesus's ministry was pastoral, combining both the diaconal and kerygmatic and should therefore motivate similar mission practice in parachurch agencies, for mission is acted out in accordance with God's justice.[158] Newbigin further asserts that mission is to be centered between action for God's justice and proclamation of the gospel.[159] Doing mission holistically contributes to the

---

du royaume, (2) guérissent les maladies et (3) chassent les mauvaises esprits." Stamps et al., *La Bible*, 1533.

155. Sunquist, *Understanding Christian Mission*, 217; see also Bosch, *A Spirituality*, 135–139; Newbigin, *The Pen Secret*, 103.

156. The term kerygmatic comes from the Greek word κήρυγμα (see Matt 12:41; Mark 16:20; Luke 11:32), which means preaching the message of God's kingdom or the proclamation of the gospel. The kerygma also means the message preached.

157. Koech, "The Spirit Motif," 156.

158. Newbigin, *The Pen Secret*, 103.

159. Newbigin, 107.

restoration of justice to people – a justice that has been stolen and destroyed by the devil and is to be restored in the image and likeness of God's kingdom and in the holism of Jesus. This is to be done in the likeness of Jesus's holistic earthly ministry and mission – as foreshadowed in Luke 4:18–19 and predicted by the prophet Isaiah (61:1–3). Following the example of Jesus Christ our lord and master, I believe that is what holistic spiritual missiology expects of Christian mission workers – his followers and disciples of today. They have to carry the gospel out in a mission that can impact this world holistically. God's spirit empowers and gives the means for that mission.

The need for divine power in proclamation of the good news and development of effective Christian spiritual missiology – also called holistic mission spirituality – is ineluctable. It is important to highlight the fact that holistic mission spirituality is a combination of the theory and praxis of spiritual dynamics with the execution of Christian mission. Lamport's definition of the concept has credence here. He says that holistic mission spirituality comes from the analysis of the truths and forces, resources and manifestations that govern the spiritual destiny of Christian organizations in the experience of divine grace and in the execution of the mission of God.[160] Lampert's observation continues with the following definition:

> Spiritual missiology is the study of how to live the Christian life in concert with the grace of God and in total commitment to His kingdom. It is the study of the correct application of Bible doctrine to experience; it is the reflection on experiential sanctification and Christian service, and most of all, it is the theology of faith application. It is the 'how-to' manual of arms or the handbook for spiritual growth, spiritual warfare, spiritual survival, spiritual power, spiritual authority, spiritual maturity, spiritual resources, and spiritual tools, to better accomplish God's mission in the world.[161]

Spiritual missiology is directly related to the commission given by Jesus to the church and to parachurch agencies to reach all nations in the world, and it operates at the most practical levels. Lamport argues that Christian

---

160. Lamport, *Encyclopedia of Christianity*, 509.
161. Lamport, 509.

spiritual missiology, most of all, has to do with the spiritual resources that God has given to equip both church and agencies for mission, such as miracles, signs and wonders, gifts of the Holy Spirit, spiritual discernment, divine power encounters, and so forth.[162] After having recapitulated the teaching, preaching and healing ministry of Jesus (Matt 9:35,) Matthew directly makes a shift to the 'mission discourse' in chapter 10 (cf. Mark 6:7–13; Luke 9:1–6). In Matthew 10:1 and 11:1 Jesus makes a reference to his disciples, thereby re-introducing the basic task of the twelve, which is mission (4:18–22). With this in mind, Garland describes how Jesus begins his speech (the second of the five key discourses in the Gospel of Matthew) with the commissioning of twelve apostles with divine authority and power (Matt 10:1) to develop his holistic ministry of teaching, preaching and healing (9:35; cf. Luke 9:1–2).[163] It is remarkable that the mission of the twelve and that of the seventy disciples are both prefaced by the same terms concerning the mission, the sending, and the need for divine power, and that they convey the same instructions and warnings (Luke 10:1–24). Jamieson, Fausset and Brown note that Jesus fully trained and authorized the disciples with heavenly power and divine authority, or even with "saintly right", to equip and prepare them for the mission ahead (Luke 9:1) – "He gave them power and authority."[164] Jesus justifies the need for the mission in Matthew 9:36–38,[165] as Blomberg states. He then gives specific mission instructions (10:5–23) and makes a reference to the nation of Israel (10:6, 23) thus emphasizing the nature and manner of their mission with a forewarning of the mission's perils,[166] as Garland argues.

Considering the application of Matthew 9:35–38 (see 4:17) and Luke 4:18–19 (see 4:14–15; 9:1–2, 19 and Acts 1:8; 10:38), it becomes evident that missiology in parachurch agencies is to be interlinked with divine power in order to be effective in touching lives and meeting people's spiritual and other needs. "Power from above" (from God) is significant in helping to fulfil the missionary task of Christian NGOs/NPOs in this world. Bosch, Newbigin, Wacker, Koech, and Skreslet indicate that the outpouring of the Holy Spirit's

---

162. Lamport, 510.
163. Garland, *Reading Matthew*, 110.
164. Jamieson, Fausset and Brown, *Critical and Explanatory Commentary*, 35.
165. Blomberg, *Matthew*, 135.
166. Garland, *Reading Matthew*, 110.

power is acknowledged in Jesus's ministry and in the promise of the coming down of the "latter rain" (Joel 2:23–29; Hos 6:3; see Isa 61:1–3) for the ripeness of the harvest (Matt 9:37–38). It takes a worldwide mission (word and deed) for the kingdom to be restored through the Spirit's empowerment.[167] In the book of Acts (1:8), the lord Jesus Christ pledges two significant things to his disciples: δύναμις (power) and μάρτυς (witness). The word used in this context is δύναμις, and one finds the same term used of Jesus's miracles in the synoptic gospels (Matt 11:23; 13:54; 14:2; Mark 6:2; Luke 10:13). It is the power of God's Holy Spirit (Acts 2:1–21) that CFB-NGOs/NPOs need in their practice of holistic mission. The apostles' role is that of μάρτυς (*martys*) and the "endowment with the Spirit is the prelude to, and the equipping for, mission,"[168] as Zerwick implies. The future tense in Act 1:8 refers to an imperative implication for better application:

1. Ἀλλὰ λήμψεσθε δύναμιν "But you will [must] receive power";
2. καὶ ἔσεσθέ μου μάρτυρες, "and you will be my witnesses."

With regard to application, Keck stresses that "the less Jesus is the core of witness, the less power we have in mission practice."[169] In a deeper development of this view, Newbigin talks about "thy kingdom come . . . as the key phrase which defines the aim of missions . . . , and the work of missions is to join with and endeavour to give effect to the work of this Spirit."[170] In my view, this is the implication and the means of application of spiritual missiology. According to Tippett, the spiritual missiology of Christian faith-based agencies involves two basic dimensions:

> Missiological theory and action may be designated as both *theological* and *anthropological* – *theological* because the message is a word from God concerning his purpose for, and promise to mankind. It is *anthropological* because it has to be communicated within the structure and organization of human societies. This message is *theological* because it concerns not only the inner life of an individual, one's spiritual experience, but also

---

167. Bosch, *Witness to the World*, 17; Newbigin, *The Pen Secret*, 24; Wacker, *Heaven Below*, 251; Koech, *Spirit Motif in Luke*, 159 and 162; and Skreslet, *Comprehending Mission*, 50.
168. Zerwick, *A Grammatical Analysis*, 350; see also Dupont, *Nouvelles Études*, 51–52.
169. Keck, "Listening to," 197; see also Koech, *Spirit Motif in Luke*, 155.
170. Newbigin, *Sign of the Kingdom*, 7.

one's external state. It is *anthropological* because this takes place in an earthly environment on which humans depend for their physical life and where these spiritual experiences have to be worked out in a series of human relationships that are culturally conditioned.[171]

Following Tippett's analysis, it would be fair to conclude that the mission of parachurch agencies involves two basic dimensions, namely, the theological aspect dealing with the spiritual dimension, and the anthropological dealing with the cultural and physical dimension.[172] When, in his prayer to God the father (John 17:11–14), Jesus said that the disciples were 'not of this world' and yet they are also 'in the world,' he was revealing a basic dichotomy in Christian mission: the spiritual (the evangelistic aspect of the gospel) and the physical (the socio-humanitarian aspect of the gospel). These two dimensions need to be kept in equilibrium as far as Christian missiology is concerned, both in its missionary policymaking and in its action regarding world mission. Zorn acknowledges that, to imitate Christ, the missiology of parachurch agencies cannot ignore the fact that the missionary enterprise was born from the charisma of people praying for the mission who were then organized into societies of "friends of the missions" independently of the churches.[173] He further asserts that these origins thus gave birth to a missionary spirituality that was perpetuated by being schooled in Protestantism, and that engendered a fundamental difference of approach from the kind of academic theology that received an ecclesial legitimacy.[174] However, Christian spiritual missiology is the driving force for all aspects of world *missio Dei*. It aims to relate the believer's personal experience to Jesus Christ, through God's spirit.

Emphasizing the spiritual missiology of parachurch agencies, Spindler and Lenoble-Bart argue that parachurch agencies must adopt Jesus's missionary

---

171. Tippett, *Introduction to Missiology*, xxi; see also Servais and Spijker, *Anthropologie et Missiologie*, 260; and Hoedemaker, and Camps, *Missiology*, 41.

172. Tippett, *Introduction to Missiology*, xxi.

173. Zorn, *La Missiologie*, 89.

174. The original text in French: "À l'imitation de Christ . . . la missiologie ne peut oublier que l'entreprise missionnaire est née du charisme des priants pour la mission qui se sont ensuite organisés en sociétés des « amis des missions » indépendants des Églises. Ces origines ont donc donné naissance à une spiritualité missionnaire qui s'est perpétuée en faisant école dans le protestantisme et en engendrant une différence fondamentale d'approche avec la théologie universitaire qui, elle, a reçu une légitimité ecclésiale." Zorn, 89.

spirituality if they want to integrate a spiritual dimension into their mission work.[175] Moreover, they suggest that CFB-NGOs/NPOs must remember that any treatise on ecclesiastical sciences can be studied according to various functions: theology, research and synthesis, pastoral work and the methodology of action, lived experience and spirituality, etc.[176] Besides, as Spindler and Lenoble-Bart aptly assert, the missionary spirituality of Christian NGOs/NPOs is an integral part of missiology since it is a study of missionary experience.[177] According to Bifet, one must always return to the figure of the good shepherd, perceptible in all the great missionaries since Peter and Paul.[178] Based on Bifet's argument, it can be noted that the life of the good shepherd, is all about personal relationship and generous fidelity to the mission received from God the father and can be seen from the incarnation of the Son (Heb 10:5–7) to the cross (John 19:30).

Faithfulness to mission requires that the church and church-related agencies must have Jesus at the center of their kerygmatic ministry and their diaconal service,[179] as Newbigin argues. This fidelity is realized in harmony with the action of God's spirit who consecrates Jesus and sends him to minister to the poor by meeting his spiritual, physical and all other needs (Matt 9:35–38; 11:5; Luke 4:18). This is the point of reference for any parachurch agency's missiological spirituality that claims to be biblical and apostolic, diaconal and kerygmatic in its way of carrying out of holistic modern mission practice. Now, after proposing an application of Matthew 9:35–38 and Luke 4:18–19 to this study, I am going to outline a theoretical framework of how to apply all these research findings.

---

175. Spindler and Lenoble-Bart, *Spiritualités Missionnaires*, 60.

176. Translated from: "Il faut adopter une spiritualité missionnaire qui est celle de Jésus. Si l'on veut intégrer la dimension spiritual dans la missiologie, il faut se souvenir que tout traité de sciences ecclésiastiques peut être étudié selon diverses fonctions: théologie, recherche et synthèse, pastorale et méthodologie de l'action, expérience vécue et spiritualité, etc." Spindler and Lenoble-Bart, 60.

177. Translated from: "La spiritualité missionnaire est partie intégrante de la missiologie en tant qu'étude du vécu des missionnaires." Spindler and Lenoble-Bart, 60.

178. Bifet, *Priestly Spirituality and Mission*.

179. Newbigin, *Sign of the Kingdom*, 33.

5.9 Applicable Guide: A Theoretical Framework Emerged from the Results

The upsurge in the growth of holistic parachurch agencies has been such that they have become a very significant faith-based means through which the followers of Christ, regardless of race, gender, or social class, can participate in holistic kingdom work all over the world. That being the case, the question of the appropriate application framework is relevant to the subject of this thesis. The whole of chapter 4 was dedicated to this research study's findings. These have resulted in several statements and proposals in the form of warnings and suggested solutions, which are raised in chapter 4 and discussed in chapter 5. It is worth recalling them here to demonstrate their applicability. The following are some examples:

1. The need for fundraising activities to be in accordance with the standards of integrity by aligning them with the gospel's message. The plight of the poor must not be exploited in order to meet funders' expectations. A stewardship responsibility of parachurch NGOs/NPOs is to significantly reduce the dependency on donors and increase their transparency in financial matters;
2. The need to safeguard ambition for growth and to ensure that publicity efforts reflect the agency's holistic mission and vision statements and the responsibility to educate both the staff and funders in the way Christian holistic transformation is achieved and fully accepted;
3. The need to demonstrate the Christian holistic organizational objectives and kingdom values, and to avoid competition with other Christian NGOs/NPOs involved in similar ministries, while avoiding conformism with secular international agencies that pursue a 'success mentality' and disregard God's integral concern for the poor;
4. The need to collaborate adequately with local churches and to listen sensitively to those in local partnership when delivering programs to the communities that are being served. A balanced 'two-way process' in communicating with local people needs to be facilitated, in order to develop a true partnership between parachurch agencies with the local people they seek to serve;

5. The need to guarantee that the legitimate accountability of parachurch agencies to external authorities (i.e. governments, donors, stakeholders, regulatory agencies, resources, suppliers, etc.) does not result in the "imposition of Western management systems on local communities,"[180] based on the assumption that Western control systems are the best to certify accountability;
6. The need to ensure recruitment of co-religionists as co-workers (most especially at the managerial level) to avoid loss of Christian identity, internal secularization and the general humanitarization of the NGO/NPO. This must be in accordance with the organization's confession of faith and vision statement;
7. The need for parachurch agencies to work humbly as "apprentices" from within their partner churches in the role of pioneers and catalysts, thus, contextualizing and facilitating the implementation of the church's public holistic theology for the whole *Missio Dei* and reaching out to the whole world with the whole gospel. In this way, the theological contribution of the church's public, holistic and contextualized mission must cover three dimensions:
    1. Connecting people in a meaningful way to achieve the increase of their holistic welfare conditions and spiritual and socio-humanitarian situations,
    2. Coming alongside them in their cultural settings so that they can adapt to their new environment of Christian faith, identity, and values,
    3. Developing and fostering a 'holistic discipleship curriculum'[181] that will help to reinforce the commitment of parachurch agencies to apply the church's public theology of holistic mission.

The role of management is to serve the holistic God by allowing practitioners to grow in their Bible-based holistic mission convictions and to use

---

180. Befus and Bauman, "*The Role of Christian NGOs*," 2004: Lausanne Movement, "Holistic Mission."

181. A sort of curriculum or roadmap that integrates and implements spiritual formation and community development all-inclusively with respect to cultural settings that tally with biblical values.

their own gifts "to prepare God's people for God's [holistic] works of service, so that the body of Christ may be built up" (Eph 4:12). Throwing themselves as holistic practitioners at the mercy of the holistic gospel by celebrating the holistic church so that the entire world might see holistic agencies bear witness to hope in Jesus must be the missional commitment of parachurch agencies. This is the aim, the ideal, the commitment that parachurch agencies must embrace with humility as an achievable goal, rather than a "statement of intent". Now, having discussed the empirical research findings of this study and having proposed an application of Matthew 9:35–38 and Luke 4:18–19 in this chapter, while outlining a framework of the application of the results, the next chapter launches with a discussion of theories and spectra that are bound up with the occurrence of mission drift.

CHAPTER 6

Interconnected Theories And Spectrums

In chapter 4, I presented some "circumstantial factors"[1] which emerged during data collection, and which are favorable to "drifting." These were then extensively discussed in considerable detail in chapter 5. Now, in this chapter I articulate the results that emerged from this empirical research in connection with existing theories and spectrums related to circumstantial factors propitious to mission drift in parachurch agencies. The outcome of this research was based on a scholarly analysis of the interconnected theories and spectrums that facilitate the occurrence of mission drift in a CFB-NGO/NPO, which I compared with the results of previous hypothetical studies and publications. This particular discussion related to the main question of the research: *In what ways do parachurch agencies face the crisis of mission drift in their mission activities?* This brings in the circumstantial and/or environmental factors surrounding the agencies.

The goal in chapter 6 is to seek a deeper theoretical understanding of the context of mission drift in parachurch agencies that are working holistically (just like hybrid ventures in microfinance), especially with connections to the seven samples of the case study. This process included discussing a wide range of varied but correlated concepts that tend to overlap so as to form a continuous sequence or series (spectrum or continuum). These analyses of

---

1. Professionalization and bureaucratization of parachurch agencies (Hiring unbelieving professionals at the managerial positions and as co-workers), out-boundary ambition for growth and fundraising, and the dechristianization (loss of Christian identity) of society and secularization of holistic mission.

theories and spectra form the basis of biblical holism for understanding "drifting" within the parachurch agency from a scholarly point of view. Throughout chapter 6, various theories and continua are elucidated, thus forming the philosophical part of this empirical study research. With my research done and findings presented, my contribution to the theoretical and academic discussions can be articulated in the following theories and spectrums.

6.1 Theory Analysis

Based on the outcome of this empirical study, I dialogue with existing theories in this chapter. Theory analysis in this research purports to explain or describe what the phenomenon of mission drift in parachurch agencies is and what it does. It predicts the events that affect the phenomenon and the possible ways it can touch other phenomena. Theory analysis objectively and systematically examines the given phenomenon for meaning, usefulness, logical adequacy, testability, workability and generalizability, which may lead to deeper understanding regarding formulations or insights that were previously undiscovered. In this study, the theory is broken down into different parts which are examined individually and as they relate to each other in terms of events affecting the phenomenon of mission drift.

6.1.1 Organization Theory

In this section, challenges that constrain the distinctiveness that a Christian faith-based NGO/NPO can experience are further explored, such as those suggested by 'organization theory' or 'institutional theory'. In this research analysis, organization theory (also called environmental theory, neo-institutional theory, or organizational fields theory) is used to reveal external forces that challenge or put pressure on Christian holistic agencies (see section 4.2.3 about these external forces). Lin, in her efficient categorization argues that one of the known ways that these external pressures challenge Christian NGOs/NPOs is through the environment of key regulatory agencies, resources, suppliers, stakeholders[2] and other institutions that produce similar services.

Church-related agencies sometimes develop relationships with organizations that are dissimilar to them and that might have a different understanding

---

2. Lin, "Countering Mission Drift" 71.

of Christian faith and of the holistic mission concept, and which therefore have a divergent impact upon the religious NGO/NPO. On the one hand, Lin further declares that parachurch agencies "have relations to their founding faith traditions. These can include church congregations, affiliates, organizations and individuals."[3] As Schneider argues, these Christian communities have a tremendous impact on the support structures of the agency as well as on the extent to which these CFB-NGOs/NPOs reflect their mission objectives and values.[4] On the other hand, these parachurch NGOs/NPOs "exist within society, and might consciously seek validation as legitimate members within their area of expertise,"[5] says Schneider. This is what one respondent reported, then went on to say that many CFB-NGOs/NPOs have drifted from their first mission, partnering with institutions and governments all over the world for the sake of legitimatization and validation.[6] There is a need for "these faith-based organizations to connect to higher levels of decision-making as well as to share information with other established organizations,"[7] asserts Lin.

Pertaining to organizational fields theory, Meyer and Rowan were the first scholars who "identified issues relating to institutional fields when they focused on how organizations were moulded by what they referred to as 'institutional rules' which are the 'taken for granted' approaches to structuring organisations."[8] In addressing these issues, Gallet argues that institutional rules may be reinforced through public expectations arising as a result of legal requirements.[9] It is from this perspective that DiMaggio and Powell strongly affirm that these rules should be broadly disseminated to the point of becoming key patterns for various NGOs/NPOs operating within the same institutional/organizational field.[10] Berger unambiguously states that the fact of "being too explicitly religious can result in the creation of legal obstacles

---

3. Lin, 71.
4. Schneider, *Social Capital*, 517–518.
5. Schneider, 518.
6. Interviewee 5.
7. Lin, 71.
8. Meyer and Rowan, "Institutionalized Organizations," 351.
9. Gallet, "Christian Mission," 98.
10. DiMaggio and Powell, "Introduction."

when applying for public funding."[11] Interviewee sixteen echoes these 'legal threats' or 'opposition to funding' in stating the following: "Our partners were very much against the term evangelize.... If donors would hear that we want to convert people to Christ then they will stop supporting financially."[12] Which is why Meyer and Rowan uphold the view that the success of these agencies is dependent on conforming to rules that are shaped by leading actors in the field, such as the dominant organizations, the governments involved and/or the various professional associations operating in the same institutional environment.[13] This has been put forward by Berger as one of the fundamental reasons why many Christian faith-based agencies try to seek formal recognition as "NGOs/NPOs"[14] in order to fit into the environment of international organizations.

As Ormerod suggests, there are potential major divergences relating to goals that can result in compromising the parachurch agency's mission in terms of what he calls a "free market competition model."[15] Cleary, commenting on these issues, states that church-related agencies have been "seduced into the rhetoric of the market, they are seduced into the agenda of elite actors."[16] This leads to the following questions: "In whose image are we providing services? Are we providing services in the image of the gospel, and what we believe to be our mandate?"[17] Furthermore, Cleary asks: Are parachurch NGOs/NPOs now simply the hand-maiden of elite actors in the organizational field, providing the kinds of mission that 'they' believe are appropriate for people?[18] In an attempt to answer this question, interviewee sixteen declares that Jesus should be the center of church-related NGOs/NPOs' relief and development works in order to stand apart from the philanthropist clubs, the humanitarian organizations and UN agencies which operate on a secular and humanitarian basis.[19] For parachurch holistic agencies, this is

---

11. Berger, "Religious Nongovernmental Organizations," 17.
12. Interviewee 16.
13. Meyer and Rowan, "Institutionalized Organizations," 340–363.
14. Berger, "Religious Nongovernmental Organizations," 17 and 20.
15. Ormerod, "Seek First the Kingdom," 435.
16. Cleary, "The Poor You."
17. Cleary.
18. Cleary.
19. Interviewee 16.

an environmental challenge or organizational field issue that may seriously constrain features that are distinctively Christian and lead to mission drift. As a consequence, the impact of these work relationships with international organizations challenges and puts pressures on the agencies, which can lead to institutional isomorphism.

6.1.2 Isomorphic Theory

The theory of "organizational isomorphism" was first elaborated in an article entitled "The Iron Cage Revisited: Institutional Isomorphism and Collective Rationality in Organizational Fields,"[20] by DiMaggio and Powell. These writers describe organizational pressure or institutional isomorphism as being the process by which church-related institutions or agencies lose their Christian distinctiveness and identity and come to the point of resembling one another.[21] These Christian faith-based agencies drift away from those original holistic mission-objectives which constituted the distinctive features and identities that made them Christian. This happens because of pressures that constrain CFB-NGOs/NPOs to homogenize their purposes and to become more like other organizations that operate in the same field. A good example of an institution to which isomorphic theory can be applied is Harvard University. Greer and Horst write that the university was established in New England as a Christian educational institution, but one that has slowly lost its Christian identity and basis[22] (see sections 2.1.5, and 5.1). Greer and Horst note that the Harvard University motto at the start was, 'Veritas Christo et Ecclesiae' (Truth for Christ and the Church), that it employed professors who were exclusively Christian, and that it rooted all its policies and practices in a Christian worldview.[23] Today, this is far from the case.

Through the process of isomorphism, little is left of the institution's spiritual heritage and the moto has been reduced simply to *Veritas*,[24] as they regretfully point out. The same history and spiritual heritage apply to Yale University, which has also significantly isomorphized. Another good example

---

20. DiMaggio and Powell, "The Iron Cage Revisited," 147–160; see also Stout and Cormode, "Institution and the Story," 67–70.
21. DiMaggio and Powell, 147; see also McKinley and Mone, "Micro and Macro," 347–372.
22. Greer and Horst, *Mission Drift*, 17–18.
23. Greer and Horst, *Mission Drift*, 17–18.
24. Greer and Horst, *Mission Drift*, 16–18.

is that of the Christian Children's Fund founded by the American missionary and Presbyterian minister J. Calvitt Clarke in 1938 in China as a Christian child development agency to help relieve global poverty among children. Lin observes that the charity "has since lost its Christian roots, and in 2009 changed its name to Childfund International"[25] in order to conform to current rules and practices for international NGOs and to gain legitimacy in that organizational field,[26] as DiMaggio contends. Obviously, McKinley and Mone; and DiMaggio, reiterate this view noting that this process improves the chances for the existential survival of Christian faith-based NGOs/NPOs, but in turn it may mean compromise involving demands that are difficult to satisfy without acting in a way that is inconsistent with their mission doctrine and belief.[27] For parachurch agencies, there is a real danger of ignoring their Christian identity and missional understanding if they are in a regular relationship with agencies that do not share their faith. It is from this perspective that one participant to this empirical research goes on to unequivocally state that some of the so-called parachurch holistic agencies have lost their Christian faith identity and mission values due to these organizational challenges.[28] Another participant revealed that many parachurch agencies choose to partner with bigger institutions and governments for survival, consequently, drifting from their first holistic mission objectives.[29] In addressing these isomorphic issues, interviewee six disclosed that their NPO experienced mission drift because they partnered with a successful humanitarian NGO in training farmers, as their mission required significant fundraising[30] that became time consuming.

As DiMaggio and Powell, and Chaves rightly note, isomorphic pressures from the organizational field can create a decline of Christian religious authority and generate the occurrence of internal secularization in church-related organizations[31] (see section 4.2.3). Wittberg, and Frumkin side with this view, highlighting the fact that isomorphism has a propensity for occurring

---

25. Lin, "Countering Mission Drift," 72.
26. DiMaggio, "The New Institutionalisms," 696–705.
27. McKinley and Mone, "Micro and Macro Perspectives" 345; and DiMaggio, 696–705.
28. Interviewee 16.
29. Interviewee 5.
30. Interviewee 6.
31. DiMaggio and Powell, "Introduction," 70–74; Chaves, "Intraorganizational Power," 3; and Chaves, "Secularization as Declining," 749–750, and 756–757.

within religious-based social welfare agencies, educational institutions, areas of the health sector and the like, causing the attenuation of their Christian worldview and culture.[32] Contrariwise, a study conducted by Vanderwoerd suggests that church-related agencies "are able to withstand isomorphic pressures and maintain their unique mission and goals, provided they have a clear sense of their God-given mission and the will to carve their own path."[33] Following the same line of thought, Pallant argues that church-related NGOs/NPOs are in fact able to shape the identity and character of their faith-based organizations – while emphasizing that isomorphism need not be inevitable and is less likely if a correlation to the faith aspects of the organization is well-preserved.[34] Nevertheless, if the connection to the Christian worldview and character is weak, it is likely that parachurch agencies will lose their Christian distinctiveness and identity.

These issues have relevance to this empirical research study particularly in relation to the extent to which the parachurch agencies under consideration are facing problems of mission drift in connection with environmental pressures and challenges. Depending on the institutional field and the context of a parachurch NGO/NPO, distinctive types of isomorphic pressures may take place. Therefore, DiMaggio and Powell have identified three sorts of mechanisms associated with isomorphism that result in agencies resembling each other.[35] These are: normative, coercive, and mimetic; and are detailed in the next three sections. According to Gallet, these pressure-induced mechanisms are Normative Isomorphism, which is associated with the issue of professionalization; Coercive Isomorphism, which pressurizes the agency to conform to government mandates;[36] and Mimetic Isomorphism, which pushes the NGO/NPO to conform to the practices and programs of other organizations.

---

32. Wittberg, *From Piety to Professionalism*, 16; and Frumkin, "After Partnership," 208.
33. Vanderwoerd, "How Faith-Based," 262.
34. Pallant, *Keeping Faith*, 20–21.
35. DiMaggio and Powell, "The Iron Cage Revisited," 147–160.
36. Gallet, "Christian Mission," 156.

6.1.3 Normative Theory

Normative isomorphic challenge is related to the issue of credentials and other influences that are correlated to professionalization.[37] These pressures are associated with "the efforts of aggregate organizations to develop the methods, conditions and codes that underpin their work."[38] This kind of isomorphism takes place when Christian faith-based agencies are pressurized to conform to established standards. To this effect, Jakobs and Jacobs vehemently argue that the normative conformity pressures related to professionalization can push an NGO/NPO into certain positions to conform to external standards related to the codes of behavior within their organizational field.[39] Moreover, Scott maintains that normative rules introduce an obligatory, prescriptive and evaluative dimension into social duties.[40] He further declares that normative schemes coerce compliance in the social sector; the 'normative pillar' comprises norms, roles and values in order to promote professionalization.[41] Normative isomorphism is strengthened by the existence of strong cultural and social expectations in relation to certain organizational and professional norms, conventions, behaviors and practices. Deviation from these norms would be likely to affect the legitimacy of an agency and thus make it difficult to deal with the issues of deviance and mission drift.

Bess and Dee argue that some NGOs/NPOs are successfully able to ignore these professional policies, credentials, systems and practices, and attempt to explore how far they can 'stretch' beyond the 'recognized canons of acceptability' set up by the more powerful and well-known organizations and "operate outside the bounds of all the normative expectations."[42] However, going too far beyond the "legitimacy frameworks" will consequently take these organizations out of the market, and "actors in the external environment

---

37. Professionalization in this study is to be understood as a character or status being built up by the different influences of policies that professional associations have put in place to regulate various codes of behaviour (policies and practices) of the organizational field.

38. DiMaggio and Powell, "The Iron Cage Revisited," 148; see also Tsoukas and Knudsen, *The Oxford Handbook*, 362; and Wittberg, *From Piety to Professionalism*, 14.

39. Jakobs, *Corporate Standardization Management*, 131; and Jacobs, *Mapping Strategic Diversity*, 165.

40. Scott, *Institutions and Organizations*, 37.

41. Scott, 37.

42. Bess and Dee, *Understanding College and University*, 143.

will consider them too different from the respectable models."[43] Following this train of thought, interviewee twenty-five asserts that many CFB-NGOs/NPOs would have to close their doors in the future if they refuse to meet the international requirements (professional standards, conventions, behaviors and practices), and a certain number may gradually put aside their Christian identity in order to continue to exist.[44] As a consequence, many holistic agencies may find it progressively problematic to work in some countries without 'shifting the paradigm' to meet international humanitarian standards and practices, thus drifting from their core Christian faith-based mission and holistic principles.[45] According to this empirical research study, all of these are examples of the process of 'normalization.'

Decisions about whether to aim for similarity with, or difference from other NGOs/NPOs chiefly depend on assumptions made by management concerning the potential of agencies to deviate from professional practices and norms in order to stay true to their God-given mission. Moreover, it is presumed that if and when holistic CFB-NGOs/NPOs' mission objectives become fully established and operate independently from 'recognized canons of acceptability' and 'legitimacy frameworks', the potential for normative isomorphism to impact them with its 'professionalized credentials' will be lessened,[46] as Gallet affirms. Although this research has discovered evidence of parachurch agencies adopting similar systems and practices to those of NGOs/NPOs operating in the same field, normative conformity is not seen as the only isomorphic pressure.

6.1.4 Coercive Theory

With 'coercive pressures', NGOs/NPOs seek to resemble each other and to align with public institutions and government directives enacted through laws in response to "the wielding of the political influence of some institutions by an explicit show of power and authority"[47] – says Lin who is equally supported by DiMaggio and Powell – and to conform to social and cultural expectations,

---

43. Bess and Dee, *Understanding College and University Organization*, 143.
44. Interviewee 25, interviewed by author, e-mail interview, May 25 2020.
45. Interviewee 25.
46. Gallet, "Christian Mission," 157.
47. Lin, "Countering Mission Drift," 72.

especially when (and where) "resource dependency" is concerned.[48] DiMaggio and Powell reiterate that this may include formal and informal pressures enforced by other agencies.[49] As an example of this dependency, following on from a seminary's adoption of accreditation standards, a more discreet form of coercion that may occur is when an institution feels constrained to adopt organizational field policies and practices that, although not required, are vital for "attractiveness" and/or "legitimacy." With this perspective in mind, Bess and Dee argue:

> Coercive conformity in higher education often comes about through the accreditation process. Accreditation associations seek to ensure that all higher education institutions meet certain standards of quality. Similarly, governing boards and coordinating boards can enforce conformity across a state's public higher education system by requiring institutions to adhere to academic and admissions policies. Institutions attempt to develop graduate programs, seek research grants, and raise admissions requirements to attain a more prestigious position in the academic hierarchy.[50]

Coercion by powerful organizations, public institutions and the state is a pertinent concept that significantly impacts church-related agencies in their holistic mission endeavors. In addressing this coercive issue, two participants in this empirical study denounce the fact that governments and institutions would set their rules and visions before funding CFB-NGOs/NPOs' programs, thus influencing them to become secular humanitarian agencies,[51] whereas non-Christian donors would quickly and purposefully impose their vision of the humanist world.[52] Some scholars such as Wittberg, Altbach, and Schmitter uphold the view that state and/or government corporatism and societal corporatism clearly suggest a possible coercive role by the government, where powerful NGOs may penetrate, influence and capture the state's legislative authority to exclude private faith-based organizations and

---

48. DiMaggio and Powell, "The Iron Cage," 148.
49. DiMaggio and Powell, 150.
50. Bess and Dee, *Understanding College and University Organization*, 142–143.
51. Interviewee 5.
52. Interviewee 26.

deny them space.[53] Altbach argues that both forms of corporatism represent official systems that are subtly integrated in the state and function as official publicly subsidized and licensed monopolies planned and coordinated for harmony, unity and coherence.[54] Those corporations whose interests are linked to coercive pressures for conformity are motivated to limit alternatives offered by the religion-based sector, either by the conviction that their system is the best or by self-interest. A common target among parachurch agencies' managements, including some hybrid ventures, is, for example, to advance 'up' their competitiveness and legitimacy norms, or change their organizational designation from 'holistic mission NGO/NPO' to the more prestigious 'humanitarian international organization'. They risk conforming by mimicking whatever features can increase their attractiveness, at the expense of drifting in their mission.

6.1.5 Conformism and Mimetic Theory

The expression 'mimetic conformity pressures' refers to the propensity of agencies to mimic or conform to the behaviors and practices of other similar yet more 'successful' NGOs in the field – especially during times of existential insecurity. Gallet lays emphasis on this description, noting that "mimetic pressures are evident during times of uncertainty and involve organizations imitating the practices of other organizations in the field.[55]" To identify the existence of conformism in parachurch agencies, Gallet has examined the following three issues:

1. How mimetic isomorphism results from mimicking the strategies of other similar NGOs in welfare service;
2. How CFB-NGOs/NPOs become indistinguishable from their secular counterparts as they further seek to legitimize themselves;
3. How conformism comes about due to difficulties in breaking through the competitive market forces of the quasi-markets of the public sector and humanitarian organizations.[56]

---

53. Wittberg, *From Piety*, 14; Altbach, *Private Prometheus*, 22; and Schmitter, "The New Corporatism," 102–105.
54. Altbach, *Private Prometheus*, 22–24.
55. Gallet, "Christian Mission," 162; see also Pallant, *Keeping Faith*, 20.
56. Gallet, 3–4 and 162.

Mimetic conformity often results from a process in which less prestigious organizations are unofficially forced to follow the more notable ones or be viewed as of lower quality and efficiency,[57] as Bess and Dee declare. This study shows that some church-related welfare NGOs/NPOs conform with and imitate secular organizations, even 'going the extra mile' by removing their Christian faith-based symbols in order to be identifiable with others in the field! Consequently, as this investigation reveals, some parachurch NGOs/NPOs end up functioning like purely social agencies, fully conforming with well-known humanitarian organizations and agreeing with the restrictions that governments put on them,[58] states interviewee sixteen. Interviewee twenty-five attests that, in fact, governments tend to establish rules that favor non-faith (non-religious) organizations in the field, thereby obliging some Christian holistic agencies to conform if they need recognition from the state.[59] In this sense, interviewee twenty-two acknowledges the fact that, at a particular point, their parachurch NPO had to adapt its statutes in order to orient itself slightly more towards the context of Swiss NGOs in terms of relief and development at the international level.[60] This was in order to meet institutional requirements – like other NGOs in the country – so as to benefit from the government's Directorate for Development and Co-operation funds.

Bretherton pertinently suggests that "the pressure to conform does not come only from external forces, but rather from the perceived need within church-related organizations to mimic what are seen to be the successful models embraced by the leading organizations in the field."[61] In addressing this issue, Wittberg argues that when church-related agencies mimic or change to conform to their secular counterparts facing identical environmental conditions, this creates drifting in terms of their core mission and results in confusion or disagreement within the broader church.[62] It is from this understanding that DiMaggio and Powell assert that the pressure to comply with the norms, rules and practices of the organizational field creates resemblance between one agency and the other, as well as similarity of

---

57. Bess and Dee, *Understanding College and University Organization*, 142.
58. Interviewee 16.
59. Interviewee 25.
60. Interviewee 22, interviewed by author, e-mail interview on April 30, 2020.
61. Bretherton, *Christianity and Contemporary Politics*, 1984.
62. Wittberg, *From Piety*, 276.

services amongst agencies operating within a similar field.[63] Following this train of thought, Wittberg implies that the significance of this for CFB-NGOs/NPOs is that they are likely to begin to comply with rules relating to the organizational field and seek to resemble their secular counterparts.[64] As a result, these parachurch agencies lose their distinctively Christian attributes and holistic mission character.

To sum up these sections on circumstantial factors in relation to this research, I would say that through isomorphic pressures, church-related agencies operating in holistic mission are constrained (officially and/or unofficially) to conform to the norms, rules and agendas set by secular welfare organizations. Parachurch organizations in the field of socio-humanitarianism are coerced into achieving the agenda of secular institutions and governments rather than that of the church. This situation has the propensity to accelerate mission drift, which eventually leads to secularization within Christian faith-based NGOs/NPOs.

6.2 Spectrum Analysis

For the purpose of this study and based on its findings, spectrums or spectra can be used in analyzing the concept of mission drift in a parachurch organization as a situation or circumstance. This is a process that has the potential to vary infinitely across a continuum, as this empirical study shows (see section 4.2.3 and Table 4.4). This spectrum or process has neither paces nor phases and is not limited to a specific set of values (e.g. Christian values). It underlies possible mechanisms that can change smoothly, generating similar disorders – in this case mission drift. In addressing the issue of spectrum analysis, Newton believes that the term 'spectrum' is mainly used in science, especially in optical physics, to study the reflecting rays of rainbow light and color going through a prism by refraction or diffraction.[65] Spectra in parachurch agencies' mission are to be understood as implying uninterrupted sequences that unfold gradually. They do not seem to cause perceptible

---

63. DiMaggio and Powell, "The Iron Cage," 148–149.
64. Wittberg, *Creating a Future*, 34.
65. Newton, "New Theory," 3076.

difficulties, yet they lead to extreme deviations in organizational behavior and ultimately in mission focus.

6.2.1 Spectrum of Bureaucratization

Bureaucratization as a regulatory spectrum in parachurch NGOs/NPOs describes a process involving managing and administering an agency by increasing controls: paying attention to every detail for the sake of filling in administrative paperwork, and opting for an increase in professional management, which involves hierarchical coordination and an adherence to rigid policies and procedures. Most church-related organizations are going through a long, slow, and yet steady drift towards more bureaucratization. This involves more controls; regulations and the apparatus of paperwork being created for them and for the voluntary practitioners who aim to offer holistic service. The system is created to maximize efficiency but has the potential to trap and negate individual and organizational freedom to do mission,[66] as Künkler, Swedberg, and Ritzer write.

Bureaucratization as a regulatory spectrum is essentially a centralized form of administration and operates in a different fashion from an 'ad hoc' approach in which supervision is decentralized. Barnett and Finnemore have defined bureaucratization as encompassing four features:

1. A hierarchy that clearly outlines the spheres of competence, expertise and divisions of workforce with a strict chain of command;
2. A structural continuity where the administrators have a full-time paid-job and an advanced position within the structure;
3. A system of impersonality and rationality which prescribes operating rules rather than arbitrary practices and actions for mission purposes,
4. A concept of "expertise," which chooses practitioners according to professional merit and prefers trained officials who hold access

---

66. Künkler, "The Bureaucratization," 195; Swedberg, *The Max Weber Dictionary*, 18–21; and Ritzer, *Enchanting a Disenchanted World*, 55.

to knowledge rather than, as is the present case, Christians with faith-based patrimonial, kinship and charismatic authority.[67]

Religious sociologists from the wider field of sociology consider faith-based NGOs as bureaucracies.[68] Studies by Harrison; Winter; Takayama; Chapman; Woolnough and Ma; and Ward have looked at the impact of the spectrum of bureaucratization over time on the church and have argued that as church-related agencies become more bureaucratic, the focus of the church's mission will tend to concentrate more on functional aspects.[69] In relation to the effects of this spectrum, interviewee twenty-two attests that their CFB-NGO has revised its administrative policies and professional procedures in order to meet international institutional requirements.[70] Consequently, this has the propensity to generate incompatible mission practices. Policymakers tend to be more and more professional, and decisions are taken grounded on the value of their professional function. As a result, theology, the substance of Christian faith, "takes a back seat to the day-to-day operations dominated by the functional issues of bureaucracy,"[71] as Lin points out.

Chang argues that incompatibility between religion-based principles and bureaucratization often motivates the professional decision-making process because "religion and rationality are antithetical to one another."[72] Using a similar logic, Grint maintains that the spectrum of bureaucratization leads to an increase in legality and rationality, in which reasonable actions (based on rational principles, expert knowledge, calculability and common sense) oppose affective traditional Christian actions (based on religious convictions and motives).[73] It should be noted that bureaucratic structures in religious institutions are both unable and unwilling to effectively and holistically

---

67. Barnett, and Finnemore. *Rules for the World*, 17–18; see also Picot, Reichwald and Wigand, *Information, Organization*, 191.

68. Lin, "Countering Mission Drift," 56.

69. Harrison, *Authority and Power*; Winter, *The Emergent American*; Takayama, "Administrative Structures," 5–37; Chapman *Faith, Power*, 20; Woolnough and Ma, *Holistic Mission*, 134; and Ward, *The Electronic Church*, 83.

70. Interviewee 22, interviewed by author, e-mail interview on April 30, 2020.

71. Lin, 56; see also Chang, "Escaping the Procrustean,127.

72. Chang, 127.

73. Grint, *The Sociology*, 108–109; see also Grint, "Problems, Problems, 1363–1390.

address the deprivation of people, as Elliot, and Woolnough and Ma have put forward.[74]

The establishment of bureaucratization in parachurch agencies may underlie the drift of Christian faith ideals through which their God-given objectives are left behind in favor of the progress of their organizations. To this effect, this case study research shows that rationalization as a spectrum of bureaucratization causes the increase of influence by a variety of investors (see section 4.2.5). This explains why Christian identity is less and less central to the processes of CFB-NGOs/NPOs. For this reason, Lin argues that Christian identity in church-related agencies has been "relegated to a supporting role that is not always prioritized."[75] The imposition of bureaucratization as a "sophisticated system" over Christian faith-based mission principles underlies the administrative mind-set in church-related holistic NGOs/NPOs, and the dominance of expertise in determining the identity of the agency, rather than sensitivity to the holistic needs of people. Mangayi notes with pertinence that "instead of religious and moral ideals guiding our lives, we are governed and controlled by economic and bureaucratic principals, resulting in a sad decline in the fabric and cohesion of social life."[76] This reality gradually becomes a counterforce that makes CFB-NGOs/NPOs navigate against the current.

However, Poloma insists that the fact that the establishment of innovative holistic ministries or parachurch holistic mission (see sections 5.3, 5.4, and 5.5) can challenge – and break with – the structures of the bureaucratic apparatus[77] and of economic rationalism. Braaten, echoing this view, emphasizes that "those unconstrained by bureaucratic roles and free from the limitations of official leadership have a distinctive call to the service of unity."[78] In terms of such a theme, Dowsett, Phiri, Birdsall, Terfassa, Yung and Jørgensen, indicate that prevailing impersonal and hierarchical systems of bureaucratization have difficulty in flourishing in person-centered traditional Christian cultures where kinship and faith-based networks play a key role in getting the mission done.[79] They further observe – as do Woolnough and Ma – that unfortunately

---

74. Elliot, *An Introduction*, 204; and Woolnough and Ma, 162–163.
75. Lin, "Countering Mission Drift," 216.
76. Mangayi, "Mission in an African city," 148.
77. Poloma, *The Assemblies of God*, 129; see also Backues, "Interfaith Development," 69.
78. Braaten, *In One Body*, 51.
79. Dowsett et al., *Evangelism and Diakonia*, 171.

this is often subject to restrictions enforced by recalcitrant bureaucracies, dominant oligarchs, popular opinion and other "militant defenders of the status quo, as well as available resources, a fractious civil society or competing political and other interests."[80] The findings of this study, gleaned from field research and according to interviewee thirty-one and interviewee thirty-two, showed a gradual move through a professional bureaucratic spectrum in several parachurch agencies,[81] something that Lin also highlights in her study.[82] It can be concluded that, in time, the bureaucratic mind-set will impact one Christian organization after another in terms of its Christian identity and cause a 'drift' away from its vision, values and holistic mission objectives.

6.2.2 Spectrum of Professionalization

The spectrum of professionalization moves through a slow process that brings professional demarcation into the agency, along with an emphasis on high social status and conformity to knowledge-authorities. This in turn creates a hierarchical social system undermining the faith-based system. Thus, professionalization establishes within the parachurch agency a narrow elite who retain power, prestige, and privileges, and who are somehow cut off from the common staff because of their elevated station in the organization, as Weeden writes.[83] As a consequence of the operation of this spectrum, managers – in contrast to staff – are seen as professionals, and decisions are taken in line with their professional function and values. Following this train of thought, interviewee sixteen declares that their church-related agency was paid and entrusted by the state to care for immigrants coming into the country.[84] Furthermore, this interview respondent added that regrettably, being accountable to the state meant that the NGO was required to hire professionals regardless of their spiritual background and, as a result, some of them (mainly atheists and Muslims) openly hindered the spiritual activities[85] and opposed the sharing of the gospel.

---

80. Dowsett et al., 173; and Woolnough and Ma, *Holistic Mission*, 178–179.
81. Interviewee 31; and Interviewee 32.
82. Lin, "Countering Mission Drift," 310.
83. Weeden, "Why Do Some Occupations," 55.
84. Interviewee 16.
85. Interviewee 16.

The spectrum of professionalization is a phenomenon in CFB-NGOs/NPOs to be interpreted in terms of the philosophical concept "telos." In this sense, Jochemsen defines that telos is the root of the modern Greek word "teleology" and is described as a "final causality", the end result or a "goal-directed process" that denotes the study of purposiveness – "a certain finality or core value as to why the practice exists."[86] From a teleological perspective, and in terms of its related ethical system (also called consequentialism or consequentialist ethics), the professional spectrum can be deemed wrong according to its own terms of reference because of its propensity to cause drifting in Christian mission and/or generate opposition to holistic mission practices, as the findings of this study show (see section 4.2.5 and particularly Table 4.4), thus contradicting its "end purpose." Furthermore, Jochemsen argues that professional spectra set 'the standards of excellence' which are meant to be

> The rules of play as understood by the practice. They are the "know how" required to realize the "telos" of the practice. These rules are embodied in professional conduct consisting in the ability to act according to a rule and to assess the correctness of this application even without making the rule explicit.[87]

In this respect, Semple maintains the view that the professionalization of church-related organizations arises not so much from the rising educational standards of mission workers as from the intertwining of religion-based and secular-oriented mission practices.[88] The end result is a conflict involving social status and vision, with radical change as a possible consequence.

From this consequential perspective, interviewee thirty-one echoes this view, noting that 'high professional' managers who have proven their performance in the business sector will definitely engage workforce for the NGO with no consideration of their spiritual background,[89] thus leading the agency down the road of dechristianization and secularization. In this respect, interviewee thirty-two affirms that their board of directors and management have decided to hire non-religionists for strategic positions in the name of

---

86. Jochemsen, "Normative Practices," 103.
87. Jochemsen, 104.
88. Semple, *Missionary Women*, 191.
89. Interviewee 31.

'professionalism.'[90] As a result, this Christian holistic agency has become more and more a professional, humanitarian, international NGO – with little or no Christian values. In addressing these issues, Larsen and Ledger-Lomas suggest that the downside of professionalization is that it threatens to subordinate the agencies to its own large-scale mission objectives,[91] thus also threatening the voluntary principles that have long been at the center of Christian mission – a mission that involves both social and spiritual ministries. In line with this view, Hiroshi and Shin note that Christianity must reject the 'institutionalization' of Christian faith and work that leads to the professionalization of Christian holistic mission.[92] Moreover, Torry argues that the spectrum of professionalization strives to institutionalize implicit and explicit professional norms, procedures, and practices in order to make Christian mission administratively more efficient.[93] Parsons echoes this view:

> The professionalization of all Christian ministries – be they Anglican, Roman Catholic, Methodist or Congregationalist – took place within a *conservative* context. The ministers concerned did not wish to deny their deep-felt religious beliefs, to risk losing the congregations they served or the souls they had brought to Christ in the interests of 'professionalization' and improved conditions for themselves. Belief that there must be a ministry was a matter of faith in a way that belief that there must be secular teachers or doctors or lawyers was not. To carry this "professionalization" too far would negate the true "vocation" of the minister.[94]

The expansion of professionalization, as Cowan argues with appositeness, has resulted in "the development of a systematic cognitive praxis" occurring in church-sponsored organizations and coalitioning NGOs such as Christian agencies and secular institutions.[95] However, according to the results of this case study research, several parachurch agencies do negotiate a complex

---

90. Interviewee 32.
91. Larsen and Ledger-Lomas, *The Oxford History*, 464.
92. Hiroshi and Shin, *Living for Jesus*, 93.
93. Torry, *Managing Religion*, 206.
94. Parsons, *Religion in Victorian Britain*, 210.
95. Cowan, *Bearing False Witness*, 95.

collaboration with well-endowed, highly-developed and deeply professionalized institutions, thus challenging their 'sacred-mission' standing. Some scholars like Barnett and Stein, and Lin argue that it is actually not difficult for the professional spectrum to become entrenched in bureaucratization and in the centrality of effective fundraising.[96] On the other hand, it should be noted that holism is a way of thinking and acting in Christian mission. In this respect, Woolnough and Ma have argued that church-related organizations must recover from their 'prideful professionalism'[97] – inventing ways to become godly, and figuring out how to become an integral part of the Christian community that supports, engages, and empowers their partners in local churches.

The implication is that CFB-NGOs/NPOs and the church must be able to collaboratively discover and respect their respective roles in God's mission of holistic transformation. Christianity needs holistic practitioners who have been professionally educated and trained to overcome these modern worldviews, who use "the Bible and theology, along with their understanding of spirituality, in order to infuse and shape their transformational development theory and practice (see sections 4.2.3, 4.3 and Table 4.2). They must be able to think theologically about their work and especially their actions: acting theologically is an important skill,"[98] as Woolnough says. Moreover, Woolnough argues that parachurch agencies are the arm of the church in terms of delivering holistic mission,[99] in the light of the earthly ministry of our lord and savior Jesus Christ.

Christian faith-based NGOs/NPOs need to professionalize their holistic mission without secularizing it,[100] as Hoggarth, MacDonald, Mitchell and Jørgensen write. To Woolnough and Ma, Christian holistic mission needs to employ professionals in sustainable agriculture, microfinance, education, community psychology, water and sanitation but must also recognize that such trained professionals operate out of the secular and modern worldview where God is no longer needed by soil scientists and hydrologists.[101] In sum-

---

96. Barnett and Stein, *Sacred Aid*, 7; and Lin, "Countering Mission Drift," 85.
97. Woolnough and Ma, *Holistic Mission*, 122.
98. Woolnough, "Christian NGOs," 200.
99. Woolnough, 200.
100. Hoggarth et al., *Bible in Mission*, 234.
101. Woolnough and Ma, *Holistic Mission*, 125.

mation, the spectrum of professionalization and its managerial model can be an immense social gift for parachurch agencies, because of its unprecedented ability to enlarge the boundaries of God's kingdom, but this necessitates detachment from its slow-moving and gradual controlling model that 'drifts' these organizations from their God-given mission. Now, I will look at the spectral impact of dechristianization on Christian agencies.

6.2.3 Spectrum of Dechristianization

The contemporary faith-crisis is favorable to mission drift, as the steady dechristianization of Western society increases the global secularization of Christian faith-based mission agencies. Speaking about dechristianization, one always thinks it is inevitably a European issue. When one speaks globally, Christianity appears to be the fastest-growing religion, while in the developed countries, the social significance of Christian faith seems to have decreased. However, Christie and Gauvreau note that the social significance of Christianity in the United States appears to have increased.[102] To grasp the significance of dechristianization and the mission drift that has taken place in Christianity since the Second World War, one should look across Christian faith to analyze the whole religious spectrum. It becomes more and more obvious that one should assess major socio-cultural changes in relation to religion and to Christianity in particular. To this effect, one participant in this empirical research aptly states that the economic-cultural context, coupled with the high bureaucratization and professionalization of institutions, the pursuit of higher levels of performance, and the obsession with growth for its own sake[103] – and without any spiritual considerations – has triggered the total dechristianization and secularization of their parachurch organization.

Following this train of thought, Bailey points to the Orthodox Church's struggle against the reality of dechristianization in Russian society and its negative impact on Christian mission.[104] In a further development of this view, van Luijk describes how, due to cultural and economic change in the West (the Western Revolution), dechristianization came to refer not only to the desertion of the Christian faith by a "growing number of individual Europeans

---

102. Christie and Gauvreau, *The Sixties and Beyond*, 367.
103. Interviewee 31.
104. Bailey, *Ernest Renan's Life*, 156 and 216.

and Americans, but also, and primarily, to the demolition of the traditional presence of the church in the public sphere."[105] Moreover, van Luijk argues that "dechristianization" also causes the abandonment of Christian faith, and that the mission of Christian institutions suffers as a result.[106] Scholars – Roy; Marthaler, Carson and Cerrito; and Saayman and Kritzinger – argue that dechristianization in Europe is associated with deep sociological trends, such as urbanization, the disappearance of the "peasantry",[107] and industrial growth correlated with the creation of proletarian areas, and the abandonment of religiosity by the sophisticated and middle working classes.[108] The speed at which this happens varies: in France it was sudden, but in Ireland the drop in commitment to faith was preceded by a long decline.

The modernization of culture and the westernization of the gospel followed by changes in the global religious landscape, have increased the lack of communication of religious identity in some Christian faith-based agencies. In this respect, the result of this study shows that faith in general, and Christianity in particular, is no longer a pillar in the life of the majority of the Western populations, who instead believe in "humanism" and "humanity" – beliefs associated with individual freedom, but which exclude faith in God,[109] as interviewee twenty-five states. This change of religious landscape can create gaps between social groups: Christians versus anti-Christians, believers versus unbelievers, and rich versus poor – a field that reveals the risks involved in the work of parachurch agencies. Christie and Gauvreau argue that "globalization, with regard to religion, often refers to the worldwide expansion of religions. That is, however, only part of it. Globalization also includes the increasingly rapid exchange of information, the appropriation and hybridization of globalized commodities, and the creation of interacting networks across the globe, which seem today to be disconnected territorially from any particular country or place of origin."[110] The French historian Michel Vovelle,

---

105. van Luijk, *Children of Lucifer*, 247.

106. van Luijk, 247.

107. The term peasantry denotes the status of peasants collectively, relating to the uneducated low social rank farmers who have little financial means. It refers to the way of life of farm laborers, as in Europe, America, and Asia.

108. Roy, *Is Europe Christian*, 31–33; Marthaler, Carson and Cerrito, *New Catholic Encyclopaedia*, 857; and Saayman and Kritzinger, *Mission in Bold Humility*, 64–65.

109. Interviewee 25.

110. Christie and Gauvreau, *The Sixties and Beyond*, 367.

who specialized in the French Revolution, describes dechristianization as a movement of detachment from the Christian faith that has consequences for Christian religious mission practice.[111] It is a phenomenon characterized by a retreat from sacred mission, holistic mission involvement, Christian life and practice, the social obligations of Christians and normative Christian values.

In relation to the effects of this spectrum, one respondent to the research questionnaire – interviewee eighteen – controversially states (based on his mission convictions) that "actions can touch people more than words" and that, with the effect of modernization and globalization, a missionary agency is no longer a parachurch humanitarian NGO because the latter functions on the basis of Christian values with the pursuit of social and humanitarian objectives only, whereas the first proclaims the gospel.[112] As a result, it affects the social significance of parachurch mission. According to Soboul, dechristianization can also be the result of a religious movement, a political ideology or a government that fights against Christianity and its faith-based mission practice (Communist Russia, China, extremist Islamic nations, France, Japan, Mexico, etc.),[113] thus oppressing church-related agencies. This kind of oppression or persecution can push holistic mission NGOs/NPOs into experiencing mission drift. On the other hand, dechristianization sometimes results from sociological mutations such as modernization.

In short, Roy asserts that "there has been a 'ratchet effect': dechristianization never takes a step backward."[114] The rapid dechristianization of British society for instance, puts the parachurch's mission (and theological schools in particular) in a different societal space – in a culture that has shifted from one of spiritual commitment to one centered on material consumption, as Fergusson and Elliot; and Davie affirm.[115] Christian parachurch missionary agencies still endure in spite of dechristianization, but this does not guarantee their continuation in the future when their Bible-based mission may be relentlessly affected by modernization and globalized secularization. At this

---

111. Vovelle, *Religion et Révolution*, 81.
112. Interviewee 18.
113. Soboul, *Dictionnaire Historique*, 327.
114. Roy, *Is Europe Christian*, 35.
115. Fergusson and Elliot, *The History*, 8; and Davie, *Religion in Britain*, 133.

juncture, I turn my attention to the question of whether the phenomenon of mission drift is a symmetric concept, a binary theory, or a spectrum.

6.3 Mission Drift: A Symmetric Idea, a Binary Theory and/or a Snowballing Spectrum?

The results of the research at hand suggest similarities between what I have studied regarding the theory of isomorphic pressures and the spectral changes. The focus on administrative efficiency (efficiency cult) as well as the rational expectations of the populace have certainly led to the establishment of spectra as well as fostering isomorphic pressures with their drive towards conformity. First and foremost, I want to define mission drift as a process of "goal displacement" that extends beyond the spiritual aspect of the parachurch agencies' missions. It is, therefore, a symmetric concept in the first place, which is one of this research's empirical findings. In terms of this question, interviewee five puts forward their agency's "holistic child development concept" that is grounded in the all-inclusive nature of the earthly ministry of Jesus as depicted in Matthew 9:35–38 and Luke 4:18–19 where genuine compassion is being demonstrated, and biblical holism revealed.[116] I welcome the way in which interviewee fourteen articulates what a "symmetric concept" might look like: "Our agency believes that Jesus's message and Jesus's deeds cannot be separated from one another."[117] Moreover, he pinpoints that Jesus shows in Matthew 9:35–39 and Luke 4:18–19 that the two are intrinsically interdependent.[118] In a similar development of this view, interviewee sixteen suggests that Mathew 9:35–39 and Luke 4:18–19 are very important texts for church-related organizations, because these two Bible statements speak about a holistic approach (body, soul and spirit) to Christian faith-based mission.[119] Based on these arguments, I therefore support the view that mission drift in a parachurch mission context is to be viewed as a concept that fits into the field of Christian holistic organizational theory – a symmetric concept – and

---

116. Interviewee 5.
117. Interviewee 14.
118. Interviewee 14.
119. Interviewee 16.

more particularly with arguments for the establishment of biblical holism, which presume that both aspects of the holistic nature are vital to the agency.

To continue in this vein, I refer to the position defended by Battilana and Lee on the hybridity of social venture projects, which argues that both commercial and social aspects are essential to hybrid organizations, and therefore neither can be treated peripherally, separated from the other or dismissed without a significant change to the entire model.[120] Furthermore, they indicate that this leads to the conclusion that their "sustainability as hybrids depends both on the advancement of their social mission and on their commercial performance."[121] Sharing this understanding, one respondent – interviewee sixteen – states with appropriateness that a parachurch NPO's practitioner who works as a physician caring only for the medical needs of the poor is not being holistic in his/her approach to Christian mission since there is no spiritual component – unless he/she collaborates with others who "care for the spiritual needs of the beneficiaries."[122] In concurring with this approach, I would like to emphasize that the mission of parachurch holistic agencies is not only about its socio-humanitarian impact but also the spiritual aspect, which leads me to define mission drift as coming about through the inability of a holistic church-related NGO/NPO to achieve its spiritual or its socio-humanitarian goals. This can be further defined as the inability of a parachurch agency to keep to its original holistic mission objectives.

Parachurch agencies are not charities that fortuitously include a spiritual aspect to their activities; they are purposeful holistic mission organizations "created and designed to address a societal problem,"[123] to borrow from Yunus. The implications of these two aspects for holistic parachurch agencies was decidedly accentuated in several of my empirical interviews, as well as appearing in previous studies and literature. In my view, the two aspects mentioned above must be seen as interdependent in order to yield a lasting impact. Finally, from the evidence of my analysis, I support the understanding that mission drift is not to be viewed as a "binary concept"[124] but as a "snowballing

---

120. Battilana and Lee, "Advancing Research," 408.
121. Battilana and Lee, 408; see also von der Heydte, *Challenges Resulting*, 22.
122. Interviewee 16.
123. Yunus, *Building Social Business*, 13–16.
124. A binary concept would constitute an analysis of 'socio-humanitarian drifting' versus 'spiritual-evangelistic drifting' – in the phenomenon of mission drift occurring in holistic

spectrum" or as a "cumulative process,"[125] lining up with previous studies by Jeter, Roche, and Cornforth. Mission drift is inherent in holistic parachurch agencies, but equally, it is predictable as a temporary or definitive occurrence, a situation that is to be explained more in terms of a spectrum than by binary theory. This evaluative understanding supports Jeter's description of mission drift as a progressive "rerouting of time, energy, and money away from an organization's values, benefits, and beneficiaries."[126] Moreover, in the context of CFB-NGOs/NPOs, this often means that socio-humanitarian activities are given greater emphasis as opposed to the agency's spiritual mission, leading to the 'drifting away' of focus, God-given vision and Christian faith-based identity. Though this current study reveals much about the reality of 'spiritual drifting' in church-related organizations, its findings also challenge the asymmetric view of mission drift that only considers the loss of the spiritual-evangelistic aspect of mission.

This empirical study research also reveals that a perfect balance between the spiritual and socio-humanitarian does not exist[127] (see section 4.2.2), according to interviewee eighteen's arguments. However, it does hold out the possibility of retaining holistic mission objectives and the God-given vision for an organization's mission. Each end of the holistic mission is a snowballing spectrum that obviously represents one type of unanswerable and unacceptable mission drift: the agency conceding or sacrificing its spiritual-evangelistic aspect or its socio-humanitarian sustainability. Both the outcome of my interviews and the evidence of the literature shows that mission drift is better seen as a spectrum rather than a binary phenomenon, and that it is not always definitely unavoidable or unresolvable. The dominant idea I wish to convey here is that the phenomenon of mission drift or 'goal displacement' is a 'snowballing spectrum' of various situations, as well as a cumulative process driven by the decisions and practices of different executives. This leads to the conclusions of this empirical research, which I have presented in the following chapter.

---

parachurch agencies – which totally excludes the two possibilities of drifting at the same time. It is a binary opposition of the two ends of a spectrum.

125. Jeter, "Exploring Mission Drift," 35; Roche, "Hybrid Nature of Social Enterprises," 44; and Cornforth, "Understanding and Combating Mission Drift," 3–20.

126. Jeter, 12.

127. Interviewee 18.

CHAPTER 7

Conclusion

This thesis focused on a multiple case study research, involved seven parachurch agencies and sought to understand the concept of mission drift. The study has addressed the main research question, termed the 'Empirical Unknown' (EU): *In what ways do parachurch agencies face the crisis of mission drift in their mission activities?* In this empirical multiple case study, I methodically investigated the real-life situations and field-services of the seven CFB-NGOs/NPOs involved in the study. After having demonstrated in the previous chapter how the major theories and spectra contribute to the understanding of the phenomenon of mission drift in a holistic organizational context, I went on to draw general conclusions applicable to this study. To do so, I first set out some viable and doable implications (theological, missiological and socio-humanitarian) in order to highlight the key findings of this present study. Secondly, I proposed some recommendations towards minimizing the occurrence of mission drift. Lastly, I closed this analysis dealing with the problem of mission drift and the holistic mission aspects of Christian NGOs/NPOs with a comprehensive summary of the research findings.

7.1 Reflecting on Research Methods

For this qualitative empirical research project, I used a multiple case design (also called collective case study) to conduct this investigation on the topic: *Dealing with Mission Drift in Parachurch Agencies: An Analysis of Holistic Mission of Christian NGOs/NPOs*. Three questions in relation to these research methods arose during the research and need some attention:

7.1.1 What have I Learned?

The main lesson learned is how multiple case study research involving several sample cases works: that is, by offering a multi-sided approach and involving various instrumental bounded situations with the participation of a range of cases involving a whole group of people. As a consequence of viewing the process as one of exploratory analysis, I was able to generate new ideas, collect in-depth data and to expand my understanding of the phenomenon of mission drift in parachurch agencies; one that can be tested by other researchers using other techniques. This approach helped shed light on people's thinking and behavior regarding the phenomenon of mission drift – enabling the description of individual situations and helping me to identify the key issues of each case within each sample and then to cross-analyze the cases in order to better understand the phenomenon. For the reasons given above, I see this research approach as giving positive results in terms of new ideas and understanding.

7.1.2 Challenges of Multiple Case Study?

This research study needed to involve several parachurch agencies and the first challenge was finding Christian NGOs and NPOs that had originally committed to a holistic kind of faith-based mission and that would consent to take part in the study. The second challenge, after having found a considerable number of agencies, was to mobilize a significant number of respondents for each sample of the study. Many people were willing to be interviewed but then declined when they saw the questionnaire. The third major challenge was to get the participants to respond to the questions and send back the data. This necessitated several back-and-forward e-mails and phone calls and was a rather negative aspect of the process.

7.1.3 Benefits of Multiple Case Study?

To the question of whether I would use the same research design for further study, my answer is definitely yes. Even though it involved challenges, the multiple case study design allowed me to conduct this empirical study research fully and successfully. My experience with this research has been that collective case study is a labour-intensive technique that takes longer to analyze data – but leads to more open-ended insights, deeper understanding, and more novel ideas. Multiple case design strives towards yielding interrelated

7.2 Implications

In this thesis, a multiple case design has been used to answer a research question located in the real-life situations and field-services of parachurch agencies. Several implications relating to this study have been considered. In addressing the issue of mission drift in parachurch agencies, these implications must be considered as involving fundamental vectors necessary to carry on holisticalization in Christian faith-based mission.

7.2.1 Biblical-Soteriological Implications

The seven agencies I investigated stand as a good example of how parachurch mission and Christian faith-based NGOs/NPOs contribute greatly to the biblical-soteriological view of Christian holistic mission. Globally, these groups have grasped a biblical understanding of Christian mission that values the coming of God's kingdom in the after-death future. Setran upholds the view that several of these faith-based missions have involved biblically based spiritual-evangelistic activities, which communicate the good news of the kingdom for the sake of their personal salvation,[1] made possible in Jesus Christ.

Mission drift occurs when a church-related agency, whose mission originally was holistically based, comes to reject even the term 'salvation' or any spiritual activity and chooses to conform to the secularization of the present-day world situation. In an illustrative development of this construal, interviewee thirty-two states that the effects of secularization within their parachurch NGO is the key factor that has brought the organization down the road of exclusively spotlighting socio-humanitarian activities – after having moved from being a small Christian NPO to becoming an international humanitarian agency.[2] With regard to an organization that 'drifts' away from the nature of Christ's holistic earthly mission (biblical holism), as exemplified in Matthew 9:35–39 and Luke 4:18–19 and diligently interpreted

---

1. Setran, "Student Religious," 6.
2. Interviewee 32.

in this research study (see sections 2.4.2, 2.4.3, 5.6 and 5.8), Edwards, citing Sommerville, notes that in terms of changes in the organization "an activity might be taking on a new function, which would be a sign of the secularization of activities."[3] Observing things from this standpoint, one can note that secularization is a very slow and exterminating process.

This changing ("drifting") view of the nature of the mission and of the kingdom of God will greatly shift the trajectory of CFB-NGOs/NPOs. This consideration contains serious biblical and soteriological implications for the objectives and activities of those agencies. Because of this, each church-related agency should be grounded on, and committed to, a biblical-doctrinal basis as its reference point in order to remain true to its mission (see sections 2.3.2, 2.3.3, 4.2.2, 5.4, 5.6.1, 5.6.2 and 5.6.3). However, while that holistic yet biblical-doctrinal basis is definitely Christ-centered – functioning as a standing point – it draws no missiological boundaries.

7.2.2 Missiological Implications

The most basic way for a parachurch agency to communicate its Christian holistic mission identity lies in the implications of the very simple words of its organizational vision statement and/or mission statement. All the parachurch agencies investigated have a written "vision statement" or "mission statement" on their website or in their literature (see section 4.1 and Table 4.1). These two statements concerning holistic mission must speak about the organization's holistic approach that seeks to cover the needs of the body, the soul, and the spirit of the people the parachurch agency serves. These statements are to be seen as motivating statements that serve as an animating force that also creates clarity and consistency in the holistic mission of the CFB-NGO/NPO. Acknowledging this, Edwards argues with aptness that "if the mission statement does not truly animate or inspire the work of the organization, then the organization might encounter a problem. Whether or not the mission statement has changed over time will also indicate a sign of mission drift."[4] Reverberating this view, Ronsen suggests that the mission of holistic parachurch agencies must be a mission that is Christ-centered both

---

3. Edwards, "Faithfull Innovation," 26; and Sommerville, "Secular Society," 250.
4. Edwards, "Faithfull Innovation," 23–24.

in statement and action,[5] making the person of Jesus Christ the ultimate end for the holistic mission of each particular Christian faith-based NGO/NPO amidst the people they serve.

Contextualization of mission requires the support of top management to enable activities that lead to spiritual transformation,[6] which Ronsen argues, is the key feature of holistic mission (see section 4.2.6). It is from this perspective that interviewee twenty-four suggests that management should promote meaningful 'contextualized holistic mission' (see sections 5.4 and 5.5, and Table 5.1) and holistic transformational development that covers the educational, health care and spiritual-evangelistic concerns of Christian mission.[7] In addressing these concerns, interviewee thirty-two observes that parachurch agencies connect the two aspects of Christian holistic NGOs/NPOs' mission while offering a contextualized contribution for the improvement of people's social, physical, and spiritual condition.[8] If church-related agencies are able to adjust, adapt and contextualize their activities to people's needs, while remaining true to the mission of God's kingdom, then they would most likely avoid mission drift. Conversely, Jones observes that if the change in mission service pulls the focus away from Christ, then the agencies may well be shifting towards mission drift and secularization.[9] It is from this perspective that Chesterton claims that "progress should mean (just now) that we are always changing the world to suit the vision."[10] Following Chesterton's argument, it might be concluded that Christian parachurch agencies must maintain the integrity of Christian holistic mission, and that progress in mission activities does not mean always changing the vision in order to suit the world.

'Drifting' is certainly a constant threat to any parachurch organization that is trying to remain 'mission true' and 'holistically relevant' in a quickly changing world. Even the ways of 'classic ministry' by the church, followed by church-related 'mission work,' are changing and adapting to societal changes. The wide acceptance of changing values in society as well as in the church leaves its mark also on the way holistic parachurch agencies operate today.

---

5. Ronsen, *Mission Drift?* 88.
6. Ronsen, 88–89.
7. Interviewee 24.
8. Interviewee 32.
9. Jones, *Christian Social Innovation*, 19.
10. Chesterton, *Orthodoxy*, 95.

CFB-NGOs/NPOs should aim clearly to live and work in a transformational and yet holistic way.

7.2.3 Socio-Humanitarian Implications

While many aspects of parachurch agencies point to the necessity of stressing their spiritual identity, other factors relating to them should indicate their socio-humanitarian identity. The latter identity refers to their focus on social justice. Socio-humanitarian issues are frequently at the heart of church-related NGOs/NPOs, and because of this, Edwards claims, holistic mission agencies risk "moving toward a more 'social justice' focus in an accommodation with a left-leaning culture."[11] Though the original objective of a Christian faith-based organization is to hold firmly to the social significance of its holistic mission, 'social justice' issues may be taking over this commitment in some parachurch agencies.

Since mission drift can arise in parachurch agencies through slow and ongoing changes, a top-management focus on socio-humanitarian issues, without balancing that emphasis with the offer Christ makes for salvation and spiritual relief (cf. Matt 9:35–38 and Luke 4:18–19), might be signs that the NGO/NPO is vulnerable to mission drift,[12] as Edwards points out. In relation to the effects of these implications, interviewee ten suggests the need for a strategic adaptation of programs, aids, understanding the culture and language by using biblical terms to reach out to people in their local cultural settings.[13] This suggestion is holistically viable and would harmonize elements of the plan for mission. It concludes these ideas on the socio-humanitarian implications of Christian faith-based NGOs/NPOs. Parachurch agencies that are engaged in social welfare (i.e. health, education, human rights, natural disaster rescue, and relief advocacy) have the propensity to grow into agents of humanitarian activism who advocate good works alone – to the detriment of their spiritual-evangelistic involvement. Now, in the second part of my concluding thoughts, I have turned my attention to some central recommendations.

---

11. Edwards, "Faithfull Innovation," 95.
12. Edwards, 95.
13. Interviewee 10.

7.3 Recommendations

This research thesis has been a multiple case empirical study which, as indicated above, I now conclude with some recommendations. Even though these recommendations have arisen from an exhaustive process developed systematically throughout the thesis, its results have not been tested. It remains a contribution to knowledge on the understanding of the phenomenon of mission drift in parachurch agencies with a holistic-purposeful mission. This thesis recommends practical steps towards minimizing the risk of drifting and for setting parachurch organizational goals. The recommendations outlined here are to be implemented through looking at the concept of "beingness and doingness," and they point towards further research opportunities for evaluation, validity, and refining.

7.3.1 Minimizing the Risk of Drifting

Organizational leadership and partnerships with the church are vital to the question of where Christian faith-based agencies see themselves positioned in terms of mission, particularly holistic parachurch NGOs/NPOs like the seven I investigated. Such leadership would be able to choose to align themselves with the agency's holistic mission and work, which in turn would be aligned with the earthly holistic mission model of Jesus. Christian faith and God-given mission must be the central concern of, and the reason for, the existence and work of parachurch agencies. Leaders of church-related organizations must integrate and preserve Christian identity in all aspects of their NGO/NPO's existence and work. This implies the passing on of biblical and spiritual distinctiveness from one generation of leadership (team and staff) to the next. Comparing the objectives of parachurch agencies with the mission model of Jesus, as exemplified in Matthew 9:35–38 and Luke 4:18–19, says a great deal about all Christian faith-based agencies established within the perspective of biblical holism, about their belief systems and their attitude to mission work.

In addressing these relations between the leadership of parachurch organizations and their partnerships with the church, Hadden and Shupe argue that in a similar way the supports offered by a church partnership have the faculty to influence the leadership and works of the church-related agency and "therefore provide an objective look into the stances and work of the organization."[14]

---

14. Hadden and Shupe, *Secularization and Fundamentalism*, 25.

When leadership is seen as part of a working partnership with the church, this allows holistic mission objectives and Christian faith-based activities to be implemented within the vision of the agency, and this gradually, over time, helps to avert drifting. To avoid mission drift, parachurch organizations must retain their core mission, Christian faith-based values, organizational identity-culture, and God-given vision in pursuit of high-quality holistic ministration. They must offer authenticity in the communication of their Christian spiritual beliefs and be wholly devoted to a Bible-based holistic mission that can benefit the poor holistically.

7.3.2 Setting Organizational Goals: "Beingness in Doingness"

The minimizing of mission drift also comes through the setting of organizational goals. What is needed is a deliberate clarification of the identity of holistic parachurch agencies through the principle of "doingness through beingness," which highlights the peculiarity of Christian mission work in achieving a holistic transformational and developmental practice. The Christian religious concept of 'beingness in doingness' provides a clearer "understanding of the structure as well as the Christian direction that the organization should move towards,"[15] as Lin writes. Precautions must be taken to internalize this Christian value of "beingness" first – that is, being "Christ-centered" followed by "doingness"; in other words, doing "Bible-based mission" – in order to concretize the uniqueness of Christian mission within the parachurch agency and differentiate it from secular humanitarian NGOs/NPOs. The concept of "beingness" comes from the fact that a parachurch agency is, first a Christian faith-based organization. This reality should be applied in the agency's doing of mission – its "doingness" of mission – which is the induction as well as the implementation of the organization's Christian DNA into its practice of mission. The agency's "doingness" must not differ from what its real "beingness" is. Therefore, what the agency does – the "doingness" – constitutes Christian faith-based mission work in a secular world.

As a word to Christian faith-based holistic agencies, I would say: "Expect mission drift to cross your path". It is sadly a reality in our current world, which is undergoing so much radical change in terms of access to news

---

15. Lin, "Countering Mission Drift," 306.

and fake news and, in terms of communication, the limitless availability of information and therefore also of philosophical influences of a magnitude never known before. At a time and season when there exists a postmodern worldview that does not really accept religious absolutes, or the simple truth of salvation in Christ, "drift" is a force to be reckoned with. The best response? To accept mission drift as a constant challenge to the Christian belief system and to holistic mission practice, and to learn to what extent we can remain humble practitioners grounded in Christ. These are also times in which it is important to listen to the "still small voice" of the Holy Spirit, staying connected with Jesus Christ and expecting God himself to allow us to see the truth, and being able to walk radically in that truth through the challenge of mission drift.

7.3.3 Further Research

Having listed key implications of this empirical study research, and suggested some recommendations, and before summarizing the thesis of this research, I realize that there are some unresolved issues that can be considered as good future research ideas and opportunities. I have therefore identified four of these areas of fertile ground that hold out the prospect of future research. They are briefly outlined here:

1. A comparative analysis between "drifting" in other faith-based organizations and Christian faith-based holistic agencies;
2. In-depth research seeking an understanding of mission drift among African churches in Europe and its influence on transnational "reverse mission;"
3. Field investigations as to how the individual on-site beneficiaries of parachurch agencies are being shaped holistically by Christian faith-based missionary organizations in a particular society;
4. Academization, accreditation, institutionalization and professionalization have the potential to lead to mission drift in theological education,[16] as appropriately suggested by Ott. This study could be done through looking diligently at the development of theological institutions and educational issues relating to theological education and the pertinence of Christian mission.

---

16. Ott, e-mail message.

7.4 Research Summary

The main findings of this research (see Figures 4.1 and 4.2) were the identification of "internal secularization" as a key factor causing mission drift in some CFB-NGOs/NPOs with, however, a high proportion (63 percent) of the agencies studied keeping their holistic mission identity and staying "mission true" (see Figure 4.2). These findings are discussed in the context of a wider body of literature from various streams. To understand the phenomenon of mission drift, the discussion involved paradigm shifts, contextualization, out-boundary fundraising, disproportionate growth ambition, hiring of professional managers and staff, loss of Christian identity and internal secularization, as well as theory and spectrum analysis (see Figures 5.1 and 5.2).

The central idea presented here is that mission drift is a 'snowballing spectrum' of various situations – a cumulative process involving different executive decisions and practices that have the combined influence of upsetting the equilibrium of the holistic aspect of mission. The underlying assumption that I propounded in this thesis was that even the most balanced managerial decisions are either slightly more spiritually or more socially-oriented and that it is the sum of those choices that – over time – can generate a likely situation for mission drift in a parachurch agency, which is either temporary or which definitely cannot be resolved. Organizational theorists and sociologists such as Philip Selznick long ago warned of hybrid types of agencies with dual goals, of the acute risk of the "cult of efficiency", of "organizational survival", and of deserting one essential aspect of the organization's mission objectives.[17] They urged parachurch organizations to transcend those risks by creating leadership structures capable of achieving their mission.

More administrative attention in these agencies has often been focused on dealing with survival, growth, and efficiency. Focusing on the organization's survival, efficiency, and conforming with the expectations of powerful leading institutions has, indeed, led church-related agencies into isomorphism as well as bureaucratization. This analysis also made it clear that "out-boundary" growth ambitions, fundraising, and involving groups and individuals ranging from governmental institutions to private investors and donors has disturbed the overall significance of Christian faith-based values within the agencies. It has also been observed that the Christian impact on the overall holistic

---

17. Selznick, *Leadership in Administration*, 134–136.

mission of the CFB-NGOs/NPOs has diminished over time due to societal challenges. Almost all the seven parachurch agencies interviewed have shared that there are tensions in the pursuit of dual goals, which often leads to daily struggles in decision-making.

By definition, the phenomenon of mission drift occurs steadily but surely over time in a parachurch agency when small decisions, adjustments, syntheses or compromises are made. The result being that its organizational Christian identity is amalgamated with that of secular culture. When a parachurch agency is set on changing its God-given vision to adapt to the needs of the world – in a passing and culturally rooted society – and becomes less committed to its holistic mission objectives, mission drift is certain to occur. This empirical multiple case study research of the seven parachurch organizations has identified that, for some, what began as a uniquely Christian faith-based missionary agency has evolved into a Christian humanitarian international NGO/NPO focused on good works, advocacy, development, and relief.

Appendix

Interview Questionnaire

Introductive Questions

1. Name and date of creation of the organization? Your Name? What is your position?
2. What are the organization's mission statement and mission objectives? Can you please provide some documents?
3. How many workers, including paid staff, volunteers, full and part-time co-workers serve in your organization?

Interview Questionnaire

1. How do you see your organization's holistic development work in the light of Jesus's earthly ministry as described in Matthew 9:35–38 and Luke 4:18–19 for instance?
2. What kind of relations does your NGO/NPO have with the local churches in the area where you work to bring hope and relief to the poor?
3. From your point of view (and experience), what distinctiveness must Christian faith-based NGOs/NPOs have in relief and development work in comparison to non-Christian international organizations?

4. What are and must be the visible signs of your organization's or any faith-based NGO/NPO's Christianness (Christian identity) and worldview?
5. How do you reconcile your organization's Christian identity and worldview with the worldview of your unbelieving funders (if you have non-Christians among your donors)? What potential risk of compromising do you foresee?
6. Since the founding of your NGO/NPO, has the organization had to undergo some 'paradigm shifts'[1]? If yes, how did that shift (or those shifts) help to counter the risk of 'mission drift'[2]?
7. How do you cultivate or foster a healthy paradigm shift to avoid mission drift in an environment with a secular worldview? Explain how a beneficial paradigm shift can be implemented.
8. Have you changed your original mission statement and have you experienced mission drift in your organization? If yes, to what extent?
9. What can be the potential changes or other evidence helping you to see that your NGO/NPO (or any parachurch agency) might be gradually sliding towards becoming a secular humanitarian organization with secular worldview?
10. What 'missionary school of thought'[3] is your organization modelled on, and why? The evangelization-only school, the

---

1. The term "Paradigm Shift" describes a fundamental change in the way a Christian organization does mission: it may change its concepts, programs and methods for the sake of contextualization – but keeps the essential values of its Christian identity.

2. The phenomenon of "Mission Drift" defines any Christian faith-based organization that has drifted away from its founding mission, its purpose for existing, and its Christian identity, and has not returned to its original intent and founding mission statement.

3. Missionary schools of thought: (1) Parachurch agencies that adhere to 'the Evangelization-only school' and believe that the ideal mission concept for 'Missio Dei' is evangelism. The only mission they do is evangelistic outreach. (2) Agencies that adhere to the "Humanitarization-only School" believe that the appropriate theory and praxis for Christian mission is through social involvment or humanitarian works: therefore, evangelism is not part of their mission statement and objectives. (3) NGOs/NPOs that adhere to the 'Holistic Transformation School' believe that the best way to do Christian mission is through 'integral gospel', that is, by engaging both in spiritual-evangelistic and socio-humanitarian activities. They defend these two activities as integral parts of the earthly ministry of Jesus and of present-day mission.

humanitarization-only school or the holistic transformation (integral missionary) school?
11. What impact does your NGO/NPO have on social development, transformation, evangelistic outreach, conversion and discipleship (on personal and community level)?
12. What are the organization's approaches to contextualization in relation to holistic transformation?
13. What might be the best meanings, models, implications and methods to use as the conceptual framework for the holistic transformation and contextualization of the Missio Dei among the people the NGO/NPO serves?
14. If you could give advice to Christian faith-based agencies who might be dealing with mission drift, what would you say to them?
15. How do you foresee the future of the Christianness (Christian identity) of your agency, and generally speaking of those Christian faith-based NGOs/NPOs which exist at present?

Bibliography

Abbott, Anthony John. "Church, Civil Society and Politics," in *Church and Civil Society: A Theology of Engagement*, edited by Francis Sullivan and Sue Leppert, 1–5. Adelaide, Australia: ATF Press, 2004.

Ajulu, Deborah, ed. *Development as Holistic Mission*. Edinburgh: Regnum Books, 2010.

———. *Holism in Development: An African Perspective on Empowering Communities*. Monrovia: MARC, 2001.

Aldrich, Howard E., and Martin Ruef. *Organizations Evolving*. Thousand Oaks: Sage Publications Inc., 2006.

Alford, Henry. *Alford's Greek Testament: An Exegetical and Critical Commentary*. Volume 1. Grand Rapids: Guardian Press, 1976.

Allison, Dale C. *Studies in Matthew: Interpretation Past and Present*. Grand Rapids: Baker Academic, 2005.

Altbach, Philip G., ed. *Private Prometheus: Private Higher Education and Development in the 21st Century*. London: Greenwood Press, 1999.

Amalraj, John, Geoffrey W. Hahn, and William D. Taylor, eds. *Spirituality in Mission: Embracing the Lifelong Journey*. Globalization of Mission Series. Pasadena: William Carey Publishing, 2018.

Anderson, Allan H. "The Contribution of David Yonggi Cho to a Contextual Theology in Korea." *Journal of Pentecostal Theology* 12, no. 1 (2003): 85–105.

Anderson, Chip M. *Wasted Evangelism: Social Action and the Church's Task of Evangelism, A Journey in the Gospel of Mark*. Eugene: Resource Publications, 2013.

Anderson, Hugh. "Broadening Horizons: The Rejection at Nazareth Pericope of Luke 4:16–30 in Light of Recent Critical Trends." *Interpretation* 18, no. 3 (1964): 259–275.

Anderson, Paul A. "Decision Making by Objection and the Cuban Missile Crisis." *Administrative Science Quarterly* 28, no. 2 (1983): 201–222.

Anthony, Michael J., and Warren S. Benson. *Exploring the History and Philosophy of Christian Education: Principles for the 21st Century*. Eugene: Wipf & Stock, 2003.

Armendáriz, Beatriz, and Ariane Szafarz. "On Mission Drift in Microfinance Institutions." Centre Emile Bernheim, working paper No. 09/015, May 2009. Viewed 03 January 2020, from https://www.solvay.edu/EN/Research/Bernheim/documents/wp09015.pdf.

Austin, James E., Howard Stevenson, and Jane Wei-Skillern. "Social and Commercial Entrepreneurship: Same, Different, or Both?" *Entrepreneurship Theory and Practice* 30, no. 1 (2006): 1–22.

Austin, Michael J. "The Changing Relationship Between Non-profit Organizations and Public Social Service Agencies in the Era of Welfare Reform." *Non-profit and Voluntary Sector Quarterly* 32, no. 1 (2003): 97–114.

Austin, P. *Salvation-Soteria: A Greek Word Study*, 2018. Viewed 4 February 2020, from https://www.preceptaustin.org/salvation-soteria_greek_word_study.

Ayres, Lioness, Karen Kavanaugh, and Kathleen A. Knafl. "Within-Case and Across-Case Approaches to Qualitative Data Analysis." *Qualitative Health Research* 13, no. 6 (2003): 871–883.

Ayton, Darshini, Gemma Carey, Helen Keleher, and Ben Smith. "Historical Overview of Church Involvement in Health and Wellbeing in Australia: Implications for Health Promotion Partnerships." *Australian Journal of Primary Health* 18, no. 1 (2012): 4–10.

Babbie, Earl R. *The Basics of Social Research*. 3rd edition. London: Thomson Wadsworth, 2005.

Backues, Lindy. "Interfaith Development Efforts as Means to Peace and Witness." *Transformation* 26, no. 2 (2009): 67–81.

Bailey, Heather L. *Ernest Renan's Life of Jesus and the Orthodox Struggle Against the De-Christianisation of Christ in Russia, 1863–1917*. Minneapolis: University of Minnesota Press, 2001.

Barker, Kenneth L. *Micah, Nahum, Habakkuk, Zephaniah*. Nashville: Broadman & Holman Publishers, 1999.

Barnett, Michael, and Janice Stein, eds. *Sacred Aid: Faith and Humanitarianism*. Oxford: Oxford University Press, 2012.

Barnett, Michael N., and Martha Finnemore. *Rules for the World: International Organizations in Global Politics*. Ithaca: Cornell University Press, 2004.

Barron, M. "The Role of Pastoral Care in Development: Is it Really Development?" *IMU Report*, March–May 2007.

Bassham, Rodger C. *Mission Theology: 1948–1975 Years of Worldwide Creative Tension*. Eugene: Wipf & Stock Pub, 2002.

Battilana, Julie, and Matthew Lee. "Advancing Research on Hybrid Organizing: Insights from the Study of Social Enterprises." *The Academy of Management Annals* 8, no. 1 (2014): 397–441.

Battilana, Julie, and Silvia Dorado. "Building Sustainable Hybrid Organizations: The Case of Commercial Microfinance Organizations." *Academy of Management Journal* 53, no. 6 (2010): 1419–1440.

Battilana, Julie, Matthew Lee, John Walker, and Cheryl Dorsey. "In Search of the Hybrid Ideal." *Stanford Social Innovation Review* 10, no. 3 (2012): 50–55.

Battilana, Julie. "Cracking the Organizational Challenge of Pursuing Joint Social and Financial Goals: Social Enterprise as a Laboratory to Understand Hybrid Organizing." *Association Internationale de Management Stratégique* 21, no. 4 (2018): 1278–1305. Viewed 07 January 2020, from https://www.cairn.info/revue-management-2018-4-page-1278.htm.

Bebbington, David W. *The Dominance of Evangelicalism: The Age of Spurgeon and Moody*. Downers Grove: IVP Academic, 2005.

Beck, Ulrich. *A God of One's Own: Religion's Capacity for Peace and Potential for Violence*. Cambridge: Polity, 2010.

Befus, David, and Stephan Bauman. "The Role of Christian NGOs and Service Agencies." Lausanne Occasional Paper 33, 2004. Viewed 23 March 2021, from https://www.lausanne.org/content/lop/holistic-mission-lop-33#trocnasa.

Bennett, Andrew, and Colin Elman. "Case Study Methods in the International Relations Subfield." *Comparative Political Studies* 40, no. 2 (2007): 170–195.

Bennett, Roger, and Sharmila Savani. "Surviving Mission Drift: How Charities Can Turn Dependence on Government Contract Funding to Their Own Advantage." *Non-profit Management and Leadership* 22, no. 2 (2011): 217–231.

Berger, Julia. "Religious Nongovernmental Organizations: An Exploratory Analysis." *Voluntas: International Journal of Voluntary and Non-profit Organizations* 14, no. 1 (2003): 15–39.

Berger, Peter L. "Secularization and De-Secularization." In *Religions in the Modern World: Traditions and Translations*, edited by Linda Woodhead, 336–344. London: Routledge, 2005.

Berger, Peter L. and Richard J. Neuhaus. *To Empower People: The Role of Mediating Structures in Public Policy*. Washington, DC: American Enterprise Institute, 1977.

Bergin, Nicholas. "A Dual Mission Challenge: Best Practices for Navigating Mission Drift in Social Enterprises." Master thesis, Norwegian Business School, 2018.

Bernard, Russell H. *Research Methods in Anthropology: Qualitative and Quantitative Approaches*. 4th edition. New York: Altamira Press, 2006.

Berthon, Hilary, and Lin Hatfield-Dodds. "Standing for Truth: Vision-Driven Advocacy." In *Church and Civil Society: A Theology of Engagement*, edited by Francis Sullivan and Sue Leppert. Adelaide: ATF Press, 2004.

Bess, James L., and Jay R. Dee. *Understanding College and University Organization: Theories for Effective Policy and Practice*. Sterling,: Stylus Publishing, 2012.

Betz, Hans Dieter, ed. *Religion Past and Present: Chu-Deu*. Leiden: Brill Publishers, 2007.

Bhatia, Manu. "Your Guide to Qualitative and Quantitative Data Analysis Methods" (2018). Viewed 14 July 2020, from https://humansofdata.atlan.com/2018/09/qualitative-quantitative-data-analysis-methods/.

Bible Hub, "Expository Greek Testament." Viewed 06 December 2024, from https://biblehub.com/commentaries/matthew/9-37.htm.

Bielefeld, Wolfgang, and William Cleveland. "Defining Faith-Based Organizations and Understanding them Through Research." *Non-profit and Voluntary Sector Quarterly* 42, no. 3 (2013): 442–467.

———. "Faith-Based Organizations as Service Providers and Their Relationship to Government." *Non-profit and Voluntary Sector Quarterly* 42, no. 3 (2013): 468–494.

Bifet, Juan E. *Priestly Spirituality and Mission: Sign of the Good Shepherd*. Roma: Pontificia Universita Urbaniana, 1995.

Billis, David, ed. *Hybrid Organizations and the Third Sector: Challenges for Practice, Theory and Policy*. Basingstoke: Palgrave Macmillan, 2010.

Birdsall, Doug S., and Brown Lindsay. "The Cape Town Commitment: A Confession of Faith and a Call to Action." *Kairos Evangelical Journal of Theology* 5, no. 1 (2011): 165–224. Viewed 03 August 2020, from https://hrcak.srce.hr/file/105064.

Blomberg, Craig L. *Matthew: An Exegetical and Theological Exposition of Holy Scripture*, The New American Commentary. Volume 22. Nashville: Broadman & Holman Publishers, 1992.

Boadt, Lawrence. *Reading the Old Testament*. New York: Paulist Press, 1984.

Bocelli, Andrea. "CV of Professor Muhammad Yunus." Viewed 18 December 2019, from https://www.andreabocellifoundation.org/wp-content/uploads/2014/08/CV-of-Professor-Muhammad-Yunus.pdf.

Bongmba, Elias K., ed. *The Routledge Companion to Christianity in Africa*. London: Routledge, 2015.

Bosch, David J. *A Spirituality of the Road*. Eugene: Wipf & Stock Publishers, 2001.

———. *Transforming Mission: Paradigm Shifts in Theology of Mission*, Maryknoll: Orbis Books, 2011.

———. *Witness to the World: The Christian Mission in Theological Perspective*. Atlanta: John Knox Press, 1980.

Bouma, Gary, Desmond Cahill, Hass Dellal, and Athlia Zwartz. *Freedom of Religion and Belief in 21st Century Australia*. Research report prepared for the Australian Human Rights Commission, 2011.

Bouma, Gary. "Religious Diversity and Social Policy: An Australian Dilemma." *Australian Journal of Social Issues* 47, no. 3 (2012): 281–295.

Braaten, Carl E. *In One Body Through the Cross: The Princeton Proposal for Christian Unity*. Grand Rapids: Wm. B. Eerdmans Publishing, 2003.

Bretherton, Luke. *Christianity and Contemporary Politics: The Conditions and Possibilities of Faithful Witness*. Chichester: Wiley-Blackwell Publishing, 2010.

Breward, Ian. *A History of the Australian Churches*. St. Leonards: Allen & Unwin, 1993.

Briley, Donnel A., and Jennifer L. Aaker. "When does Culture Matter? Effects of Personal Knowledge on the Correction of Culture-Based Judgments." *Journal of Marketing Research* 43, no. 3 (2006): 395–408.

Brown, Alice W. *Staying the Course: How Unflinching Dedication and Persistence Have Built a Successful Private College in a Region of Isolation and Poverty*. Bloomington: AuthorHouse, LLC, 2014.

Brown, Candy G., and Mark Silk. *The Future of Evangelicalism in America*. New York: Columbia University Press, 2016.

Bruce, Alexander B. *The Synoptic Gospels*. New York: George H. Doran Company, 2009.

Bryman, Alan. *Social Research Methods*. 3rd edition. Oxford: Oxford University Press, 2008.

Buckley, Christian, and Ryan Dobson. *Humanitarian Jesus: Social Justice and the Cross*. Chicago: Moody Publishers, 2010.

Burtness, James H. "Innovation as the Search for Probabilities: To Re-Contextualize the Text." In *Learning in Context: The Search for Innovative Patterns in Theological education*, edited by The Theological Education Fund, 13. Monroe: New Life Press, 1973.

Bush, Luis. "Paradigm Shifts in World Missions." *International Journal of Frontier Missions* 16, no. 3 (1999): 111–118.

Butler, Trent C. *Holman New Testament Commentary: Luke*. Volume 3. Nashville: Broadman and Holman Publishers, 2000.

Buttmann, Philipp. *A Catalogue of Irregular Greek Verbs: With all the Tenses Extant, their Formation, Meaning and Usage*. Second edition. Translated by J.R. Fishlake, Charleston: Forgotten Books, 2019.

Byrnes, Rita M. *Religion and Apartheid*. Washington, DC: US Library of Congress, 1996.

Campbell, Ernest T. *Christian Manifesto*. New York: Harper and Row, 1970.

Campbell, Ian D. *Opening up Matthew's Gospel*. Leominster: Day One Publications, 2008.

Campbell, Jonathan. "Releasing the Gospel from Western Bondage." *International Journal of Frontier Missions* 16, no. 4 (2000): 166–172.

Campbell, L. "Church and Civil Society: A Social Compact." In *Church and Civil Society: A Theology of Engagement*, edited by Francis Sullivan and Sue Leppert. Adelaide: ATF Press, 2004.

Canda, Edward R., Leola D. Furman, and Hwi-Ja Canda. *Spiritual Diversity in Social Work Practice: The Heart of Helping*. Oxford: Oxford University Press, 2019.

Carlsen, Arne. "On the Tacit Side of Organizational Identity: Narrative Unconscious and Figured Practice." *Culture and Organization* 22, no. 2 (2016), 107–135.

Cassell, Catherine, and Gillian Symon. *Essential Guide to Qualitative Methods in Organizational Research*. Thousand Oaks: SAGE Publications, Inc., 2004.

Chambers, Liudmila. "Growing a Hybrid Venture: Toward a Theory of Mission Drift in Social Entrepreneurship." PhD diss., Dept. of Management, Economics, Law, Social Sciences and International Affairs, University of St. Gallen, 2014.

Chambers, Robert. *Rural Development: Putting the Last First*. London: Longman, 1983.

Chang, Patricia M.Y. "Escaping the Procrustean Bed: A Critical Analysis of the Study of Religious Organizations, 1930–2001." In *Handbook of the Sociology of Religion*, edited by Michele Dillon, 123–135. New York: Cambridge University Press, 2003.

Chapman, Audrey R. *Faith, Power, and Politics: Political Ministry in Mainline Churches*. Cleveland: Pilgrim Press, 1991.

Chaves, Mark. "Intraorganizational Power and Internal Secularization in Protestant Denominations." *American Journal of Sociology* 99, no. 1 (1993): 1–48.

———. "Secularization as Declining Religious Authority." *Social Forces* 72, no. 3 (1994): 749–774.

Chester, Tim. "What makes Christian Development Christian?" Paper presented at the Global Connections Relief and Development Forum, May 16, 2002. Viewed 07January 2020. http://www.globalconnections.org.uk/papers/what-makes-christian-development-christian.

———. *Good News to the Poor: Social Involvement and the Gospel*. Wheaton: Crossway, 2013.

Chesterton, Gilbert Keith. *Orthodoxy*. Scotts Valley: CreateSpace Independent Publishing Platform, 2015.

Christie, Nancy, and Michael Gauvreau, eds. *The Sixties and Beyond: Dechristianization in North America and Western Europe, 1945–2000*. Toronto: University of Toronto Press, 2013.

Clarke, Gerard, and Michael Jennings. *Development, Civil Society and Faith-Based Organizations: Bridging the Sacred and Secular*. New York: Palgrave Macmillan, 2008.

Clarke, Gerard. "Faith Matters: Development and the Complex World of Faith-Based Organizations." Paper presented at the annual conference of the Development Studies Association, Milton Keynes, Open University, 7–9 September, 2005.

Claydon, David, ed. *A New Vision, A New Heart: A Renewed Call Lausanne Occasional Papers from the 2004 Forum for World Evangelization*. Pasadena: William Carey Library, 2005.

Cleary, Ray. "The Poor You Will Always Have with You." *Radio Interview, ABC The Religion Report* (1999). Viewed 8 August 2020, from https://www.abc.net.au/radionational/programs/archived/religionreport/the-poor-you-have-with-you-always/3557252#transcript.

———. *Reclaiming Welfare for Mission: Choices for Choice*. Canberra: Barton Books, 2012.

Cnaan, Ram A., and Charlene C. McGrew. "Social Welfare." In *Handbook of Religion and Social Institutions*, edited by Helen Ebaugh, no pages. Springer, NY: Kluwer Academic/Plenum Publishers, 2005.

Colquitt, Jason A., and Cindy P. Zapata-Phelan. "Trends in Theory Building and Theory Testing: A Five-Decade Study." *Academy of Management Journal* 50, no. 6 (2007): 1281–1303.

Copestake, James, Martin Greely, Susan Johnson, Naila Kabeer, and Anton Simanowitz. *Money with a Mission: Microfinance and Poverty Reduction*. Bourton-on-Dunsmore: ITDG Publishing, 2005.

Copestake, James. "Mainstreaming Microfinance: Social Performance Management or Mission Drift?" *World Development Journal* 35, no. 10 (2007): 1721–1738. Viewed 06 January 2020. https://doi.org/10.1016/j.worlddev.2007.06.004.

———. "Mission Drift: Understand It, Avoid It." *Journal of Microfinance/ESR Review* 9, no. 2 (2007): 20–25, viewed 06 January 2020, from https://scholarsarchive.byu.edu/esr/vol9/iss2/6.

Cornforth, Christopher. "Understanding and Combating Mission Drift in Social Enterprises." *Social Enterprise Journal* 10, no. 1 (2014): 3–20.

Cowan, Douglas E. *Bearing False Witness? An Introduction to the Christian Countercult*. Westport: Praeger, 2003.

Creswell, John W. *Educational Research: Planning, Conducting, and Evaluation Quantitative and Qualitative Research*. 4th edition. Lincoln, NE: Pearson, 2012.

———. *Qualitative Inquiry and Research Design: Choosing Among Five Traditions*. Thousand Oaks: Sage Publications, Inc., 2017.

———. *Research Design: Qualitative, Quantitative, and Mixed Methods Approaches*. 3rd edition. Thousand Oaks: Sage Publications, Inc., 2009.

Cueva, Samuel. *Mission Partnership in Creative Tension: An Analysis of the Relationships in Mission within the Evangelical Movement with Special Reference to Peru and Britain between 1987 and 2006*. Carlisle: Langham Academic, 2015.

Cull, Robert, Asli Demirguç-Kunt, and Jonathan Morduch. "Financial Performance and Outreach: A Global Analysis of Leading Microbanks." *Economic Journal, Royal Economic Society* 117, no. 517 (2007): 107–133.

Curtius, Georg. *The Greek Verb: Its Structure and Development*, Riverside: Library of University of California, 2014.

Dahle, Margunn Serigstad, Lars Dahle and Knut Jørgensen. *The Lausanne Movement: A Range of Perspectives*. Oxford: Regnum Books International, 2014.

Davie, Grace. *Religion in Britain: A Persistent Paradox*. Hoboken: Wiley-Balckwell, 2015.

Davies-Kildea, Jason. *Faith in Action: A Study of Holistic Models of Care for Highly Disadvantaged People Which Have Been Established in Faith-Based Communities*. Melbourne, Australia: The Winston Churchill Memorial Trust and The Salvation Army, 2007.

Davies, M. "A Missional Miss." *Onfire* 15, no. 6 (2014): 4–5.

Davies, William David, and Dale C. Allison. *A Critical and Exegetical Commentary on the Gospel According to Saint Matthew*, International Critical Commentary, Volume 3, London: T&T Clark, 2000.

Davis, Tom. *Centers for Faith-Based and Community Initiatives: Promise and Progress*. Washington, DC: U.S Government Printing Office, 2004.

De Gruchy, John W. "Grappling with a Colonial Heritage: The English-speaking Churches under Imperialism and Apartheid." In *Christianity in South Africa: A Political, Social, and Cultural History*, edited by R. Elphick and R. Davenport, 150–167. Berkeley: University of California Press, 1997.

———. "The Great Evangelical Reversal: South African Reflections." *Journal of Theology for Southern Africa* 9, no. 24 (1978): 45–57.

———. *Theology and Ministry in Context and Crisis: A South African Perspective*. Grand Rapids: Eerdmans, 1987.

De Gruchy, John W., and Steve de Gruchy. *The Church Struggle in South Africa: Twenty-fifth Anniversary Edition*. Minneapolis: Fortress Press, 2005.

Dempsey, K. "Microfinance Mission Drift – A Study of Microfinance Institutions in Asia and Latin America." Master of Arts thesis, Dept. of Development Economics, University of Northern British Columbia, 2011.

Denscombe, Martyn. *The Good Research Guide: For Small-Scale Social Research Projects*. 4th edition. Maidenhead: Open University Press, 2010.

Denzin, Norman Kent, and Yvonna S. Lincoln. *Handbook of Qualitative Research*. London: Sage Publications Ltd, 1984.

Dewitt, Calvin B., and Ghillean T. Prance, eds. *Missionary Earth Keeping*. Macon: Mercer University Press, 1993.

Dickey, Brian. *No Charity There: A Short History of Social Welfare in Australia*. Melbourne: Thomas Nelson, 1980.

Dillon, R.J. "Easter Revelation and Mission Program in Luke 24:46–48." In *Sin, Salvation and the Spirit*, edited by D. Durken. Collegeville: Liturgical Press, 1979.

DiMaggio, Paul J. "The New Institutionalisms: Avenues of Collaboration." *Journal of Institutional and Theoretical Economics* 154, no. 4 (1998): 696–705.

DiMaggio, Paul J., and Walter W. Powell. "Introduction." In *The New Institutionalism in Organizational Analysis*, edited by Walter W. Powell and Paul J. DiMaggio, No pages. Chicago: The University of Chicago Press, 1991.

———. "The Iron Cage Revisited: Institutional Isomorphism and Collective Rationality in Organizational Fields." *American Sociological Review* 48, no. 2 (1983): 147–160.

Doherty, Bob, Helen Haugh, and Fergus Lyon. "Social Enterprises as Hybrid Organizations: A Review and Research Agenda." *International Journal of Management Reviews* 16, no. 4 (2014): 1–21.

Dowsett, Rose, Isabel Phiri, Doug Birdsall, Dawit Olika Terfassa, Hwa Yung, and Knud Jørgensen, eds. *Evangelism and Diakonia in Context*. Volume 32. Oxford: Regnum Books International, 2015.

Dudley-Smith, Timothy. *John Stott: A Global Ministry*. Leicester: Inter-Varsity Press, 2001.

Dudovskiy, John. *The Ultimate Guide to Writing a Dissertation in Business Studies: A Step-by-Step Assistance*, Research Methodology, 2018. Viewed 19 March 2020, from https://research-methodology.net/sampling-in-primary-data-collection/purposive-sampling/.

Dupont, Jacques. *Nouvelles Études Sur Les Actes des Apôtres*. Lectio Divina 118. Paris: Édition Cerf, 1984.

———. *The Salvation of the Gentiles: Essays on the Acts the Apostles*. New York: Paulist Press, 1979.

Durbin, Mary Ellen, Cathy Katoski, Elvira Kelley, Carol Simler, and Susan R. Stolfa. *The Empowerment Process: Centering Social Ministry in the Life of the Local Christian Community*. New York: Paulist Press, 1994.

Duriez, Bruno, François Mabille, and Kathy Rousselet. *Les ONG confessionnelles: Religions et action internationale*. Paris: Éditions L'Harmattan, 2007.

Dyrness, William A., and Veli-Matti Kärkäinen, eds. *Global Dictionary of Theology: A Resource for the Worldwide Church*. Downers Grove: IVP Academic, 2009.

Earley, Dave, and David Wheeler. *Evangelism is . . . How to Share Jesus with Passion and Confidence*. Nashville: Academic Publishing Group, 2010.

Ebaugh, Helen Rose, Janet S. Chafetz, and Paula F. Pipes. "Faith-Based Social Service Organizations and Government Funding: Data from a National Survey." *Social Science Quarterly* 86, 2 (2005): 273–292.

Ebrahim, Alnoor, Julie Battilana, and Johanna Mair. "The Governance of Social Enterprises: Mission drift and Accountability Challenges in Hybrid Organizations." *Research in Organizational Behaviour* 34 (2014): 81–100. Viewed 06 January 2020, from https://www.sciencedirect.com/science/article/abs/pii/S0191308514000082.

Edmondson, Amy C., Richard M. Bohmer, and Gary P. Pisano. "Disrupted Routines: Team Learning and New Technology Implementation in Hospitals." *Administrative Science Quarterly* 46, no. 4 (2001): 685–716.

Edwards, Emmy. "Faithfull Innovation and Mission Drift in Christian Parachurch Student Organizations." Master thesis, Baylor University, 2017.

Eims, Leroy, and Randy Eims. *Laboring in the Harvest*. Saybrook: Christianaudio, 2011.

Eisenhardt, Kathleen M. "Building Theories from Case Study Research." *The Academy of Management Review* 14, no. 4 (1989): 532–550.

Eisenhardt, Kathleen M., and Melissa E. Graebner. "Theory Building from Cases: Opportunities and Challenges." *The Academy of Management Journal* 50, no. 1 (2007): 25–32.

Elliot, Jennifer A. *An Introduction to Sustainable Development: Routledge Perspectives on Development*. Brighton: Routledge, 2006.

Elphick, Richard, and Rodney Davenport. *Christianity in South Africa: A Political, Social, and Cultural History*. Berkeley: University of California Press, 1998.

Engel, James F., and William A. Dyrness, *Changing the Mind of Missions: Where Have We Gone Wrong?* Downers Grove: InterVarsity Press, 2000.

Engels, Pim. *Mission Drift in Microfinance: The Influence of Institutional and Country Risk Indicators on the Trade-off between the Financial and Social Performance of Microfinance Institutions*. Stuttgart: Ibidem-Verlag, 2010.

Engelsviken, Tormod. "*Missio Dei*: The Understanding and Misunderstanding of a Theological Concept in European Churches and Missiology." *International Review of Mission* 92, no. 367 (2003): 481–497.

English, J.T. Deep Discipleship: How the Church Can Make Whole Disciples of Jesus. Nashville: B&H Publishing Group, 2020.

Erickson, Millard J. *Christian Theology*. 2nd edition. Grand Rapids: Baker Academic, 2003.

Escobar, Samuel. "Missiology Faces the Lion." *Missiology* 17, no. 3 (1989): 347–349.

———. La Mission: A l'Heure de la Mondialisation du Christianisme. Beaubourg: Editions Farel, 2006.

———. *The New Global Mission: The Gospel from Everywhere to Everyone.* Downers Grove: InterVarsity Press, 2003.

Eurich, Johannes. "Diaconia under Mission Drift: Problems with its Theological Legitimation and its Welfare State Partnership." *Vandenhoeck & Ruprecht Verlage* 3, no. 1 (2012): 58–65. Viewed 25 July 2019, from https://www.vr-elibrary.de/doi/10.13109/diac.2012.3.1.58#.XhiNFBd7kRZ.

Fagerli, Beate, Knud Jørgensen, and Frank-Ole Thoresen, eds. *Witnessing to Christ in a Multi-Religious Context.* Oxford: Regnum Books International, 2015.

Fath, Sébastien. *Une Autre Manière d'être Chrétien en France: Socio- Histoire de L'implantation Baptiste (1810–1950).* Histoire Et Société no. 41. Genève: Labor et Fides, 2001.

Fergusson, David, and Mark W. Elliot, eds. *The History of Scottish Theology: Celtic Origins to Reformed Orthodox.* Volume 1. Oxford: Oxford University Press, 2019.

Ferris, Elizabeth. "Faith-Based and Secular Humanitarian Organizations." *International Review of the Red Cross* 87, no. 858 (2005): 311–325.

Finn, Nathan A., and Keith S. Whitfield, eds. *Spirituality for the Sent: Casting a New Vision for the Missional Church.* Downers Grove: InterVarsity Press, 2017.

Fitzmyer, Joseph A. *The Gospel According to Luke I-IX: Introduction, Translation, and Notes.* The Anchor Bible. Volume 28. New Haven: Yale University Press, 2008.

Flemming, Dean. *Recovering the Full Mission of God: A Biblical Perspective on Being, Doing and Telling.* Downers Grove: InterVarsity Press, 2013.

Floyd, J.D. "Is Personal Evangelism Passé." *Journal of Evangelism and Missions* 1 (2006): 40–56.

Ford, David F. *Christian Wisdom: Desiring God and Learning in Love.* Cambridge: Cambridge University Press, 2007.

France, Richard Thomas. *The Gospel of Matthew.* Grand Rapids: William B. Eerdmans Publishing Company, 2007.

Franklin, Kirk. "Mission Spirituality" (2018). Viewed 08 July 2020, from https://www.academia.edu/40033149/Mission_and_Spirituality.

Free Conference Told. "Church's Role is Spiritual, not Social, Free Conference Told." *The Lutheran Layman* 37, no. 8 (1966): 16.

Freeman, Dena. *Pentecostalism and Development: Churches, NGOs, and Social Change in Africa.* Basingstoke: Palgrave Macmillan, 2012.

Friedman, John. *Empowerment: The Politics of Alternative Development.* Cambridge: Blackwell, 1992.

Fritsch, Brittany, Becky Rossi, and Tessa Hebb. "An Examination of the Tension Between Business and Mission among Social Enterprises." Paper presented at the ANSER-ARES conference, Victoria, Canada, 5–7 June, 2013.

Frumkin, Peter, and Alice Andre-Clark. "When Missions, Markets, and Politics Collide: Values and Strategy in the Non-profit Human Services." *Non-profit and Voluntary Sector Quarterly* 29, (2000): 141–163.

Frumkin, Peter. "After Partnership: Rethinking Public-Nonprofit Relations." In *Who Will Provide? The Changing Role of Religion in American Social Welfare*, edited by Mary J. Bane, Brent Coffin, and Ronald Thiemann. Centre for the Study of Values in Public Life, Harvard Divinity School. Westpress, Boulder, 2000.

———. *On Being Non-profit: A Conceptual and Policy Primer.* Cambridge: Harvard University Press, 2002.

Fujino, Gary. "Lausanne III at Cape Town 2010: God's Glory Church on Mission." *Japan Harvest*, 2011. Viewed 03 August 2020, from https://www.lausanne-japan.org/app/download/4151504467/God%27s%2BGlobal%2BChurch%2Bon%2BMission.pdf?t=1312357579.

Gallagher, Robert L., and Paul Hertig, eds. *Mission in Acts: Ancient Narratives in Contemporary Context.* Maryknoll: Orbis Books, 2004.

Gallet, Wilma. "Christian Mission or an Unholy Alliance?: The Changing Role of Church-Related Organizations in Welfare-to-Work Service." PhD thesis, Dept. of Social and Political Sciences, University of Melbourne, 2016.

Galunic, Charles, and Kathleen M. Eisenhardt. "Architectural Innovation and Modular Corporate Forms." *The Academy of Management Journal* 44, no. 6 (2001): 1229–1249.

Garland, David E. *Reading Matthew: A Literary and Theological Commentary on the First Gospel.* Macon: Smyth & Helwys Publishing, 2012.

Gatewood, Willard B. *Controversy in the Twenties: Fundamentalism, Modernism, and Evolution.* Nashville: Vanderbilt University Press, 1969.

Geertz, Clifford. *After the Fact: Two Countries, Four Decades, One Anthropologist.* Cambridge: Harvard University Press, 1995.

George, Sherron Kay. "Joined and Knit Together . . . Each Part Working Properly: A Missiological Reflection on Practices of God's Holistic Mission in Ephesians." *Missiology: An International Review* 37, no. 3 (2009): 397–409.

Gibbert, Michael, and Winfried Ruigrok. "The 'What' and 'How' of Case Study Rigor: Three Strategies Based on Published Work." *Organizational Research Methods* 13, no. 4 (2010): 1–63.

Gibbert, Michael, Winfried Ruigrok, and Barbara Wicki. "What Passes as a Rigorous Case Study?" *Strategic Management Journal* 29, no. 13 (2008): 1465–74.

Gilbert, Clark G. "Unbundling the Structure of Inertia: Resource Versus Routine Rigidity." *The Academy of Management Journal* 48, no. 5 (2005): 741–763.

Gilliland, Dean. "Contextualization." In *Evangelical Dictionary of World Missions*, edited by A. Scott Moreau, Harold Netland and Charles Van Engen, 225–28. Grand Rapids: Baker Book House, 2000.

Gittins, B. "The Nature of Mission." *Onfire* 15, no. 9 (2014): 4–5.

Glasser, Arthur Frederick, and Donald Anderson McGavran. *Contemporary Theologies of Mission*. Grand Rapids: Baker Book House, 1983.

Gooding, David W. *According to Luke: A New Exposition of the Third Gospel*. Grand Rapids: Eerdmans, 1987.

———. *According to Luke: The Third Gospel's Ordered Historical Narrative*. Coleraine: Myrtlefield House, 2013.

Gove, Philip Babcock, ed., *Webster's Third New International Dictionary*, Springfield: Merriam-Webster Inc., 1986.

Graham, Billy. "What we Expect at the Berlin Congress." *World Vision Magazine* 10, no. 9 (1966): 3–9.

Grant, Don, K.M. O'Neil, and L.S. Stephens. "Neosecularization and Craft Versus Professional Religious Authority in a Nonreligious Organization." *Journal for the Scientific Study of Religion* 42, no. 3 (2003): 479–487.

Green, Joel B. *The Gospel of Luke*. Grand Rapids: William B. Eerdmans Publishing Company, 1997.

———. *The Theology of the Gospel of Luke*. New Testament Theology. Cambridge: Cambridge University Press, 1995.

Green, Judith L., Gregory Camilli, Patricia B. Elmore, Audra Skukauskaiti, and Elizabeth Grace, eds. *Handbook of Complementary Methods in Education Research*. Washington, DC: Lawrence Erlbaum Associates, Inc., 2006.

Green, Michael E. *The Message of Matthew*. Downers Grove: InterVarsity Press, 2000.

Greer, Peter, and Chris Horst. *Mission Drift: The Unspoken Crisis Facing Leaders, Charities, and Churches*. Minneapolis: Bethany House Publishers, 2014.

Greer, Peter, and Philip Smith. *The Poor will be Glad: Joining the Revolution to Lift the World out of Poverty*. Grand Rapids: Zondervan, 2009.

Gregg, Samuel. "Playing with Fire: Churches, Welfare Services and Government Contracts." *Issue Analysis [CIS]* 14, no. 1 (2000): 1–8.

Grigg Viv. *Companion to the Poor: Christ in the Urban Slums*. Tring: Lion Books, 1984.

Grimes, Matthew G., Trenton Alma Williams, and Eric Yanfei Zhao. "Anchors Aweigh: The Sources, Variety, and Challenges of Mission Drift." *The Academy of Management Review* 10, no. 1 (2018): 1–63.

Grint, Keith. "Problems, Problems, Problems: The Social Construction of 'Leadership.'" *Sage Journals* 58, no. 11 (2005): 1363–90.

———. *The Sociology of Work: Introduction*. Cambridge: Polity Press, 2005.

Gros, Jeffrey, Thomas F. Best, and Lorelei F. Fuchs. *Growth in Agreement III: International Dialogue Texts and Agreed Statements, 1998–2005*. Geneva: WCC Publications, 2007.

Guinness, Os. *Dining with the Devil: The Megachurch Flirts with Modernity*. Grand Rapids: Baker Publishing Group, 1993.

Gurus, B. "Bio Professor Muhammad Yunus – African Development Bank." Viewed 18 December 2019, from https://www.afdb.org/fileadmin/uploads/afdb/Documents/Generic-Documents/Biography%20Professor%20Muhammad%20Yunus.pdf.

Gustafson, James W. "The Church and Holistic Ministry in Culture." *Tokyo Christian University Journal* 84, no. 1 (2004): 80–85.

Gutierrez, Gustavo. *A Theology of Liberation: History, Politics, and Salvation*. Maryknoll: Orbis Books, 1988.

Hadden, Jeffrey K., and Anson D. Shupe. *Secularization and Fundamentalism Reconsidered*. New York: Paragon House, 1989.

Hahn, Roger L. *Matthew: A Commentary for Bible Students*. Indianapolis: Wesleyan Publishing House, 2007.

Haigh, Nardia, John Walker, Sophia Bacq, and Jill Kickul. "Hybrid Organizations: Origin, Strategies, Impacts and Implications." *California Management Review* 57, no. 3 (2015): 5–12.

Harmon, Steve R. *Ecumenism Means You, Too: Ordinary Christians and the Quest for Christian Unity*. Eugene: Wipf & Stock Publishers, 2010.

Harries, Jim. "Encouraging Western People to Engage in Global Mission in a Vulnerable Way" (2020). Viewed 28 December 2020, from https://vulnerablemission.org/.

Harris, Robert Geoffrey. *Mission in the Gospels*. Werrington: Epworth Press, 2004.

Harrison, Paul Mansfield. *Authority and Power in the Free Church Tradition*. Princeton: Princeton University Press, 1959.

Harrison, Philip. *South Africa's Top Sites: Spiritual*. Cape Town, South Africa: New Africa Books Ltd, 2004.

Hart, Darryl G. *From Billy Graham to Sarah Palin: Evangelicals and the Betrayal of American Conservatism*. Grand Rapids: William B. Eerdmans Publishing Company, 2011.

Hartley, Jean. "Leading and Managing the Uncertainty of Strategic Change." In *Managing Strategic Implementation*, edited by Patrick C. Flood, Stephen Carroll, Liam Gorman and Tony Dromgoole, 109–122. Oxford: Blackwell, 2000.

Hastings, Adrian, Alistair Mason, and Hugh Pyper. *The Oxford Companion to Christian Thought: Intellectual, Spiritual, and Moral Horizons of Christianity*. Oxford: Oxford University Press, 2000.

Heist, Dan and Ram A. Cnaan. "Faith-Based International Development Work." *Religions* 7, no. 3 (2016): 1–17. Viewed 16 April 2020, from https://doi.org/10.3390/rel7030019.

Heldt, Jean-Paul A. "Revisiting the 'Whole Gospel': Toward a Biblical Model of Holistic Mission in the 21st Century." *Missiology: An International Review* 32, no. 2 (2004): 149–172.

Hendrickson, Craig S. "Charismatic Leadership and Missional Change: Mission-Actional Ministry in a Multi-ethnic Church." PhD diss., School of Intercultural Studies, Fuller Theological Seminary, 2017.

Hesselgrave, David J. "Missiology Faces the Lion." *Missiology* 17, no. 3 (1989): 347–349.

———. *Communicating Christ Cross-Culturally: An Introduction to Missionary Communication*. Grand Rapids: Zondervan Publishing House, 1991.

Hesselgrave, David J., and Ed Stetzer, eds. *Mission Shift: Global Mission Issues in the Third Millennium*. Nashville: B&H Publishing Group, 2010.

Hesselgrave, David J., and Edward Rommen. *Contextualization: Meanings, Methods, and Models*. Pasadena: William Carey Library, 2013.

Hiebert, Paul G. "Critical Contextualization." *International Bulletin of Missionary Research* 11, no. 3 (1987): 104–112.

Hiebert, Paul G., R. Daniel Shaw, and Tite Tiénou. "Responding to Split-Level Christianity and Folk Religion." *International Journal of Frontier Missions* 16, no. 4 (2000): 166–172. Viewed on 26 June 2020, from http://www.ijfm.org/PDFs_IJFM/16_4_PDFs/ijfm_16_4.pdf.

Higgs, Joy, Barbara Richardson, and Madeleine A. Dahlgren. *Developing Practice Knowledge for Health Professionals*. Edinburgh: Butterworth Heinemann, 2004.

Hiroshi, Shibuya, and Chiba Shin, eds. *Living for Jesus and Japan: The Social and Theological Thought of Uchimura Kanzo*. Grand Rapids: William B. Eerdmans Publishing Company, 2013.

Hockerts, Kai, and Rolf Wüstenhagen. "Greening Goliaths Versus Emerging Davids: Theorizing about the Role of Incumbents and New Entrants in Sustainable Entrepreneurship." *Journal of Business Venturing* 25, no. 5 (2010): 481–492.

Hoedemaker, L.A., and A. Camps. *Missiology: An Ecumenical Introduction*. Grand Rapids: Wm. B. Eerdmans Publishing Company, 1995.

Hoek, Marijke, and Justin Thacker, eds. *Micah's Challenge: The Church's Responsibility to the Global Poor*. Milton Keynes: Paternoster Press, 2008.

Hoggarth, Pauline, Fergus MacDonald, Bill Mitchell and Knud Jørgensen, eds. *Bible in Mission*. Volume 18. Oxford: Regnum Books International, 2013.

Holder, W.K. "A Vertical and Horizontal Gospel." Viewed 16 April 2020, from https://www.gbcbryansroad.com/hp_wordpress/wp-content/uploads/2017/07/A-Vertical-and-Horizontal-Gospel.pdf.

Hoover, Sharon R. *Mapping Church Missions: A Compass for Ministry Strategy*. Downers Grove: IVP Books, 2018.

Hopkins, Dwight N. *Black Theology of Liberation*. Maryknoll: Orbis Books, 2001.

———. *Introducing Black Theology of Liberation*. Maryknoll: Orbis Books, 2004.

Houston, Bill. "Biblical Holism: Three Helpful Theological Approaches." *South African Journal of Theology* (2014): 1–19. Viewed 27 March 2021 from https://www.academia.edu/14961880/BIBLICAL_HOLISM_Three_Helpful_Theological_Approaches p.8-16.

Howe, Brian, and Renate Howe. "The Influence of Faith-Based Organizations on Australian Social Policy." *Australian Journal of Social Issues* 47, no. 3 (2012): 319–333.

Howe, Brian. "The Church and Markets." In *The Church and the Free Market: Dilemmas in Church Welfare Agencies Accepting Contracts from Government*, edited by Alan Nichols and Maureen Postma. Melbourne: Victorian Council of Churches, Theological Forum, 2002.

Hugen, Beryl, and Rachel M. Venema. "The Difference of Faith: The Influence of Faith in Human Service Programs." *Journal of Religion & Spirituality in Social Work: Social Thought* 28, no. 4 (2009): 405–429.

Hughes, Philip. "Theology and Welfare: Literature Review." *Christian Research Association* 2, no. 12 (2013): 1–20.

Hughes, R. Kent. *Luke: That You May Know the Truth*. Wheaton: Crossway Books, 1998.

Hughes, V. "The Third Sector, Civil Society and Government: Beginning Afresh." In *Supping with the Devil? Government Contracts and the Non-Profit Sector*, edited by Peter Saunders and Martin Stewart-Weeks, CIS Policy Forum 16, St. Leonards, New South Wales, Australia: The Centre for Independent Studies, 2009.

Hulme, David, and Paul Mosley. *Finance Against Poverty*. Volume 2. London: Routledge, 1996.

Hurley, Douglas. "The U.S. Workplace is an Essential Environment for Christians to Evangelize Their Co-workers Who Do Not Know Jesus." DMin. diss., George Fox University, 2019.

Hutchinson, Mark, and John Wolffe. A Short History of Global Evangelicalism. Cambridge: Cambridge University Press, 2012.

Industry Commission. *Charitable Organizations in Australia*, Industry Commission. Melbourne: Australian Government Publishing Service, 1995.

Ireland, Dennis J. *Stewardship and the Kingdom of God: An Historical, Exegetical, and Contextual Study of the Parable of the Unjust Steward in Luke 16:1–13.* Leiden: Brill, 1992.

Ireland, Jerry M. "The Secularizing and Anti-Secularizing Potential of African Pentecostals." Paper presented at the Southeast Regional Meeting of the Evangelical Missiological Society, Raleigh, N.C, March 24, 2018.

———. *Evangelism and Social Concern in the Theology of Carl F. H. Henry.* Eugene: Pickwick Publications, 2015.

———., ed. *For the Love of God: Principles and Practice of Compassion in Missions.* Eugene: Wipf & Stock, 2017.

Jacobs, D. *Mapping Strategic Diversity: Strategic Thinking from a Variety of Perspectives.* London: Routledge, 2009.

Jakobs, Kai. *Corporate Standardization Management and Innovation.* Hershey: IGI Global, 2019.

Jambrek, Stanko. "Christian Witness in a Multi-Religious World in the Light of God's Word." *KAIROS – Evangelical Journal of Theology* 8, no. 2 (2014): 187–215.

James, Rick. *What is Distinctive about FBOs? How European FBOs Define and Operationalize their Faith.* Oxford: INTRAC, Praxis Paper 22, 2009.

Jamieson, Robert, Andrew Robert Fausset, and David Brown. *Critical and Explanatory Commentary on the Whole Bible.* Volume 2. Harrington: Delmarva Publications, 2013.

Jeavons, Thomas H. *When the Bottom Line is Faithfulness: Management of Christian Service Organizations.* Bloomington: Indiana University Press, 1994.

Jeter, Teresa M. "Exploring Mission Drift and Tension in a Nonprofit Work: Integration Social Enterprise." PhD thesis, College of Social and Behavioral Sciences, Walden University, 2017.

Jochemsen, Henk. "Normative Practices as an Intermediate between Theoretical Ethics and Morality." *Philosophia Reformata* 71, no. 1 (2006): 96–112.

Johnson, David, ed. *Politics, Modernization and Educational Reform in Russia: from Past to Present.* Oxford: Symposium Books Ltd, 2010.

Johnson, Neil C. *Business as Mission: A Comprehensive Guide to Theory and Practice.* Downers Grove: IVP Academic, 2009.

Johnson, Susan, and Ben Rogaly. *Microfinance and Poverty Reduction.* Oxford: Oxfam and Action Aid, 1997.

Jones, L. Gregory. *Christian Social Innovation: Renewing Wesleyan Witness.* Nashville: Abingdon Press, 2016.

Jones, Marshall B. "The Multiple Sources of Mission Drift." *Non-profit and Voluntary Sector Quarterly* 36, no. 2 (2007): 299–307. Viewed 6 January 2020, from https://journals.sagepub.com/doi/abs/10.1177/0899764007300385.

Jørgensen, Knud. "Edinburgh 2010 In Global Perspective" (2010). Viewed 29 November 2019, from https://www.academia.edu/24458786/Edinburgh_2010_in_Global_Perspective?email_work_card=view-paper.

Judd, Stephen, Anne Robinson, and Felicity Errington. *Driven by Purpose: Charities that Make a Difference,* Greenwich, New South Wales: Hammond Press, 2012.

Jung, Musung. "Toward A Theology of Pareo Dei: Exploring A Contextual Theology of Missio Dei for the Missiological Reconciliation of the Korean Protestant Church." PhD diss., Asbury Theological Seminary, 2012.

Kaoma, Kapya J. "Post Edinburgh 2010 Christian Mission: Joys, Issues and Challenges" (2010). Viewed 30 November 2019, from https://www.academia.edu/30577331/Post_Edinburgh_2010_Christian_Mission_Joys_Issues_and_Challenges?auto=download.

Kapolyo, Joe. "Matthew." In *Africa Bible Commentary,* edited by Tokunboh Adeyemo. Nairobi: WordAlive Publishers, 2010.

Kar, Ashim Kumar. "Sustainability and Mission Drift in Microfinance: Empirical Studies on Mutual Exclusion of Double Bottom Lines." PhD diss., Dept. of Economics, Hanken School of Economics, 2010.

Kärkkäinen, Veli-Matti. "Pentecostal Missiology in Ecumenical Perspective: Contributions, Challenges, Controversies." *International Review of Mission* 88, no. 350 (1999): 1–19.

Katz, Art. "Apostolic Service: The Mystery of Priestliness – New Mission Commitments." *International Journal of Frontier Missions* 16, no. 4 (2000): 205–220. Viewed on 25 June 2020, from http://www.ijfm.org/PDFs_IJFM/16_4_PDFs/ijfm_16_4.pdf.

Keck, Leanderr E. "Listening to and Listening for: From Text to Sermon (Acts 1:8)." *Interpretation* 27, no. 2 (1973): 184–202.

Keener, Craig S. *The IVP Bible Background Commentary: New Testament.* Downers Grove: InterVarsity Press, 2014.

Keil, Carl Friedrich, and Franz Delitzsch. *Commentary on the Old Testament.* Volume 7. Peabody: Hendrickson Publishers, 1996.

Kesis, Rei Towet. "Wholistic or Holistic? Does it Matter?" *Asia-Africa Journal of Mission and Ministry* 65, no. 5 (2012): 63–70.

Keum, Jooseop, ed. *Together Towards Life: Mission and Evangelism in Changing Landscapes,* Geneva, Switzerland: WCC Publications, 2013. Viewed 03 August 2020, from https://www.oikoumene.org/en/resources/documents/commissions/mission-and-evangelism/together-towards-life-mission-and-evangelism-in-changing-landscapes.

Klaits, Frederick. The Request and the Gift in Religious and Humanitarian Endeavours. Springer: Palgrave Macmillan, 2017.

Koech, Joseph. "The Spirit Motif in Luke 4:14–30; Acts 1:8 and the Church Today." *Transformation – Africa Journal of Evangelical Theology* 27, no. 2 (2008): 154–176.

Krippendorf, L. Klaus. *Content Analysis: An Introduction to its Methodology*. 3rd edition. Thousand Oaks: SAGE Publications, Inc., 2013.

Kühl, Stefan. *Ordinary Organisations: Why Normal Men Carried Out the Holocaust*. Cambridge: Polity Press, 2016.

———. *Organisationen: Eine sehr kurze Einführung*, Dordrecht: Verlag für Sozialwissenschaften, 2011.

Kuhn, Wagner. "Toward a Holistic Approach to Relief, Development, and Christian Witness." PhD diss., School of Intercultural Studies, Fuller Theological Seminary, 2004.

Künkler, Mirjam. "The Bureaucratization of Religion in Southeast Asia: Expanding or Restricting Religious Freedom?" *Journal of law and Religion* 33, no. 2 (2018): 192–197.

Künneth, Walter, and Peter Beyerhaus. *Reich Gottes oder Weltgemeinschaft?* Bad Liebenzell: Telos Dokumentation, 1975.

Kvale, Steinar. *InterViews: An Introduction to Qualitative Research Interviewing*. Thousand Oaks: SAGE Publications, Inc., 1996.

Lamport, Mark A., ed. *Encyclopedia of Christianity in the Global South*. London: Rowman and Littlefield Publishers, 2018.

Landau, Christopher. "China Invests in Confident Christians." *BBC Report*, 2010. Viewed 17 January 2020, from http://www.bbc.co.uk/news/world-asia-pacific-11020947.

Lange, John Peter, and Johannes Jacobus van Oosterzee. *A Commentary on the Holy Scriptures: Luke*. Translated by Philip Schaff. Bellingham: Logos Bible Software, 2008.

Lange, John Peter, and Philip Schaff. *A Commentary on the Holy Scriptures: Matthew*. Bellingham: Logos Bible Software, 2008.

Lange, John Peter, Philip Schaff, Paul Kleinert, and George R. Bliss. *A Commentary on the Holy Scriptures: Micah*. Bellingham: Logos Bible Software, 2008.

Laqueur, Walter. *Harvest of a Decade: Disraelia and Other Essays*. Oxford: Routledge, 2017.

Larsen, Timothy, and Micheal Ledger-Lomas, eds. *The Oxford History of Protestant Dissenting Traditions*. Volume 3. Oxford: Oxford University Press, 2017.

Lausanne Movement. *Evangelism and Social Responsibility: An Evangelical Commitment*. Lausanne Occasional Paper 21, 1982. Viewed 07 September 2020, from https.//www.lausanne.org/content/lop/lop-21.

Lawson, LeRoy. *Matthew: Unlocking the Scriptures for You*. Cincinnati: Standard Bible Studies, 1986.

Ledesma, Jesila M., and David-Casis. *Mission First: SPM Advocacy in the Philippines*. Pasig City: Microfinance Council of the Philippines, Pasig, 2010.

Lenski, Richard C.H. *The Interpretation of St. Matthew's Gospel*. Minneapolis: Augsburg Publishing House, 1961.

Lessing, Doris, and John Elkington. "Banker to the Poor." Viewed 18 December 2019, from https://pdfs.semanticscholar.org/7098/12bbd9c1deb067d6e7f3f9d e8a492d669e4f.pdf.

Lewis, Jonathan, ed. *World Mission: An Analysis of the World Christian Movement*. 2nd edition. Pasadena: William Carey Library, 2013.

Lewis, Jonathan, Meg Crossman, and Stephen Hoke, eds. *World Mission Manual: An Analysis of the World Christian Movement*. Pasadena: William Carey Library Publishers, 1994.

Lin, Peirong. "Countering Mission Drift in a Faith-based Organization: An Interdisciplinary Theological Interpretation Focused on the Case Study of World Vision's Identity Formation." PhD diss., Dept. of Missiological Studies, Evangelische Theologische Faculteit, 2019.

Lindlof, Thomas R., and Bryan C. Taylor. *Qualitative Communication Research Methods*. 2nd edition. Thousand Oaks: Sage Publications, Inc., 2002.

Little, Christopher R. "What Makes Mission Christian?" *Evangelical Missions Quarterly* 9, no. 3 (2006): 1–161.

Long, W. Meredith. *Health, Healing and God's Kingdom: New Pathways to Christian Health Ministry in Africa*. Oxford: Regnum Books, 2000.

Longfield, Bradley J. *The Presbyterian Controversy: Fundamentalists, Modernists, and Moderates*. Oxford: Oxford University Press, 1991.

Longman III, Tremper, David E. Garland, D. A. Carson, Walter W. Wessel, and Mark L. Strauss. *The Expositor's Bible Commentary: Matthew and Mark*. Grand Rapids: Zondervan Academic, 2010.

Lonsdale, David. *Eyes to See, Ears to Hear: An Introduction to Ignatian Spirituality*, Traditions of Christian Spirituality. Maryknoll: Orbis Books, 2000.

Lord, Andrew. *Spirit-Shaped Mission: A Holistic Charismatic Missiology*, Studies in Pentecostal and Charismatic Issues. Bletchley: Paternoster, 2005.

Love, Mark. "*Missio Dei*, Trinitarian Theology, and the Quest for a Post-Colonial Missiology." *Journal of Missional Theology and Praxis* 1 (2010): 56–64.

Luneau, René. *Paroles et silences du Synode Africain, 1989–1995*. Paris: Karthala, 1997.

Luz, Ulrich. *Studies in Matthew*. Translated by R. Selle. Grand Rapids: William B. Eerdmans Publishing Company, 2005.

———. *The Theology of the Gospel of Matthew*. Translated by J.B. Robinson. Cambridge: Cambridge University Press, 1995.

Lynn, Chad. *The DNA of a Disciple: Imparting the Life of Christ in the 21st Century*. Bloomington: Xlibris Corporation, 2011.

Ma, Ji, Elise Jing, and Jun Han. "Predicting Mission Alignment and Preventing Mission Drift: Do Revenue Sources Matter?" *Chinese Public Administration Review* 9, no. 1 (2018): 24–33. Viewed 07 January 2020, from https://www.researchgate.net/publication/326012761_Predicting_Mission_Alignment_and_Preventing_Mission_Drift_Do_Revenue_Sources_Matter.

Ma, Wonsuk, and Kenneth R. Ross. *Mission Spirituality and Authentic Discipleship*. Oxford: Regnum Books International, 2013.

MacArthur, John F. *The MacArthur Bible Commentary: Unleashing God's Truth, One Verse at a Time*. Nashville: Thomas Nelson, 2005.

Maddox, Marion. "An Argument for More, Not Less, Religion in Australia Politics." *Australian Religious Studies Review* 22, no. 3 (2009): 322–323.

———. "Blackleg churches? The Changing Relationship Between Religion and Executive Government." *Australian Religion Studies Review* 14 no. 2, (2001): 5–16.

———. "God, Caesar and Alexander." *Australian Quarterly* 75, no. 5 (2003): 4–39.

———. *God under Howard: The Rise of the Religious Right in Australian Politics*. Crows Nest, New South Wales, Australia: Allen and Unwin Book Publishers, 2005.

Mangayi, Lukwikilu Credo. "Conversions in Context: Insights from an Autobiographical Narrative of a Congolese-born Missionary at Stinkwater." *Missionalia* 45, no. 1, (2017): 77–91.

———. "Mission in an African city: Discovering the Township Church as an Asset Towards Local Economic Development in Tshwane." PhD diss., Dept. of Christian Spirituality, Church History and Missiology, University of South Africa, 2016. Viewed 26 June 2020, from http://hdl.handle.net/10500/22674.

———. "The Baptist Union of South Africa's Mission Orientation Needs Transformation: A Scrutiny by an Insider." *HTS Teologiese Studies / Theological Studies* 75, no. 4 (2019): 1–9.

———. "Township Churches of Tshwane as Potential Change Agents for Local Economic Development: An Empirical Missiological Study." *HTS Teologiese Studies / Theological Studies* 75, no. 3 (2018): 1–12.

Margull, Hans Jochen. *Hope in Action: The Church's Task in the World*. Philadelphia: Muhlenberg Press, 1962.

Marshall, Ian Howard. *New Testament Theology: Many Witnesses, One Gospel*. Downers Grove: InterVarsity Press, 2010.

Marshall, Katherine, and Lucy Keough, eds. *Mind, Heart and Soul in the Fight Against Poverty*, Washington, DC: The World Bank, 2004.

Marshall, Tina, Charles A. Rapp, Deborah R. Becker, and Gary R. Bond. "Key Factors for Implementing Supported Employment." *Psychiatric Services* 59, no. 8 (2008): 886–92.

Marthaler, Berard L., Thomas Carson, and Joann Cerrito, eds. *New Catholic Encyclopaedia*. Volume 14. Washington, DC: Catholic University of America Press, 2003.

Martikainen, Tuomas. "Changes in the Religious Landscape: European Trends at the Dawn of the Twenty-First Century." *Swedish Missiological Themes* 95, no. 4 (2007): 365–85.

Martin, J.A. "Luke." In *The Bible Knowledge Commentary: An Exposition of the Scriptures*, edited by John F. Walvoord and Roy B. Zuck, 214. Volume 2. Wheaton: Victor Books, 1985.

Mashau, Thinandavha Derrick. "A Reformed Missional Perspective on Secularism and Pluralism in Africa: Their Impact on African Christianity and the Revival of Traditional Religion," *Calvin Theological Journal* 44, no. 1 (2009): 108–126.

McConnell, D. "Holistic Mission." In *Evangelical Dictionary of World Mission*, edited by A. Scott Moreau, 448–49. Carlisle: Paternoster Press, 2000.

McCrae, I.J. "Good News to the Poor: The Challenge of the Poor in the History of the Church." *Mid-Stream* 20, no. 1 (1981): 519–22.

McGrath, Alister E. *Christianity: An Introduction*. Volume 2. Malden: Blackwell Publishing, 1997.

McGravran, Donald A. "Missiology Faces the Lion." *Missiology* 17, no. 3 (1989): 335–41.

McKinley, William, and Mark A. Mone. "Micro and Macro Perspectives in Organization Theory: A Tale of Incommensurability." In *The Oxford Handbook of Organization Theory*, edited by Haridimos Tsoukas and Christian Knudsen, 345–72. Oxford: Oxford University Press, 2003.

McNiff, Jean, and Jack Whitehead. *All You Need to Know about Action Research: Living Theory*. London: Sage Publications Ltd, 2006.

Mendes, Philip. "Empowering the Poor: Towards a Progressive Version of Welfare Reform." *Australian Quarterly* 75, no. 2 (2003): 23–26.

———. *Australia's Welfare Wars: The Players, the Politics and the Ideologies*. Sydney: University of New South Wales Press, 2003.

Mennillo, Giulia, Thomas Schlenzig, and Elmar Friedrich, eds. *Balanced Growth: Finding Strategies for Sustainable Development*, Berlin: Springer-Verlag, 2012.

Mersland, Roy, and R. Øystein Strøm. "Microfinance Mission Drift?" Viewed 03 January 2020, from https://www.efmaefm.org/0EFMSYMPOSIUM/Nantes%202009/paper/bankdrift.pdf.

Meyer, John W., and Brian Rowan. "Institutionalized Organizations: Formal Structure as Myth and Ceremony." *American Journal of Sociology* 83, no. 2 (1977): 340–63.

Miller, Darrow L. *Discipling Nations: The Power of Truth to Transform Cultures*. Seattle: YWAM Publishing, 2001.

Mintzberg, Henry. "An Emerging Strategy of 'Direct' Research." *Administrative Science Quarterly* 24, no. 4 (1979): 582–89.

Mintzberg, Henry, and James A. Waters. "Tracking Strategy in an Entrepreneurial Firm." *Academy of Management Journal* 25, no. 3 (1982): 465–99.

Moberg, David. *The Great Reversal: Reconciling Evangelism and Social Concern*. Eugene: Wipf & Stock Pub., 2007.

Monsma, Stephen. *When Sacred and Secular Mix: Religious Non-profit Organizations and Public Money*. Lanham: Rowman & Littlefield Publishers Inc., 1996.

Moon, Jay. *Intercultural Discipleship: Learning from Global Approaches to Spiritual Formation*. Grand Rapids: Baker Academic, 2017.

Morley, Jean-Paul. *La mission polaire évangélique: Les surprises d'un engagement*. Paris: Les Bergers et les Mages, 1993.

Moser, Marc. "Commercial Investments and Mission Drift in Microfinance: A Qualitative Analysis of Stakeholder Perceptions in Switzerland." PhD diss., Faculty of Business and Law, University of Southern Queensland, 2013.

Murphy, John. "Church and State in the history of Australia welfare." *ReasearchGate* 51, no. 2 (2011): 261–85. Viewed 16 January 2020, from https://www.researchgate.net/publication/292886074_Church_and_state_in_the_history_of_Australian_welfare/citation/download.

———. *A Decent Provision: Australia Welfare Policy, 1870 to 1949*. Farnham: Ashgate Publishing Limited, 2011.

Myers, Bryant L. "Modernity and Holistic Ministry." In *Serving with the Poor in Asia*, edited by Tetsunao Yamamori, Bryant L. Myers, and David Conner, 179–91. Monrovia: MARC, 1995.

———. *Walking with the Poor: Principles and Practices of Transformational Development*. Maryknoll: Orbis, 2008.

Myung, Sunghoon. "Spiritual Dimension of Church Growth as Applied in Yoido Full Gospel Church." PhD thesis, Fuller Theological Seminary, 1990.

Nazarkina, Liudmila. "The Big Green Sell Out: Setting a Research Agenda to Explore and Explain Growth Strategies of Ethical Businesses." Paper presented at the Academy of Management Conference, San Antonio, USA, 12th–16th August 2011.

Newbigin, Lesslie. *Sign of the Kingdom*. Grand Rapids: Eerdmans, 1980.

———. *The Gospel in a Pluralist Society*. Grand Rapids: Eerdmans, 1989.

———. *The Pen Secret: An Introduction to the Theology of Mission*. Grand Rapids: Eerdmans, 1995.

———. *The Pen Secret: Sketches for a Missionary Theology*. Grand Rapids: Eerdmans, 1983.

Newton, Isaac. "New Theory about Light and Colours." *Philosophical Transactions of the Royal Society of London* 6, no. 80 (1671/72): 3075–87. Viewed

28 January 2020, from http://www.newtonproject.ox.ac.uk/view/texts/normalized/NATP00006.

Nida, Eugene A., and Johannes P. Louw. *Greek-English Lexicon of the New Testament Based on Semantic Domains.* Volume 1. New York: United Bible Societies, 1989.

Nodia, Ghia. *Civil Society Development in Georgia: Achievements and Challenges,* Tbilisi, GA: Caucasus Institute for Peace. Democracy and Development, 2005.

Noll, Mark A. *The Rise of Evangelicalism: The Age of Edwards, Whitefield and the Wesleys.* Downers Grove: IVP Academic, 2018.

Noll, Mark A., David W. Bebbington, and George A. Rawlyk, eds. *Evangelicalism: Comparative Studies of Popular Protestantism in North America, the British Isles, and Beyond, 1700–1990.* Oxford: Oxford University Press, 1994.

Nsi, Michel Assoumou. *L'Église catholique au Gabon: de l'entreprise missionnaire à la mise en place 1844–1982.* Saint-Denis: Éditions Connaissance et Savoirs, 2017.

Numagami, Tsuyoshi. "The Infeasibility of Invariant Laws in Management Studies: A Reflective Dialogue in Defense of Case Studies." *Organization Science* 9, no. 1 (1998): 2–15.

O'Halloran, Kerry. *Religion, Charity and Human Rights.* Cambridge: Cambridge University Press, 2014.

Obeng-Amoako, Abraham. "The History of Assemblies of God Relief and Development Services in Ghana from 1948 to 2016: Tracing their Origins, Growth and Influence on the Ghanaian Society." PhD diss., Theological Studies, Pan-Africa Theological Seminary, 2019.

Olarinmoye, Omobolaji Ololade. "Faith-Based Organizations and Development: Prospects and Constrains." *Transformation* 29, no. 1 (2012): 1–14.

Olson, Gordon C. *What in the World Is God Doing: The Essentials of Global Missions.* Moundridge: Global Gospel Publishers, 2003.

Olson, Roger E. *The Westminster Handbook to Evangelical Theology.* London: Westminster John Knox Press, 2004.

Ormerod, Neil. "Seek First the Kingdom: The Mission of the Church and Publicly Funded Welfare." *Australasian Catholic Record* 77, no. 4 (2000): 428–37.

Osborn, Ronald E. *The Faith We Affirm: Basic Beliefs of Disciples of Christ.* St. Louis: Chalice Press, 1979.

Oslington, Paul. "Guest Blog: Keep Christian Social Service Delivery Christian." *ABC Religion and Ethics* (2012): 1. Viewed 27 July 2020, from https://www.abc.net.au/religion/guest-blog-keep-christian-social-service-delivery-christian/10100690.

Ott, Bernhard. "Evangelical Theology in Western Europe – An Anabaptist Perspective." *Mission Focus* 13 (2005): 141–54.

———. "Matthew 28:16–20 and the Holistic-Mission-Debate." Paper presented at the IBTS Directors' Conference: Anabaptism and Mission, Prague, Czech Republic, 2006.

———. *Beyond Fragmentation, Integrating Mission and Theological Education: A Critical Assessment of Some Recent Developments in Evangelical Theological Education*. Studies in Mission, Regnum Books, Oxford, 2001.

———. *Understanding and Developing Theological Education*. Carlisle: Langham Global Library, 2016.

Padilla, René C. "Holistic Mission," *A New Vision, A New Heart: A Renewed Call Lausanne Occasional Papers from the 2004 Forum for World Evangelization*. Pasadena: William Carey Library, 2005.

———. *Mission Between the Times*. Grand Rapids: William B. Eerdmans Publishing Company, 1985.

———. *The Local Church, Agent of Transformation: An Ecclesiology for Integral Mission*. Numància, Barcelona, Spain: Ediciones Kairos, 2004.

Palinkas, Lawrence A., Sarah M. Horwitz, Carla A. Green, Jennifer P. Wisdom, Naihua Duan, and Kimberly Hoagwood. "Purposeful Sampling for Qualitative Data Collection and Analysis in Mixed Method Implementation Research." *Administrative and Policy in Mental Health and Mental Health Services Research* 42, no. 5 (2015): 533–44.

Pallant, Dean. *Keeping Faith in Faith-Based Organizations: A Practical Theology of Salvation Army Health Ministry*. Eugene: Wipf & Stock, 2012.

Park, Eung Chun. *The Mission Discourse in Matthew's Interpretation*. Tubingen, Germany: Mohr Siebeck Verlag, 1995.

Parris, Matthew. "As an Atheist, I Really Believe Africa Needs God." *The Times*. 27 December, 2008.

Parsons, Gerald, ed. *Religion in Victorian Britain*. Manchester: Manchester University Press, 1988.

Patton, Michael Q. *Qualitative Evaluation and Research Methods*. 2nd edition. Newbury Park: Sage Publications, Inc., 1990.

———. *Qualitative Research and Evaluation Methods*. 3rd edition. Thousand Oaks: Sage Publications, Inc., 2002.

Pauw, J. Christoff. "Anti-apartheid Theology in the Dutch Reformed Family of Churches: A Depth-Hermeneutical Analysis." PhD diss., VU Amsterdam, Amsterdam, Netherlands, 2007.

Pellowe, John. "Mission Drift: Who's On Guard?" Viewed 12 June 2020, from https://www.cccc.org/news_blogs/john/2015/09/21/mission-drift-whos-on-guard/.

Phills, James A. *Integrating Mission and Strategy for Non-profit Organizations*. New York: Oxford University Press, 2005.

Picot, Arnold, Ralf Reichwald, and Rolf Wigand. *Information, Organization and Management: The Corporation without Boundaries*. Berlin, Germany: Springer-Verlag, 2008.

Pinfield, Lawrence T. "A Field Evaluation of Perspectives on Organizational Decision Making." *Administrative Science Quarterly* 31, no. 3 (1986): 365–388.

Poloma, Margaret M. *The Assemblies of God at the Crossroads: Charisma and Institutional Dilemmas*. Knoxville: University of Tennessee Press, 1989.

Pope Francis. "*Evangelii Gaudium: An Apostolic Exhortation.*" Libreria Editrice Vaticana (2013). Viewed 03 August 2020, from http://www.vatican.va/content/francesco/en/apost_exhortations/documents/papa-francesco_esortazione-ap_20131124_evangelii-gaudium.html.

Potocan, Vojko, and Zlatko Nedelko. *Handbook of Research on Managerial Solutions in Non-Profit Organizations: Advances in Public Policy and Administration*. Hershey: Information Science Reference, 2017.

Prince, Andrew James. *Contextualization of the Gospel: Towards an Evangelical Approach in the Light of Scripture and the Church Fathers*. Eugene: Wipf & Stock, 2017.

Prudhomme, Claude. "Mission religieuse et action humanitaire: quelle continuité ?" *Annales de Bretagne et des Pays de l'Ouest* 112, no. 2 (2005): 11–29.

Putnam, Robert. *Bowling Alone: The Collapse and Renewal of American Community*. New York: Simon and Schuster, 2000.

Rabi, Abdi Rahman Jama. "How Social Enterprises Manage Mission Drift: A Systematic Review." Master thesis, Dept. of Business and Administration, Örebro University, 2016.

Radio Télévision Suisse (RTS). *Le navire-hôpital d'une ONG suisse offre des soins à Madagascar*, 2015. Viewed the 20 January 2020, from https://www.rts.ch/info/monde/6500352-le-navire-hopital-d-une-ong-suisse-offre-des-soins-a-madagascar.html#timeline-anchor-Historique.

Ragin, Charles C. "'Casing' and the Process of Social Inquiry." In *What is a Case? Exploring the Foundations of Social Inquiry*, edited by Charles C. Ragin and Howard S. Becker, 217–26. Cambridge: Cambridge University Press, 1992.

Ramia, Gaby, and Terry Carney. "New Public Management, the Job Network and Non-profit Strategy." *Australian Journal of Labour Economics* 6, no. 2 (2003): 253–75.

Rauschenbusch, Walter. *Christianity and the Social Crisis in the 21st Century: The Classic that Woke Up the Church*. Revised and edited by P. Rauschenbusch. New York: HarperCollins, 2008.

Reid, Alvin. *Introduction to Evangelism*. Nashville: Broadman & Holman Publishing Group, 1998.

Reiling, J., and J.L. Swellengrebel. *A Handbook on the Gospel of Luke*. New York: United Bible Societies, 1993.

Reimer, Anselm. "How Do We Maintain a Credible Diaconia for the Future? Some Thoughts from a German Protestant Perspective." *Diaconia* 2, no. 2 (2011): 170–74.

Rice, Christopher Paul. "Toward a Framework for a Practical Theology of Institutions for Faith-based Organizations." DMin diss., Department of Divinity, Duke University, 2014.

Ringenberg, William C. *The Christian College: A History of Protestant Higher Education in America*. Grand Rapids: Baker Academic, 2006.

Ritzer, George. *Enchanting a Disenchanted World: Revolutionizing the Means of Consumption*. Newbury Park: Pine Forge Press, 2004.

Roberson, Ronald G. *Oriental Orthodox-Roman Catholic Interchurch Marriages: And Other Pastoral Relationships*. Washington DC: United States Catholic Conference Publishing, 1995.

Robertson, Archibald T. *Word Pictures in the New Testament: The Gospel According to Luke*. 2nd edition. Grand Rapids: Kregel Academic & Professional, 2005.

Robson, Colin, and Kieran McCartan. *Real World Research: A Resource for Users of Social Research Methods in Applied Settings*. 4th edition. West Sussex: John Wiley & Sons Ltd., 2016.

Roche, Jeanne. "The Hybrid Nature of Social Enterprises: Exploring Possible Tensions and Sources of Mission Drift." Master thesis, School of Management, Université Catholique de Louvain, 2017.

Rodriguez, Miguel. "Confrontational Christianity: Contextual Theology and Its Radicalization of the South African Anti-Apartheid Church Struggle." Master of Arts thesis, University of Central Florida, Orlando, 2012.

Ronsen, Oddvar Sten. *Mission Drift? Exploring a Paradigm Shift in Evangelical Mission with Particular Reference to Microfinance*. Carlisle: Langham Global Library, 2016.

Rothschild, Steve. *The Non-Nonprofit: For-Profit Thinking for Nonprofit Success*. San Francisco: Jossey-Bass Inc., 2012.

Rowdon, Harold H. "Holistic Mission." *Christian Mission Society* 32, no. 1 (no date): 32–40. https://biblicalstudies.org.uk/pdf/cbr/40_032.pdf.

Roy, Olivier. *Is Europe Christian?* Translated by C. Schoch. Oxford: Oxford University Press, 2020.

Russell, Mark. "Christian Mission Today: Are we on a Slippery Slope? Christian Mission is Holistic." *International Journal of Frontier Missiology* 25, no. 2 (2008): 23–98.

Saayman, Willem, and Klippies Kritzinger. *Mission in Bold Humility: David Bosch's Work Considered*. Eugene: Wipf & Stock Publishers, 1996.

Saidul, Islam M.D. "The Role of NGOs in Promoting Christianity: The Case of Bangladesh." *Intellectual Discourse* 9, no. 2 (2001): 183–202.

Salmi, Asta. "Collective Case Studies and Research Processes: How Do Research Teams Tackle the Dynamics?" 2010. Viewed 17 Marsh 2020, from https://www.impgroup.org/uploads/papers/7416.pdf.

Sanders, Ed Parish. *Judaism: Practice and Belief, 63 BCE – 66 CE*. Minneapolis: Fortress Press, 2016.

Sanneh, Lamin O. *Translating the Message: The Missionary Impact on Culture*. Maryknoll: Orbis Books, 1989.

Sarantakos, Sotirios. *Social Research*. 3rd edition. Basingstoke: Palgrave Macmillan, 2005.

Saunders, Peter. "Supping with the Devil." In *Supping with the Devil? Government contracts and the Non-Profit Sector*, edited by Peter Saunders and Martin Stewart-Weeks, 1–16, CIS Policy Forum 16. The Centre for Independent Studies. New South Wales, Australia: St. Leonards, 2009.

Scheitle, Christopher P. *Beyond the Congregation: The World of Christian Non-profits*. New York: Oxford University Press, 2010.

Scherer, James A. "Missiology Faces the Lion." *Missiology* 17, no. 3 (1989): 347–49.

Schmitter, Philippe C. "The New Corporatism: Social and Political Structures in the Iberian World." *The Review of Politics* 36, no. 1 (1974): 85–131.

Schneider, Jo Anne. "Comparing Stewardship Across Faith-Based Organizations." *Non-profit and Voluntary Sector Quarterly* 43, no. 3 (2012): 517–39.

———. *Social Capital and Welfare Reform*. New York: Columbia University Press, 2006.

Schulz, Klaus Detlev. "Tensions in the Pneumatology of the 'Missio Dei' Concept." *Concordia Journal* 23, no. 2 (1997): 99–107.

Schwandt, Thomas A. *Dictionary of Qualitative Inquiry*. 3rd edition. Thousand Oaks: SAGE Publications, Inc., 2007.

Scott, J.D. *The Roundtable on Religion and Social Welfare Policy: The Scope and Scale of Faith-Based Social Services*. New York: State University of New York Press, 2003.

Scott, W. Richard. *Institutions and Organizations: Ideas, Interests, and Identities*. Newbury Park: SAGE Publications, 2013.

Selznick, Philip. *Leadership in Administration: A Sociological Interpretation*. Berkeley: University of California Press, 1984.

Semple, Rhonda Anne. Missionary Women: Gender, Professionalism and the Victorian Idea of Christian Mission. Woodbridge, Suffolk: Boydell Press, 2003.

Servais, Olivier, and Gérard Van't Spijker. *Anthropologie et Missiologie: XIXe-XXe Siècles, entre Connivence et Réalité*. Paris: Éditions Karthala, 2004.

Setran, David P. "Student Religious Life in the Era of Secularization: The Intercollegiate YMCA, 1877–1940." *History of Higher Education Annual* 21, no. 1 (2001): 1–46.

———. *The College "Y": Student Religion in the Era of Secularization*, New York: Palgrave MacMillan, 2007.
Shingadia, Ashwin. "Modern Canadian Universities, Mission Drift and Quality of Education." Master thesis, Faculty of Political Science, University of Ottawa, 2012.
Shults, F. LeRon. "Tending to the Other in Late Modern Missions and Ecumenism." *Swedish Missiological Themes* 95, no. 4 (2007): 415–34.
Sider, Ronald J. "Evangelizing the World: Reflections on Lausanne III." *Prism Magazine* 18, no. 1 (2011): 1–58. Viewed 15 August 2020, from https://issuu.com/prismmagazine/docs/ron_sider_prism_articles.
———. *Cup of Water, Bread of Life: Inspiring Stories About Overcoming Lopsided Christianity*. Eugene: Wipf & Stock Pub, 2010.
———. *Evangelism and Social Action: Rich Christians in an Age of Hunger in a Lost and Broken World*. London: Hodder & Stoughton, 1993.
———. *Good News and Good Works: A Theology for the Whole Gospel*. Grand Rapids: Baker Books, 1999.
Silverman, David. *Doing Qualitative Research: A Handbook*. 4th edition. London: Sage Publications Ltd, 2013.
———. *Interpreting Qualitative Data*. 5th edition. London: Sage Publications Ltd, 2015.
Sincero, Sarah Mae. "Types of Survey Questions." *Explorable* 104, no. 8 (2013): 1–3. Viewed 30 March 2020, from https://explorable.com/types-of-survey-questions.
Skreslet, Stanley H. *Comprehending Mission: The Questions, Methods, Themes, Problems, and Prospects of Missiology*. Maryknoll: Orbis Books, 2012.
Small Business Administration. "Faith-Based Organizations: Frequently Asked Questions Regarding Participation of Faith-Based Organizations in the Paycheck Protection Program (PPP) and the Economic Injury Disaster Loan Program (EIDL)." Viewed 27 July 2020, from https://www.sba.gov/.
Smith, John Merlin Powis. *A Critical and Exegetical Commentary on the Books of Micah*. Edinburgh: T&T Clark, 1911.
Smith, Kevin Gary E. *Writing and Research: A Guide for Theological Students*. Carlisle: Langham Global Library, 2016.
Smith, Steven Rathgeb, and Michael R. Sosin. The Varieties of Faith-Related Agencies." *Public Administration Review* 61, no. 6 (2001): 651–670.
Smuts, Jan C., *Holism and Evolution*, Arvada: Macmillan Publications Inc., 1926.
Soboul, Albert. *Dictionnaire Historique de la Révolution Française*. Paris: Presses Universitaires de France-Quadrige, 2005.
Sommerville, John C. "Secular Society/Religious Population: Our Tacit Rules for Using the Term 'Secularization,'" *Journal for the Scientific Study of Religion* 37, no. 2 (2000): 240–252.

Spindler, Marc, and Annie Lenoble-Bart. *Spiritualités Missionnaires Contemporaines: Entre Charismes et Institutions*. Paris, France: Éditions Karthala, 2007.

Stake, Robert E. "Qualitative Case Studies." In *Strategies of Qualitative Inquiry*, edited by N.K. Denzin and Y.S. Lincoln, 134–164. Thousand Oaks: Sage Publications, Inc., 2003.

———. *The Art of Case Study Research*. Thousand Oaks: SAGE Publications, Inc., 1998.

Stamps, Donald C., J.W. Adams, J. Gerbore and S. d'Orazio Berkley, eds. *La Bible Esprit et Vie*. Springfield: Life Publishers International, 1992.

Stanley, Brian. *The Global Diffusion of Evangelicalism: The Age of Billy Graham and John Stott*. Downers Grove: IVP Academic, 2018.

Steensland, Brian, and Philip Goff. *The New Evangelical Social Engagement*. Oxford: Oxford University Press, 2014.

Stein, Robert H. *Luke: An Exegetical and Theological Exposition of Holy Scripture*, The New American Commentary. Volume 24. Nashville: Broadman & Holman Publishers, 1992.

Steward, John H. *Biblical Holism: Where God, People and Deeds Connect*. Burwood: World Vision Australia, 1994.

Stiller, Brian, ed. *Evangelicals Around the World: A Global Handbook for the 21st Century*. Nashville: Thomas Nelson Publishing Company, 2015.

Stott, John R.W., and Timothy Dudley-Smith. *Authentic Christianity: From the Writings of John Stott*. Downers Grove: Inter-Varsity Press, 1996.

———. *Christian Mission in the Modern World: What the Church Should Be Doing Now*. Downers Grove: Inter-Varsity Press, 1975.

———. *The Lausanne Covenant: Complete Text with Study Guide*. Carol Stream: Hendrickson Publishers, 2012.

Stout, H.S., and D.S. Cormode. "Institution and the Story of American Religion." In *Sacred Companies Organizational Aspects of Religion and Religious Aspects of Organizations*, edited by N.J. Demerath III, Peter Dobkin Hall, Terry Schmitt and Rhys H. Williams, 62–78. Oxford: Oxford University Press, 1998.

Stronstad, Roger. *The Charismatic Theology of St. Luke*. Peabody: Hendrickson Publishers, Inc., 1984.

Summers, Lawrence H. "Convocation of the Divinity School of Harvard University." Harvard University, 2002. Viewed 10 January 2020, from https://www.harvard.edu/president/speeches/summers_2002/convocation.ph.

Sunquist, Scott W. *Understanding Christian Mission, Participation in Suffering and Glory*. Grand Rapids: Baker Academic, 2013.

Swain, Shurlee. "Do you Want Religion with that? Welfare History in a Secular Age." *History Australia* 2, no. 3 (2005): 78.1–78.8.

Swart, Jannie, Scott Hagley, John Ogren, and Mark Love. "Toward a Missional Theology of Participation: Ecumenical Reflections on Contributions to Trinity, Mission, and Church." *Missiology* 37, no. 1 (2009): 75–87.

Swedberg, Richard. *The Max Weber Dictionary: Key Words and Central Concepts*. Palo Alto: Stanford University Press, 2005.

Takayama, K.P. "Administrative Structures and Political Processes in Protestant Denominations." *Publius* 4, no. 2 (1974): 5–37.

Talbert, Charles H., and Mikeal C. Parsons. *Paideia Commentary on the New Testament: Matthew*. Grand Rapids: Baker Publishing, 2010.

Tannehill, Robert C. *The Narrative Unity of Luke-Acts: A Literary Interpretation*. Volume 1. Philadelphia: Fortress Press, 1991.

———. *The Shape of Luke's Story: Essays on Luke-Acts*. Eugene: Cascade Books, 2005.

Tatomir, Alexandru, Christopher McDermott, Jocob Bensabat, Holger Class, Katriona Edlmann, Reza Taherdangkoo, and Martin Sauter. "Conceptual Model Development Using a Generic Features, Events, and Processes (FEP) Database for Assessing the Potential Impact of Hydraulic Fracturing on Groundwater Aquifers." *Advances in Geosciences* 45 (2018): 185–92.

Tennent, T.C. "Paradigm Shifts in the Global Revitalization of Christianity." *Bibliotheca Sacra* 175, no. 699 (2018): 338–49.

Thayer, Joseph H. *Greek-English Lexicon of the New Testament*. Charleston: Forgotten Books, 2011.

The Cape Town Commitment. Cape Town, South Africa, 2010. Viewed 17 August 2020, from https://www.lausanne.org/content/ctcommitment#p1-10.

Thiessen, Elmer John. *The Scandal of Evangelism: A Biblical Study of the Ethics of Evangelism*. London: Hodder & Stoughton Publishers, 2018.

Thomas, Norman E. *Classic Texts in Mission and World Christianity: A Reader's Companion to David Bosch's Transforming Mission*. Maryknoll: Orbis Books, 1995.

Thorpe, Richard, and Robin Holt, eds. *The SAGE Dictionary of Qualitative Management Research*. London: Sage Publications Ltd, 2007.

Tippett, Alan R. *Introduction to Missiology*. Pasadena: William Carey Library, 2013.

Tizon, Al. "Evangelism and Social Responsibility: The Making of a Transformational Vision." In *The Lausanne Movement: A Range of Perspectives*, edited by M.S. Dahle, L. Dahle, and K. Jørgensen, 170–82. Oxford: Regnum Books International, 2014.

———. *Transformation After Lausanne: Radical Evangelical Mission in Global-Local Perspective*. Wipf & Stock, Eugene: Regnum Studies in Mission series, 2008.

———. *Whole and Reconciled: Gospel, Church and Mission in a Fractured World*. Grand Rapid: Baker Academic, 2018.

Torry, Malcolm. *Citizen's Basic Income: A Christian Social Policy.* London: Darton, Longman and Todd, 2016.

———. *Managing Religion: The Management of Christian Religious and Faith-Based Organizations.* Volume 1. Basingstoke: Palgrave MacMillan, 2014.

Treloar, Geoffrey R. *The Disruption of Evangelicalism: The Age of Torrey, Mott, McPherson and Hammond.* Downers Grove: IVP Academic, 2017.

Trones, Maren. "Hybrid Organizations: Defining Characteristics and Key Factors for Organizational Sustainability." Master Thesis, Dept. of Economics and Business, Norwegian University of Life Sciences, 2015.

Tsoukas, Haridimos, and Christain Knudsen, eds. *The Oxford Handbook of Organization Theory: Meta-theoretical Perspectives.* Oxford: Oxford University Press, 2005.

Turner, David L. *Cornerstone Biblical Commentary: The Gospel of Matthew.* Carol Stream,: Tyndale House Publishing, Inc., 2005.

Ukpong, Justin. "What is Contextualization." In *Readings in World Mission*, edited by Norman Thomas, 179–80. London: SPCK, 1995.

Unruh, Heidi Rolland, and Ronald J. Sider. *Saving Souls, Serving Society: Understanding the Faith Factor in Church-Based Social Ministry.* Oxford: Oxford University Press, 2005.

Uwaegbute, Kingsley Ikechukwu. "A Challenge of Jesus' Manifesto on Luke 4:16–21 to Nigerian Christian." *International Journal of Theology & Reformed Tradition* 5, no. 1 (2013): 143–59.

Vähäkangas, Auli. "Comments 'Postcolonial Mission: Oxymoron or Paradigm Shift' – A Response to Maluleke." *Swedish Missiological Themes* 95, no. 4 (2007): 529–32.

Van den Brink, Gijsbert, Eveline van Staalduine-Sulman, and Maarten Wisse. *The Spirit is Moving: New Pathways in Pneumatology.* Leiden: Brill, 2019.

Van Luijk, Ruben B. *Children of Lucifer: The Origins of Modern Religious Satanism.* Oxford: Oxford University Press, 2016.

Van Rad, Gerhard. *Old Testament Theology.* Translated by D.M.G. Stalker. Volume 2. New York: Harper & Row Publishers, 1695.

———. *The Message of the Prophets.* Volume 20. London: SCM Press, 1968.

Van Rheenen, Gailyn. "From Theology to Practice: Participating in the *Missio Dei*." *Journal of Missional Theology and Praxis* 1, no. 10 (2010): 1–89.

Vanderwoerd, James R. "How Faith-Based Social Service Organisations Manage Secular Pressures Associated with Government Funding." *Non-profit Management and Leadership* 14, no. 3 (2004): 239–62.

———. "Religious Characteristics of Government-Funded Faith-Related Social Service Organizations." *Social Work & Christianity* 35, no. 3 (2008): 258–286.

Ver Beek, Kurt Alan. "Spirituality: A Development Taboo." *Development in Practice* 10, no. 1 (2000): 31–43. Viewed 08 July 2020, from http://www.informaworld.com/smpp/content~db=all?content=10.1080/09614520052484.

Verna, Gérard. "Le comportement des ONG engagées dans l'aide humanitaire: Selon leur culture d'origine et les pressions politiques subies." *Anthropologie et Sociétés* 31, no. 2 (2007): 25–44.

Verwer, George. *Sortir de la Zone de Confort: XXIe siècle et la Mission Continue.* Marne-La-Vallée Cedex: Éditions Farel, 2000.

Vieira, G. *La Religion Africaine Réhabilitée: Regards Changeants sur le Fait Religieux Africain.* Paris: Karthala éditions, 2007.

Vincent, Marvin R. *Word Studies in the New Testament.* Volume 4. Peabody: Hendrickson Publishers, 1985.

Vine, William Edwy. *The Expanded Vine's Expository Dictionary of New Testament Words.* Minneapolis: Bethany House Publishing, 1984.

Von der Heydte, Lisa. *Challenges Resulting from Multiple Institutional Logics in Hybrid Organizations: The Case of Social Business Hybrids.* Wiesbaden: Springer Gabler, 2020.

Vovelle, Michel. *Religion et Révolution: La Déchristianisation de l'an II.* Paris: Édition Hachette, 1976.

Wacker, Grant. *Heaven Below: Early Pentecostals and American Culture.* Cambridge: Harvard University Press, 2001.

Währisch-Oblau, Claudia, and Fidon Mwombeki. *Mission Continues: Global Impulses for the 21st Century.* Oxford: Regnum Books International, 2010.

Ward, Mark. *The Electronic Church in the Digital Age: Cultural Impacts of Evangelical Mass Media.* Westport: Praeger Publishers, 2015.

Ward, William Reginald. *Early Evangelicalism: A global Intellectual History, 1670–1789.* Cambridge: Cambridge University Press, 2006.

Waweru, Rebecca. "Integral Mission: An Overview of Four Models and Its Role in Development." *International Journal of Novel Research in Humanity and Social Sciences* 1, no. 2 (2015): 13–18.

Weaver, Dorothy J. *Matthew's Missionary Discourse: A Literary-Critical Analysis.* London: Bloomsbury Academic, 2015.

Weber, Stuart K. *Holman New Testament Commentary: Matthew.* Nashville: Broadman & Holman Publishers, 2000.

Webster, Merriam. *Collegiate Dictionary.* 10th edition. Springfield: Merriam-Webster Incorporation, 2000.

Weeden, Kim A. "Why Do Some Occupations pay more than Others? Social Closure and Earnings Inequality in the United States." *American Journal of Sociology* 108, no. 1 (2002): 55–101.

Weiss, E.R. *The Four Gospels: The Gospel According to St. Matthew, St. Mark, St. Luke and St. John.* Leipzig: Poeschel & Trepte, 1932.

Wells, Samuel. *Incarnational Mission: Being with the World*. Grand Rapids: William B. Eerdmans Publishing Company, 2018.

Weren, Wilhelmus Johannes Cornelis. *Studies in Matthew's Gospel: Literary Design, Intertextuality, and Social Setting*. Biblical Interpretation Series. Volume 130. Leiden: Brill, 2014.

White, Reginald Ernest Oscar. *Listening Carefully to Jesus*. Grand Rapids: William B. Eerdmans Publishing Company, 2000.

Whiteman, Darrell L. "Contextualization: The Theory, the Gap, the Challenge." *International Bulletin of Missionary Research* 21, no. 1 (1997): 2–7.

Wiersbe, Warren W. *The Bible Exposition Commentary*. Volume 1. Wheaton: Victor Books, 1996.

———. *The Wiersbe Bible Commentary: The Complete New Testament in One Volume*. Colorado Springs: David C. Cook edition, 2007.

Wietzke, Joachim, ed. *Mission erklärt: Ökumenische Dokumente von 1972 bis 1992*, Leipzig: Evangelische Verlagsanstalt, 1993.

Wink, Walter. *Unmasking the Powers: The Invisible Forces that Determine Human Existence*. Minneapolis: Fortress Press, 2004.

Winkworth, Gail, and Peter J. Camilleri. "Keeping the Faith: The Impact of Human Services Restructuring on Catholic Social Welfare Services." *Australian Journal of Social Issues* 39, no. 3 (2004): 315–28.

Winter, G. *The Emergent American Society: Large Scale Organization*. New Haven: Yale University Press, 1967.

Wittberg, Patricia. *Creating a Future for Religious Life: A Sociological Perspective*. Mahwah: Paulist Press, 1991.

———. *From Piety to Professionalism and Back? Transformations of Organized Religious Virtuosity*. Lanham: Rowman & Littlefield, 2006.

Wolffe, John. *The Expansion of Evangelicalism: The Age of Wilberforce, More, Chalmers and Finney*. Downers Grove: IVP Academic, 2007.

Woodward, J.R. "A Holistic Gospel: What God Has Joined Together, Let No One Separate." MTh. thesis, Fuller Theological Seminary, 2007.

Woolnough, Brian E. "Christian NGOs in Relief and Development: One of the Church's Arms for Holistic Mission." *Transformation* 28, no. 3 (2011): 195–205.

Woolnough, Brian, and Wonsuk Ma, eds. *Holistic Mission: God's Plan for God's People*. Edinburgh: Regnum Books, 2010.

World Council of Churches. Pontifical Council for Inter-Religious Dialogue. World Evangelical Alliance (2011). *Christian Witness in a Multi-Religious World: Recommendations for Conduct*. Viewed 07 September 2020, from https://www.oikoumene.org/en/resources/documents/wcc-programmes/interreligious-dialogue-and-cooperation/christian-identity-in-pluralistic-societies/christian-witness-in-a-multi-religious-world.

Wright, Christopher J. H., Lindsay Brown, Las Newman et al. *John Stott: Pastor, Leader and Friend, A Man Who Embodied 'the Spirit of Lausanne'*. Peabody: Hendrickson Publishers, 2012.

Yale University. "About History," 2013. Viewed 10 January 2020, from https://www.yale.edu/about/history.html.

Yamamori, Tetsunao, and Kenneth A. Eldred, eds. *On Kingdom Business: Transforming Missions through Entrepreneurial Strategies*. Wheaton, Illinois: Crossway, 2003.

Yeh, Allen. "Tokyo 2010: Global Mission Consultation." *International Bulletin of Missionary Research* 35, no. 1 (2011): 1–25.

Yin, Robert K. *Application of Case Study Research: Applied Social Research Methods*. 2nd edition, Volume 4. Thousand Oaks: Sage Publications, Inc., 2003.

———. *Case Study Research: Design and Methods*, Applied Social Research Methods Series. 4th edition. Thousand Oaks: Sage Publications, Inc., 2009.

———. *Case Study Research: Design and Methods*. 5th edition. Thousand Oaks: Sage Publications, Inc., 2013.

Young, Dennis R. "The State of Theory and Research on Social Enterprises." *Social Enterprises* (2012): 19–46. Viewed 08 January 2020, from https://link.springer.com/chapter/10.1057%2F9781137035301_2.

Young, N. "Army Walking a Spiritual Tightrope." *Pipeline* 17, no. 4 (2013): 6–7.

Youngblood, Ronald F. Frederick Fyvie Bruce, and Ronald Kenneth Harrison. *Nelson's New Illustrated Bible Dictionary*. Nashville: Thomas Nelson, 1997.

Yunus, Muhammad. *Building Social Business: The New Kind of Capitalism that Serves Humanity's Most Pressing Needs*. New York: PublicAffairs, 2011.

———. *Creating a World Without Poverty: Social Business and the Future of Capitalism*. New York: PublicAffairs, 2009.

Zerwick, Max. *A Grammatical Analysis of the Greek New Testament*. Subsidia Biblica 39. Rome: Biblical Institute Press, 2010.

Zoba, Wendy Murray. *The Beliefnet Guide to Evangelical Christianity*. New York: Three Leaves Press, 2005.

Zorn, Jean-François. *La Missiologie: Émergence d'une Discipline Théologique*. Genève: Éditions Labor et Fides, 2004.

Langham Literature, with its publishing work, is a ministry of Langham Partnership.

Langham Partnership is a global fellowship working in pursuit of the vision God entrusted to its founder John Stott –

> *to facilitate the growth of the church in maturity and Christ-likeness through raising the standards of biblical preaching and teaching.*

Our vision is to see churches in the Majority World equipped for mission and growing to maturity in Christ through the ministry of pastors and leaders who believe, teach and live by the word of God.

Our mission is to strengthen the ministry of the word of God through:
- nurturing national movements for biblical preaching
- fostering the creation and distribution of evangelical literature
- enhancing evangelical theological education

especially in countries where churches are under-resourced.

Our ministry

Langham Preaching partners with national leaders to nurture indigenous biblical preaching movements for pastors and lay preachers all around the world. With the support of a team of trainers from many countries, a multi-level programme of seminars provides practical training, and is followed by a programme for training local facilitators. Local preachers' groups and national and regional networks ensure continuity and ongoing development, seeking to build vigorous movements committed to Bible exposition.

Langham Literature provides Majority World preachers, scholars and seminary libraries with evangelical books and electronic resources through publishing and distribution, grants and discounts. The programme also fosters the creation of indigenous evangelical books in many languages, through writer's grants, strengthening local evangelical publishing houses, and investment in major regional literature projects, such as one volume Bible commentaries like the Africa Bible Commentary and the South Asia Bible Commentary.

Langham Scholars provides financial support for evangelical doctoral students from the Majority World so that, when they return home, they may train pastors and other Christian leaders with sound, biblical and theological teaching. This programme equips those who equip others. Langham Scholars also works in partnership with Majority World seminaries in strengthening evangelical theological education. A growing number of Langham Scholars study in high quality doctoral programmes in the Majority World itself. As well as teaching the next generation of pastors, graduated Langham Scholars exercise significant influence through their writing and leadership.

To learn more about Langham Partnership and the work we do visit langham.org

www.ingramcontent.com/pod-product-compliance
Lightning Source LLC
Chambersburg PA
CBHW070235240426
43673CB00044B/1796

In *Sermon Listening: A New Approach Based on Congregational Studies and Rhetoric*, Enoh Šeba provides one of the finest intellectual histories of the "turn to the listener" in recent homiletics, and an overview of preaching practices and homiletical scholarship among Croatian Baptists. He takes the reader on a journey into the ways that sermon listeners are processing the sermons they hear as he summarizes the results of his empirical and ethnographic study of sermon-listening among Croatian Baptists. The results are remarkably insightful and consistently helpful. This is an important contribution to listener-oriented scholarship in homiletics, and to the broader fields of rhetoric and communication theory.

John S. McClure, PhD
Charles G. Finney Professor of Preaching and Worship,
Vanderbilt Divinity School, Nashville, Tennessee, USA

Preaching is essential to our life together as the people of God. Yet, as Dr. Šeba recognizes, there is often a missing element. Preachers listen to God, but do they listen to their listeners? In this engaging exploration of preaching in Croatia, Dr. Šeba provides preachers with ways to make listeners an important and enduring part of the preaching conversation.

Lucy Lind Hogan, PhD
Hugh Latimer Elderdice Professor of Preaching, Emerita
Wesley Theological Seminary, Washington, DC, USA

Enoh Šeba offers a rich and multi-faceted study in homiletics which extends and develops our understanding of the contemporary "turn to the listener." He mines classical traditions of rhetoric and draws them into a rich dialogue with his own context, while also making a contribution to the fertile ground of "baptistic" theology within the contemporary academy. To invert Paul's question, we could ask, "How shall they preach unless there is a hearer?" Šeba offers important insights into how people listen to preaching and this book makes a unique and valuable contribution to contemporary homiletics literature.

Doug Gay, PhD
Principal of Trinity College,
Lecturer in Practical Theology, University of Glasgow, UK

In this groundbreaking study, Enoh Šeba describes and reflects on a unique research project which investigated the expectations, experiences and responses of those who listen to sermons in Croatian Baptist churches. It thus offers a unique snapshot of the dynamics at play in a particular religious setting. It makes a fascinating ethnographic study, but it is far more than that. Dr Šeba draws on key theological themes, including the Free Church emphasis on the priesthood of all believers, to argue for a much more participatory conception of the sermon. Drawing on a wide knowledge of the fields of homiletics, rhetoric, congregational studies and practical theology, his book will help congregations, pastors, denominational leaders and theologians anywhere in the world take more seriously the importance of respecting those who listen to sermons, and develop practices of preaching and hearing which truly build up the people of God on the foundation of his word.

Stephen I. Wright, PhD
Vice Principal and Academic Director,
Spurgeon's College, London, UK

For centuries preachers have acted as if what they want to *say* is the goal of the sermon. In fact, the real goal of the sermon is to help people *hear* a convicting, redeeming, empowering word from God. Only in the last few years have scholars of preaching asked the question "How do people *listen* to sermons? And what we preachers learn from them about how to communicate better?" Professor Enoh Šeba is one of the first scholars in the world to take this "turn to the listener" by studying how actual people listen to sermons in five congregations in four Croatian communities. The results show what people *really* value in sermons, what works in communication between pulpit and pew, and how preachers can shape their sermons to enhance listening, and hence, deepen Christian life and witness.

Ronald J. Allen, PhD
Professor of Preaching, and Gospels and Letters, Emeritus,
Christian Theological Seminary, Indianapolis, Indiana, USA

With this book on Croatian Baptist preaching, Enoh Šeba adds a rich homiletical study to the growing number of empirical studies in the field. His choice to combine rhetoric and congregational studies builds upon existing research and emphasizes the significance of studying preaching in relation to its local context.